2005

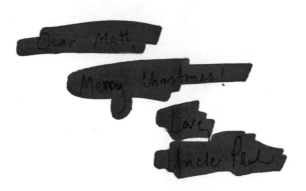

Dear Matt,

Merry Christmas!

Love
Uncle Paul

THE DEVIL'S HORN

THE
DEVIL'S
HORN

THE STORY OF THE SAXOPHONE,

FROM NOISY NOVELTY TO KING OF COOL

MICHAEL SEGELL

FARRAR, STRAUS AND GIROUX

NEW YORK

Farrar, Straus and Giroux
19 Union Square West, New York 10003

Copyright © 2005 by Michael Segell
Distributed in Canada by Douglas & McIntyre Ltd.
Printed in the United States of America
First edition, 2005

Library of Congress Cataloging-in-Publication Data
Segell, Michael, 1951–
    The devil's horn : the story of the saxophone, from noisy novelty to king of cool /
Michael Segell.— 1st ed.
        p.   cm.
    Includes bibliographical references (p.   ).
    ISBN-13: 978-0-374-15938-2
    ISBN-10: 0-374-15938-6
    1. Saxophone—History.   I. Title.

ML975.S44 2005
788.7'09—dc22

                                                                                    2004065454

www.fsgbooks.com

10   9   8   7   6   5   4   3   2   1

CONTENTS

THE DEVIL'S HORN

INTRODUCTION

Wynton made me play tenor," Branford Marsalis is saying as he sleepily jabs a spoon at a cumulus of milk froth that tops his cappuccino. "I was playing alto in Art Blakey's band, and he says, 'Man, you don't play the alto. Listen to the way you play. You never play in the upper register, you're always down around the bottom of the horn. The bottom of the alto is the top of the tenor, so you should just play tenor.'"

He takes a sip and licks the froth from his lower lip, which is creased in the middle and looks like the perfect home for a buzzing saxophone reed. "A couple weeks go by. He's starting a new band and asks me to help him find musicians. He says, 'I need a piano player,' and I say, 'Kenny Kirkland.' 'I need a drummer,' and I say, 'Jeff Watts.' He says, 'I need a tenor player, who do you know?' I say, 'I know a guy.' He says, 'Really? What's his name?' I say, 'He doesn't have a tenor yet, but he'll have one in two weeks.' So that's how I started playing tenor, and he was totally right."

We're sitting in a Starbucks in New Rochelle, a cozy suburb of New York not far from Branford's home, where he lives with his wife, a teenage son, and a toddler daughter. It's late morning and he's agreeably rolled out of bed, thrown on a New Jersey Nets T-shirt, light red workout shorts, and a pair of hybrid golf shoe/sneakers, and met me for coffee.

"It was like finally meeting the right woman," says Branford, who told his friends he would marry his wife, his second, after their first meeting. "The alto was like a first love affair and soprano like a first marriage. Now playing tenor is an extension of my personality. It's up to me what I want to project—happiness, sorrow, existential dread, whatever. It shows me all my limitations and strengths. It's really good at that. And for jazz music, nothing beats the depth and range of the tenor. I can't imagine songs like 'Alabama' by Coltrane, or the last movement of *A Love Supreme*, or the second movement of *Freedom Suite* by Sonny Rollins being played on alto."

Branford played piano as a kid, but "it was a bitch to carry around a Fender Rhodes" to the gigs he played with his R&B band. He learned the clarinet, but couldn't imagine a career for himself other than in an orchestra. At fifteen, he talked his father into buying him an alto saxophone, a Yamaha student model that he promptly disassembled. Why? "Why not?" he says. "I just wanted to know how it worked." Like everyone else in his brilliant family, he got good fast, but the alto never felt totally right. "For one thing, Charlie Parker already did everything one could do on the alto." So he spent time mastering the soprano, considered by many to be the most difficult of the saxophones, a tutorial that culminated in a 1986 hit record, *Romances for Saxophone*. Like many modern tenor players, he now routinely moves between the big and little horns—both B-flat instruments—and rarely plays the alto.

"The soprano can come off like an operatic voice," he says. "When I worked on that record, all I listened to were singers—Kiri Te Kanawa, Kathleen Battle, Maria Callas. It amazed me how much I could approximate how they sing. And as I started working more on the instrument, I found I could make it sound like an English horn, a clarinet, or an oboe. It's real malleable that way."

Branford's wife, their little girl in tow, has dropped by to pick up his car, so I tell him I'll give him a ride home. He spots a saxophone case in the back of the car; it contains my newly rented Armstrong student-model tenor. He has to see it, obeying a superstition he says is too complicated to explain. He rigs up the horn, plays a furious string of notes through the entire natural compass, and the sax-o-phone, the voice of Adolphe Sax, booms across the parking lot, dodging buses and SUVs and slipping around moms with strollers before dispersing into the woods of a golf course across the highway. "This will do until you get your own horn," he pronounces.

A natural pedagogue—he is a Marsalis, after all—Bradford can't resist giving a beginner a little lesson. "Here's what I want you to practice," he says, tuning the horn by pushing the mouthpiece a little farther onto the crook. He hands it to me. "It's a tonguing exercise. Set your metronome to 130, then articulate each note three times before rising to the next on the last quarter note and pausing. Then do the same with the next note. Go through all two and a half octaves, or until your tongue just quits."

I start with D and clumsily tongue my way up to the next octave. "Not bad," Branford says as he writes down his telephone number on a piece of paper. "Call me if you have any questions."

Thus ended my first lesson on the saxophone, the first of several tutorials that would spontaneously break out as I explored the horn's glorious and often controversial history with some of its finest practitioners. Saxophonists, I've learned, are a generous and agreeable lot, enormously sympathetic to a new convert. Immediately, they know something compelling and personal about the neophyte—namely, that he's been seduced by a power he can't quite understand and yet is helpless to resist. They're happy to help in any way they can.

Since meeting Branford, I've talked to hundreds of saxophone players—brilliant young stylists such as Marcus Strickland, Vincent Herring, and Ron Blake; middle-aged virtuosos such as Michael Brecker and Joe Lovano; and emeritus lions such as Jimmy Heath and the late Illinois Jacquet. Almost every one of them describes his virgin encounter with the horn as some kind of epiphany, conversion, mystical event—or, more prosaically, a mugging. Not long before he died, Benny Carter told me that the first time he played the saxophone, at fourteen, he felt "extraordinary joy" and that every day since had been a "religious experience." David Murray, who grew up in the Pentecostal Church, described his initial encounter as an experience not unlike that of being "saved." Sonny Rollins said that when his mother gave him his horn and he first put it to his lips, "I got that buzz. After that, any time I practiced I was in heaven, another place. It was more like it took me over." Lee Konitz recalls the transfixing golden sparkle of the horn set off against the dense purple velvet lining of the case, and the narcotic smell—like that of Proust's madeleine: "Ah, the smell." Claude Delangle remembers the feeling of being "invaded by a virus" after first tracing with a small finger the keyboard's beautiful, complex architecture. Phil Woods can vividly picture his mother pulling the cased instrument from its bedroom hiding place, as though it was a dirty family secret that he was now old enough to understand, and his hands trembling as his fingers magically assumed a perfect position on the sleek, sexy, serpentine vessel.

For me, it was a thunderbolt, a lightning strike that instantly and permanently rearranged my brain chemistry. Not long before I met Branford, a friend of mine, Ortley, strapped his Selmer Mark VI alto saxophone around my neck and showed me where to rest my fingers and how to form my embouchure—the recruitment of several dozen facial muscles that support the lips, tongue, and teeth around the mouthpiece. I took a long breath and blew. The horn responded with a rich, resonant, low E-flat. I blew again, extending the note—my first long tone—and my whole body seemed to shape-shift into a musical instrument, my cells breaking down into their component atoms and gluons and reconstructing themselves with a unified mission: to produce a perfect tone. I noodled for another five minutes, found a simple three-note melody, and repeated it, now convinced that some long-dormant past-life musicianship had been unshackled.

Since that first long tone, I've been in the throes of an infatuation that grows deeper day by day. The object of the only obsession that has exceeded this one is now the mother of my children. Perhaps you've experienced the feeling: there's a primitive recognition, it's all so deeply familiar. *I know you, this is not new, we go way back.*

In the two years since my conversion, I've come a long way toward understanding why Adolphe Sax's extraordinary creation, the most recent important musical instrument to have been invented, was so quickly embraced by the world, why millions of players and listeners have so willingly submitted to its spell—and why so many others, frightened by its diabolical charm, have tried throughout its short history to malign or suppress it. After an innocent first kiss—a perfect long tone, say—its mysterious energy envelops and overwhelms you. You enter into some strange unwritten devotional contract, helplessly announce your allegiance to the cult of Adolphe, and become a loyal advocate for the voice of Sax.

You become, you could say, an instrument of the devil.

He's tall, wears a cowboy hat and a scowl, clearly miffed by the intrusion as he lowers a long fluorescent bulb—a light that detects leaks—down the tube of an old saxophone in his dingy second-floor rental and repair shop on West Forty-eighth Street. Why the hell do I want to rent a saxophone?

I expected this to be a more joyful event. A couple of days ago, my son's guitar teacher called and recommended a teacher, Michel Gohler, who has agreed to give me lessons. After talking for an hour or so on the phone, Michel convinced me that I should learn on the big, ballsy tenor. So here I am on New York's famous Music Row, looking for an instrument I can rent for a while before buying one of my own.

But the man in the cowboy hat couldn't be more discouraging. Without looking up, he points toward a row of student models hanging on a wall. Nestled among the slinky glistening horns, apparently mounted there as a deterrent to misguided beginners like me, is a picture of a strung-out Stan Getz holding a handgun outside a Los Angeles drugstore he's trying to rob. The saxophone has corrupted the souls of many who have fallen under its sway, but none more thoroughly than that of Getz, an alcoholic, drug addict, ex-con, tax dodger, wife beater, failed suicide (twice)—and a brilliant balladeer who had a tone, people used to say, you'd be happy to go home to. Before I can sign the lease for my Armstrong tenor, Mr. Cowboy Hat makes me listen to his Stan Getz story— a convoluted tale about his flying to California to tune up one of Stan's horns and their ending up in jail after Stan made lewd advances on a diner waitress who was married to the state trooper who just happened to be idling in his cruiser in the parking lot. This is a cautionary tale, he seems to imply. The saxophone can lead straight to a world of trouble and pain and constant sorrow. Look what happened to Getz. Look what happened to its inventor.

I. THE GHOST CHILD

He was known as *Le petit Sax, le revenant* (the ghost-child) to the citizens of his village, Dinant, in Belgium. After one of his many nearly fatal accidents, his mother lamented, "The child is doomed to suffer; he won't live." Almost before he could walk, little Adolphe Sax, christened Antoine Joseph in 1814, was fascinated with the alchemical magic performed every day in his father's workshop, where the most elemental materials were recombined into the finest brass, which was in turn fashioned into an exquisite musical instrument. Although Charles Joseph Sax, who had been appointed Belgium's chief instrument maker by William I of Orange, was eager to pass on his skills to his firstborn son, agents of misfortune conspired relentlessly to remove the boy from the land of the living. When he was two Adolphe fell down a flight of stairs, smashed his head on a rock, and lay comatose for a week. A year later, toddling around his father's atelier, he mistook sulfate of zinc for milk, gulped it down, and nearly expired. Subsequent poisonings involved white lead, copper oxide, and arsenic. He swallowed a needle, burned himself severely on a stove, and was badly scorched again by exploding gunpowder, which blew him across the workshop floor. He was again rendered comatose by a heavy slate tile that dislodged from a roof and landed on his head. When he was ten, a villager happened to spot the drowning lad when, after falling into a river, he was eddying, facedown and unconscious, in a whirlpool above a miller's gate. The villager just managed to pluck him from the water. Before he entered adolescence, his head was scarred by the repeated blows, and one side of his body was badly disfigured by burns.

But his misadventures proved instructive, hardening him for the nasty battles that would plague him as he tried to launch an ingenious musical invention, a serpentine horn whose provenance he secured by naming it after himself. From the moment his lips first touched his saxophone prototype, Adolphe Sax would face a juggernaut of slander, theft, litigation, forced bankruptcies, and attempts on his life that tried to suppress his new sound, a sound never before heard in nature, a sound that promised to change the timbre and soul of music wherever it was played.

By 1842, the twenty-eight-year-old Adolphe Sax was widely recognized as one of the world's top acoustical craftsmen. Far more skilled and ambitious than his brilliant father, he set out on a late-winter day from Brussels for Paris, then the musical-instrument manufacturing center of the world. In addition to his personal belongings, he carried with him an enormous brass horn, almost as tall as he, that he had fabricated in his father's workshop, where he had thrived after surviving his calamitous childhood. It was the most recent creation of his already remarkable career. At fifteen he had fabricated a clarinet and two flutes from ivory, considered exquisite specimens by judges at the 1830 Brussels Industrial Exposition. Before he was twenty he had created a new fingering system on the soprano clarinet and reinvented the bass clarinet, transforming the unreliable and mostly unplayable instrument into a regal, elegant woodwind that provided a rich bottom to any instrumental configuration and, remarkably, played in tune. The newly rehabilitated instrument had quickly been adopted as a standard member of the woodwind group and its inventor acknowledged as an engineer of great promise in the musical capitals of Europe.

Despite his success, Sax was feeling grossly maligned and unappreciated. For several years the judges of the Belgian national exhibition had refused to grant him the first prize for his innovations, reasoning that though the precocious designer may have deserved them, were he to receive the exhibition's highest honors at such a young age, he would have nothing else to aspire to. The year before, in 1841, Sax had prepared to submit for review his new bass horn, the as-yet-unnamed saxophone, the first in a proposed family of seven that would reconfigure the sonic organization of military and symphonic orchestras. After glimpsing the instrument—a brass-and-reed hybrid that joined the body of an ophicleide, a sinuous conical horn, with a clarinet-style mouthpiece—the first wholly new one to emerge since the clarinet had been invented a hundred years before, a jealous competitor apparently booted it across the floor, damaging it so badly it was unfit for exhibition. Disappointed and disgusted, Sax had packed his belongings, carefully wrapped up his mangled creation, and fled Brussels. When he arrived in Paris he had thirty francs in his pocket.

It was the first of many attempts to suppress this intrusive latecomer, this interloper, which, unlike wind instruments with ancient roots, could trace its lineage only as far as the revolutionary design specifications of a visionary acoustical scientist. Like every subsequent injunction over the next century against the saxophone and its "carnal," "voluptuous" sound—by heads of state, local police, educators, symphonic conductors, film censors, and a host of other moral arbiters, including the Vatican—it failed.

Brash, arrogant, handsome, with a lush, full beard and bedroom eyes, Adolphe Sax was the embodiment of the fiery nineteenth-century Romantic. Enormously self-confident—"In life there are conquerors and the conquered; I most prefer to be among the first," he often said—Sax was sure that his invention would have profound and everlasting repercussions for music and its practitioners. A brief trip to Paris in the spring of 1839 had strengthened his conviction; the well-regarded composers François-Antoine Habeneck, Giacomo Meyerbeer, and Jacques Fromental Halévy, to whom he had shown the new bass clarinet and a few of his retooled brass instruments, praised him lavishly during his visit. Sax was convinced he would find a learned and appreciative audience in the salons and conservatories of France and receive the recognition he had been denied in Brussels.

Paris represented a fresh start in other ways, too. As a young man, Sax had shown a remarkable ability to develop enemies. Not long after he reinvented the bass clarinet, a jealous artist at the Brussels Grande Harmonie declared he would quit the orchestra if it adopted the new instrument by the designer, who was also a highly talented musician. Sax challenged him to a musical duel—a strategy he deployed frequently with his critics. In his adopted city of Paris, he decided on a new tack. He invited the composer Hector Berlioz, who wrote a feuilleton for the highbrow *Journal des débats*, to review his instruments, including the improved clarinets and the prototype for his new bass horn. On June 12, 1842, Berlioz devoted much of his column to Sax, "a man of lucid mind, far-seeing, tenacious, steadfast and skilled beyond words." He called the new instrument *le Saxophon*, an eponym the egomaniacal young genius wholly endorsed, and predicted the instrument would "meet with the support of all friends of music." Attempting to describe the unique effects the horn has on the human ear, Berlioz wrote elsewhere, "It cries, sighs and dreams. It possesses a crescendo and can gradually diminish its sound until it is only an echo of an echo of an echo—until its sound becomes crepuscular." In another article, he said, "The timbre of the saxophone has something vexing and sad about it in the high register; the low notes to the contrary are of a grandiose nature, one could say pontifical. For works of a mysterious and solemn character, the saxophone is, in my mind, the most beautiful low voice known to this day."

Other composers echoed the praise, even though they had heard the instrument before it underwent its final refinements. The opera composer Gioacchino Rossini declared that "it produced the finest blending of sound that I have met with." Claude Lavoix described its "particular color of sadness and resignation." A couple of months after Sax arrived in Paris, Fromental Halévy exhorted him, "Hurry and finish your new family of instruments and come and succour to the poor composers that are looking for something new and to the public that is demanding it, if not to the world itself." By 1843, Sax had put the final touches on his first prototype, a B-flat bass with a main body that was still shaped like an ophicleide.

The bombastic Berlioz, perhaps recognizing a kindred spirit in his feisty, irritable new friend, helped promote the instrument in every way he knew how. He scored his *Chant Sacre* for an ensemble of Sax's instruments, including the B-flat bass saxophone. In early 1844 the work was performed as *Hymne pour les instruments de Sax* at the Salle Herz, with Sax playing his bass prototype in what was probably the first public performance of the colossal new instrument. Later that year, Georges Kastner used the saxophone, this time a bass in C, in his biblical opera *The Last King of Juda*, performed at the Paris Conservatory, its only performance ever.

Sax also wooed French royalty. A conservatory student for much of his youth, Sax could play, and play well, virtually every woodwind and brass instrument. At the Paris Industrial Exhibition in 1844, he kept his invention hidden from view (because it was not yet patented, he was then calling it a contrabass clarinet), quietly reveal-ing it to only a few trusted acquaintances. One of them was Lieu-tenant General Comte de Rumigny, the king's aide-de-camp, who arranged a showcase for Sax and a quartet of musicians before King Louis Philippe, Queen Marie Amélie, and two of their sons at court.

Sax envisioned a major role for his new family of instruments in both the symphonic orchestra and military bands. As an acoustical technician and player, he was aware of the tonal disparity between the winds and the strings. In an orchestra, the strings were often overwhelmed by the woodwinds, which in turn were overpowered by the brasses. His saxophone, originally called an ophicleide *à bec* (that is, an ophicleide with a clarinet-like mouthpiece instead of the customary cup mouthpiece), harmonically fused the traits of all three instrumental groups into one. By joining reed and mouthpiece to the metal tube of the ophicleide, a large, conical brass instrument that was the most widely used bass horn of the day and was the forerunner of the tuba, Sax had created an instrument with the tonal qualities of the woodwinds, the projection of the brasses, and the flexibility of the strings. As a family within an orchestra—Sax envisioned the seven members as ranging from the tiny sopranino to the monstrous contrabass—the saxophones would be able to pass along the melodic line as smoothly as the members of a string quartet or the voices of a choir. (The lowest-sounding pitch on the E-flat contrabass, D-flat, is a third, or four keys, from the lowest pitch on the modern, 88-key piano. The highest-sounding pitch on the E-flat sopranino, A-flat, is an octave and a third, or fifteen keys, below the piano's top note.) Each horn was designed with the same fingering system, which allowed a musician to play all of them with only slight changes in his embouchure. The saxophones also overblew by a perfect octave, as opposed to the clarinet's more complicated twelfth. This meant that by pressing an octave key, a musician could play a scale in the first and second octaves using virtually the same fingering. The efficient harmonic design of the instrument permitted vastly simplified notation.

Sax wisely perceived an opportunity to launch the production of his player-friendly new instruments: he would persuade French military officials to include them, as well as brass instruments he had improved, in their regimental bands. In the early nineteenth century, France's military bands, which refused to hire professional players and were poorly subsidized, were humbled by the proud and noble ensembles of Prussia and Austria. After Poland and Austria repelled the last Ottoman invasion in the late seventeenth century, the victors seized complete sets of instruments from the mehter, the rousing janissary bands that accompanied the campaign songs of the Turkish armies as they strode from one bloody battle to the next. Spicing up their Western instrumentation with the exotic additions—mostly percussion instruments like cymbals and bells, but also the yiragh, a form of oboe, and the bur, a piercing horn—the Europeans formed their own versions of janissary bands, which became famous for their ability to whip fighting regiments into a patriotic froth. The slack French bands, however, suffered poorly in comparison. According to an article in *L'Illustration*, "Whoever heard an Austrian or Prussian band surely broke into laughter upon hearing a French regimental band."

Beyond the lassitude of its members, the military orchestra, in Sax's analysis, suffered from a variety of problems that could be remedied by the introduction of saxophones and reworked and improved brass instruments, most prominently his saxhorns. In addition to making them sound better, Sax designed his saxhorns and the smaller saxotrombas (throughout his life, the possessive Sax attached his name to everything he invented or redesigned) so that a soldier could play one while riding a horse. The horn could be held under the left elbow while the left hand held all four regulation reins. The right hand was free to work the valves; the instrument's vertical design protected it from the horse's head.

At the urging of his friend Lieutenant General de Rumigny, Sax sent a long letter to the French war minister in 1844 proposing a reorganization of the country's military bands. The high-pitched piccolos and clarinets and oboes, and the instruments used to carry the bass lines—the bassoons and ophicleides—were not suited to open-air performances, he argued. They were fair-weather instruments; rain rendered most of them unplayable. And many of the intermediary instruments were lost amid the competing sounds. He suggested a solution: the introduction of his new saxhorns—a family of bugles with piston valves—and, of course, his booming bass saxophones.

Virtually no one connected to the military bands—musicians, instrument makers, conductors, military brass—favored the proposed reforms of the Belgian, whom they regarded as an opportunistic interloper. The cliquish Parisian instrument makers argued loudly against the saxophone, which threatened the way they did business. As the industrial revolution progressed, they relied increasingly on artisans in outlying villages to provide interchangeable parts to be assembled and packaged in Paris. Though a boon to all involved, the process tended to stifle innovation. Advances in design tended to come from bright young upstarts, such as Adolphe Sax, who made all the parts for their own instruments. His saxophone threatened to cut the parts suppliers out of the production chain.

But Sax had developed enough influential friends, most significantly Lieutenant General de Rumigny, to force the naming of a commission to decide the matter. Michele Carafa, the director of the Gymnase de Musique Militaire, which trained most of the army's musicians, had also proposed reforming the bands, simply by adding more conventional instruments. To decide the matter, the commission, made up of acoustical experts from the army and France's foremost composers, decided to take the issue to the people. It would hold an outdoor concert, a battle of the bands, and let popular opinion decide.

On April 22 the two rival groups gathered on the Champ de Mars, a drill ground next to the École Militaire (now the gardens surrounding the Eiffel Tower), surrounded by more than 20,000 music-loving Parisians. Both Carafa and Sax had proposed bands of forty-five players, but seven of Sax's musicians had been bribed not to show up, including the two bass saxophonists. But Sax, who loved a pitched battle and was never so dangerous as when infuriated, strapped two instruments to his side, including, some historians believe, his B-flat bass saxophone. Each band was to play a piece selected by the commission in addition to one of its own choosing. But after the first round had been completed, the crowd erupted, overwhelmingly favoring Sax's band and demanding more. His ensemble, though 20 percent lighter than the competition, projected its sound throughout the assembled crowd, while the sound Carafa's group produced faded after only a short distance. The members of the commission agreed that Sax's new configuration, featuring his bold new and reworked instruments, was far superior to the old.

Sax was the talk of Paris for days. The prospect of reform within the louche and pathetic military bands excited great national pride. In September the commission issued its report: it recommended the inclusion of Sax's baritone and bass saxophones and his resonant sax-horns. Within months, regimental bands organized according to Sax's system were winning first prizes in contests. Even proud Prussia asked Sax to undertake a reform of its regimental bands. Sax had finally achieved his consecration.

And the saxophone received a quick launch. The Belgian's sax-horns were most responsible for his victory on the Champ de Mars, but it was his unusual new instrument with the serpentine shape, elaborate fingerboard, and distinct new sound that went on to capture the public's imagination. Sax won his patent for the instrument in 1846; his application listed eight members of the family, ranging from "*bourdon*," a subcontrabass, to the high soprano "*sur aigu*" ("above acute"), a piccolo instrument an octave above the soprano.*

---

*Painstaking investigations by Robert Howe, a collector of vintage instruments and an organologist (and a gynecologist by day), have revealed that Sax's early models were shaped like ophicleides. In 1845, probably in response to one of the many challenges to his patent, he altered the instrument's shape into the saxophone form. Howe has also found that by the time Sax was granted his patent in 1846, his "family" of saxophones was still something of a pipe dream. In a document summarizing his research, Howe writes, "This patent is often misinterpreted to show that Sax had invented a complete family of saxophones. Rather, it suggests eight *potential* species of saxophones having similar bore dimensions, fingerings, and tonal characteristics." They are the bass in C or B♭; E♭ baritone (in his patent, Sax called it an E♭ tenor); subcontrabass; B♭ tenor; E♭ alto; B♭ soprano; E♭ sopranino, and the soprano *sur aigu* (above acute). However, the designs for all but the bass and baritone are so different from the actual instruments—the tenor and alto had triply curved necks, for instance—that it's unlikely they actually existed at the time of the patent. Sax eventually introduced the alto, soprano, tenor, sopranino, and contrabass saxophones (he never built a subcontrabass, or *bourdon*, although others have) between 1848 and 1855. Parallel families of band and orchestral saxophones were envisioned but proved redundant, as the instrument is fluent in most keys. The *sur aigu*, a whole octave above the soprano, never made

By then, the E-flat baritone was the ascendant instrument, and it was quickly adopted into Italian, Spanish, and Hungarian military bands, bringing it instant international exposure. Within just a few years it was deploying its powers of seduction on every continent in the world. Everywhere it landed, it was recognized as the sound of modernity and independence—an instrument that gave voice to the common man, whose creative spirit was being stifled by the depersonalizing forces of the industrial revolution. In almost every new musical idiom that would emerge over the next century and a half, whether bebop, merengue, rhythm and blues, or rock, and even when the instrument was introduced to cultures whose musical traditions had been established for hundreds of years, the saxophone would assert its dominance, romancing and beguiling millions of new players on its way to becoming the most popular woodwind in the world.

For all its brilliance, and despite its almost instantaneous impact on the world's music, the saxophone was never kind to its creator. After winning a contract from the French military and receiving an infusion of cash from investors, Sax hired and trained a crew and began production of his horns in Paris. Almost immediately his competitors, now facing substantial losses of revenue, formed a coalition, the Association of United Instrument Makers, replete with president, treasurer, and a dues-paying membership, to ensure that Sax spent much of his working day challenging their specious claims in court. They sued him for patent infringement, asserting that his new instrument was a copy of many others. They supported their accusations by producing a saxophone from which they'd erased Sax's proprietary engravings and serial numbers and

---

it to production, and the only modern equivalents are a few custom-made horns from the German instrument maker Benedikt Eppelsheim (who has also built a monstrous subcontrabass saxophone).

on which they'd inscribed their own. In response to the attacks, Sax slightly altered the shape of his instrument, changing it from its original ophicleide shape to the form of the modern saxophone.

His opponents schemed to undermine him financially: after Sax sold stock in his company, they bought much of it and resold it at half the price, hoping to scare away other investors. They even resorted to stirring up jingoistic pride by inflaming the Germans, who were always looking for an excuse to express their hostility toward the French. The instrument makers' association duped the eminent German producer Wilhelm Wieprecht to challenge Sax regarding the authenticity of his invention. Although he'd never actually seen it, Wieprecht wrote to Sax, he had been persuaded (perhaps a victim of his own pride) that the saxophone was a shameless imitation of his superior bathyphone, a swollen, squawking bass horn that would go on to have a mercifully short life. Both parties, and their outraged supernumeraries, were duly offended by the accusations and both demanded satisfaction.

The issue was settled in Germany just a few months after Sax's victory on the Champ de Mars. In July 1845 many eminent musicians and composers gathered in Bonn to honor Ludwig van Beethoven, who had died in poverty two decades before. At a kind of high summit meeting in Coblenz, attended by Franz Liszt, the two craftsmen presented their instruments to each other. Sax handed Wieprecht a saxophone and invited him to play. Not only could Wieprecht produce no sound from the horn, he admitted it was a complete mystery to him. The only thing the bathyphone shared with Sax's invention was its aspiration to gain a seat in the conventional symphonic orchestra, a goal that the saxophone, despite its enormous worldwide popularity, has yet to achieve.

In a measure of the saxophone's ability to stir controversy—a talent it would reveal repeatedly over the ensuing century—the intrigues worked their way into the highest offices of government. In 1848, when Sax's benefactor, King Louis Philippe, was deposed, one of the first orders of the new republic was to remove saxophones, as well as all other Sax-built instruments, from military bands. In 1852, when Napoleon III overthrew the Second Republic and seized dictatorial powers, the first law he passed, two days after he took power, restored saxophones to the army's ensembles.

Meanwhile, the lawsuits brought by the well-funded Association of United Instrument Makers, which fittingly had its offices at 11, rue Serpent, continued to hobble Sax. His enemies deployed covert strategies as well. Sax's plans and special tools were stolen, his instruments counterfeited, and his employees bribed to abandon his service at crucial points in the production process. A mysterious fire destroyed his workshop. Some of these efforts were less subtle: thanks to a faulty fuse, Sax's life was spared when a bomb that had been placed under his bed exploded prematurely. He escaped assassination again when a loyal and trusted employee of similar height and build arrived unexpectedly one night at Sax's house after midnight. Mistaken for his boss, who was not home, the employee was fatally stabbed through the heart.

In 1853 the mysterious good fortune that had repeatedly rescued young Adolphe from the catastrophes of his childhood and blunted the attempts on his life by his enemies again exerted its influence. At the height of his battles with rival instrument makers, a hard, dark spot appeared on Sax's lower lip. Five years later, the cancerous tumor, which resisted all treatments, had grown to a grotesque size. Eating had become impossible. Sax, fed through a tube, had to decide between surgery, which would leave him hideously disfigured, or slow suffocation. From the medical underworld emerged an Indian doctor, a man formally called Dr. Vries but better known as *le docteur noir* because of the color of his skin (and, perhaps, his otherworldly associations), who treated him with secret herbal extractions from the subcontinent. Six months after the first treatment, in early 1859, the enormous tumor started to shrink. By the following February it had disappeared completely.

———

The cancer, legal assaults, and suspicious fires—not to mention the attempts on his life—exhausted him physically and financially. Sax was forced to declare bankruptcy in 1852, 1873, and finally 1877, when he turned over his declining factory to his sons and sold off his collection of nearly 500 rare instruments and handmade tools. By then his protective patents had long since expired and several other manufacturers were producing saxophones.

But the euphonious genie had been set loose upon the world. Its adoption into the military bands of neighboring countries ensured broad exposure; by the mid-1850s the saxophone had made its way to Belgium, England, Italy, Portugal, Russia, Spain, Switzerland, Turkey, and the United States, where Henri Wuille demonstrated the instrument, which he called the corno musa (or bagpipe). In 1847, Sax began teaching the instrument at the Gymnase Musical; a few years later, Georges Kastner, a minor composer and friend, wrote a method book for it. Sax commissioned repertoire—slight, light-hearted pieces that showed off the instrument's versatility, as well as transcriptions of classical pieces from eighteenth-century masters. Composers, at first baffled about how to use it, began including it in new scores.*

Not surprisingly, the bizarre new instrument with the unusual sound and impressive fingerboard architecture attracted some quirky early proponents who quickly capitalized on its potential as a novelty. One was Charles Jean-Baptiste Soualle, who was born in Ares, studied at the Paris Conservatory, where he won a first prize in 1844, and became director of the Marine Musical Troops of Senegal. A clarinetist, Soualle took refuge in England when Louis Philippe was deposed in 1849 (and the decree of 1844 admitting Sax's instruments to regimental bands was repealed) and studied the saxophone. He made a few adjustments to the instrument—most importantly, he fabri-

*On his autograph, or handwritten, score, Berlioz, Sax's great fan, included two blank staves, intended for E-flat and B-flat saxophones, in the last movement of *The Damnation of Faust*, but that was as close as he came to writing an original composition for the instrument.

cated a single octave key that replaced two separate octave keys, anticipating a design change that would become permanent forty years later. He renamed the modified instrument the turcophone, which reviewers said was capable of producing a sound "soft and suave." Occasionally, Soualle, a master of self-promotion, called the instrument the zouave.

In 1850, Soualle, a large man with fierce dark eyes, began touring the capitals of Europe with his soprano and alto turcophones, then wandered through Australia, New Zealand, Manila, Java, Canton, Macau, Shanghai, and Calcutta, showing off his mysterious instrument to enchanted listeners, who often attributed spiritual power to it. He settled in Radjah, India, where he converted to Islam and, because of his bewitching abilities on his clever new horns, was named the area's musical director. Now known as Ali Ben Soualle, the adventurer took his show back on the road—he had written forty compositions for his turcophones—and played to audiences in Isle Morris, Reunion, Cape of Good Hope, and Cape Natal before returning to Mysore, India, where he was awarded the title Chevalier de Mysore. As it had years earlier in Paris, revolution forced him to flee India in 1858; the Muslim turcophonist returned to Paris, where the royal family, headed by Napoleon III, had been reinstated.

Another clarinetist, Edward A. Lefebre, saw an opportunity to capitalize on the novelty instrument. The son of the owner of a musical-instrument store in Holland, Lefebre met Adolphe Sax in Paris, was apparently rendered spellbound by both instrument and inventor, and vowed that he would make it his life's mission to promote the saxophone's sound around the world. He traveled to Cape Town in 1859, where he set up a music store, introduced the saxophone to South African dignitaries, most of whom were Dutch, and sold the horn to music-loving merchant seamen on their way to the Far East.* After moving back to Holland for a few years, he took a job in London as a saxophonist in a sixty-two-piece orchestra. He then joined the Parepa

*A soprano cost about $40, the alto, tenor, and baritone about $50.

Rosa Opera Company, which brought him to America, where, start-ing in 1873, he found fame as the Saxophone King, first with the hugely popular Patrick Gilmore band, the country's premier concert band, which had just introduced a saxophone quartet to its ensemble, and later as a soloist. Over the course of his career, Lefebre transcribed about a hundred well-known pieces for solo saxophone and quartet and performed thousands of times across America and Canada.

Thanks to French military bands, which accompanied troops wherever they were posted, saxophones premiered in Mexico in the early 1860s and quickly migrated into new territory. In fact, the first saxophonist to take up residence in New Orleans is thought to have been a Mexican, Florencio Ramos, a former member of the Eighth Cavalry Mexican Band, which played at the World's Industrial and Cotton Centennial Exposition in New Orleans in 1884 and broke up soon thereafter. Many of the defectors became members of the city's first jazz generation and had a strong south-of-the-border in-fluence on the emerging polyglot idiom. (For instance, pizzicato, the plucking method of playing the string bass, had been incorporated into popular music by Mexicans, and it became the accepted tech-nique for jazz bassists. And the popular "Sobre las Olas" [Over the Waves] by Juventino Rosas was adopted as a standard in New Or-leans jazz performances, even though it was a waltz.) By the turn of the century, the saxophone could be heard in every urban center in America. It was strategically positioned to play a leading role in the radical new musical idioms to come.

Near the end of his life, which sadly guttered out in 1894, Adolphe Sax launched a final attack against his rivals, publishing an apologia of his life in the journal *Le Musique de Familles*. Alternately despon-dent and blustering, the inventor felt it necessary to provide a last ac-count of the many injustices he had suffered at the hands of his litigious and murderous enemies, many of whom were now dead. Appealing to the public, "this great avenger of just causes . . . from whom a sympathetic gesture has often sufficed to hasten justice too slow in coming," Sax boasted that "before me, I am proud to say, the musical instrument industry was nothing, or next to nothing, in France. I created this industry; I carried it to an unrivaled height: I developed the legions of workers and musicians, and it is above all my counterfeiters who have profited from my work." Despite being "blessed by the moral satisfaction my work has brought me," he admitted to having been brought low by "the scandalous role of the counterfeiters united against me, who have had sufficient means—as the debates have always proven—to ruin me." He concluded his *appel au publique* by begging the government for a regular stipend so that he would be able to "give myself a few hours of peace in a life consumed by trouble." Impoverished and depressed, the inventor whose grandiose visions had motivated him for a lifetime now wished only to be freed of the worry about where his next meal would come from.

It was a sad ending for a proud man who, despite all the legal hassles, bankruptcies, and attacks on his character and body, somehow remained a prolific producer of brass instruments and improved the design of virtually every woodwind in use today. Between 1843 and 1860, he and his workers made more than 18,000 pieces, 945 of which were saxophones.* In 1851 alone he exhibited eighty-five instruments at the Industrial Exhibition of London. By then his saxophone family had grown to include five members—bass, baritone, tenor, alto, and soprano. Although he had fabricated prototypes of a sopranino and a contrabass, they never made it into production.† Sax

---

*About 170 saxophones made during Sax's working years have survived. The earliest is an E♭ baritone made in 1848; the earliest surviving bass saxophone was made in 1868. Robert Howe believes that the dearth of surviving bass and baritone saxophones can be blamed on the Franco-Prussian War and the two world wars, fought in France: "Large old saxophones would be tempting sources of scrap metal."

†According to Howe, Berlioz, in his 1855 revision of *Grand traité d'instrumentation et d'orchestration modernes*, notes the existence of six voices of saxophone (the sixth being sopranino) in eleven species, "repeating the half-truth that the species were made in pairs pitched in E♭/F or B♭/C." While Sax did create altos in F and sopranos, tenors, and basses in C, Howe says, he apparently abandoned the idea of creating the "orchestral" family in C and F, deciding that it was redundant.

apparently decided that the need for the lower orchestral bass voices was met by deep saxhorns and tubas and by the new sarrusophone, essentially a bass saxophone with a double reed. The instrument was developed in 1854 by Pierre Louis Gautrot, a lifelong enemy of Sax, whom Sax, characteristically, sued for patent infringement.

Sax's creative talents transcended instrument making. By 1894, the year of his death, when he was living off the small pension he had been granted after his *appel au publique* and laboring as a stage manager at the Paris Opera House, he had been granted thirty-five patents. Some had practical applications, some were spectacular fantasies, and the rest appeared to be the musings of a deranged mind. He invented devices to reflect and correct sound. Intrigued by the parabola—the parabolic shape of the saxophone bore was the most distinctive feature of Sax's patent application—he envisioned parabolic music halls that offered a perfect acoustical experience to every member of the audience. He designed a device that achieved "an improvement of the whistle-signal of railway engines." He also invented the Goudronnier Sax, a fumigation box that infused the air of a room with the scent of tar or antiseptics, several of which were ordered by Louis Pasteur.

Sax designed a number of hybrid instruments and was often mocked in cartoons for the huge size of his musical inventions. The ribbing only motivated him to magnify his already grandiose visions. He threatened to design an instrument "with the diameter of the Colonne de Juillet [the bronze column on the place de la Bastille]," which he planned to call the Saxontonnerre (Sax-thunder). He drew up plans for a giant organ, to be erected on a hillside and powered by a locomotive steam engine, that he could use to play the music of Meyerbeer for all of Paris. The *Revue Gazette Musicale de Paris* said the instrument was "operated by vibrating blades, submitted to a pressure of four or five atmospheres. The blades are really huge steel bars, vibrating under high pressure." Sax's friend, Berlioz, deploying the era's Romantic hyperbole, declared that the monstrosity would "sing from the top of the highest towers the joys and the sorrows of a metropolis, immersing the whole populace in its harmonies."

In one of his apocalyptic moods, Sax conceived of a giant mortar bullet, eleven yards wide and weighing 550 tons, that could level an entire city. An admirer promised that the missile would "tear apart, smash entire walls, ruin fortifications, explode mines, blow up powerhouses—in a word, exert an irresistible devastation in a wide range, not to mention the horrible fright this explosion would provoke."

It's likely that when dreaming up the device that would launch this monstrous agent of destruction, which he called the Saxocannon, the eccentric inventor kept his lifelong antagonists, the Association of United Instrument Makers, firmly in his imaginary sights.

2. ANARCHISTE DE DROITE

The broad doors of the maisonette on rue du Mulhouse swing open, and there, with arms wide and a big grin, is the great Jean-Marie Londeix, recitalist, historian, teacher, and one of the twentieth century's most energetic missionaries of the "concert" saxophone. "Bonjour, bonjour," says Jean-Marie. "Welcome to Bordeaux." He seems profoundly delighted, as though he has discovered that an old friend, long missing and presumed dead, has found his way to his doorstep. A spry seventy-two years old, with crenellated gray hair, sparkling eyes, and a muscular face articulated by decades of embouchure training, he bounds across the marble foyer and directs me to an overstuffed chair looking out onto his small garden, an overgrown tangle of vines and flowers now in retreat from the impending winter. Almost before I get settled, he produces cheese, chocolate, and a sweetly fragrant but deceptively potent liqueur he has distilled from the fruit of an orange tree in the rear courtyard. For himself he chooses a nip of Scotch. "I love the whiskey," he says. It's not quite 11 a.m.

Jean-Marie, who gave his farewell performance in 1994 and hasn't picked up the horn since, has spent the intervening years contemplating and researching the complicated life of Adolphe Sax and his invention. His quest has taken him deep into the matrices of Sax's fervid brain and made him something of an expert on musical anthropology and nineteenth-century French political history. In trying to locate the source of the "voice of Sax," it's even left him probing the realm of the supernatural for answers.

In his youth, Jean-Marie underwent a rigorous musical education, first learning and practicing solfège, the torturous vocal exercise that hones both sight-reading and singing, or "sight-singing." One of six children from a musical family in Port-du-Noyer, a village along the Dordogne not far from Bordeaux, he was given a saxophone when he was eight by his father, Jems, an amateur gymnast and violinist who played accompaniments to silent films. His athletic training had convinced the elder Londeix that there was no substitute for practice and discipline. Accordingly, each of his children practiced his instrument three hours a day, often under his supervision. He also had some unusual ideas about how to perfect technique. After observing a lesson in which Jean-Marie was instructed to take in less mouthpiece, Jems constructed a ligature (which attaches the reed to the mouthpiece) ringed with sharp pins that delivered a prickly, painful reminder whenever the young student failed to heed his teacher's advice. "Some teachers say, Okay, we work for one month, two month, to change the embouchure," says Londeix with an excited, high-pitched laugh. "My father says, Okay, puts the pins in, and . . . Voilà! In three days he change my embouchure!"

Londeix began studying with Marcel Mule ("a good player, but not a good teacher—and a bad musician") in Bordeaux when he was fifteen. Over the next fifty years, he performed more than 600 engagements around the world, recorded extensively, exhaustively indexed new and old repertoire (*150 Years of Music for Saxophone*), wrote many volumes of pedagogical method and exercise books, penned hundreds of essays on the history of particular compositions, and became a magnet for international students in his lively class at the Bordeaux Conservatory. He continues to document newly published music for the saxophone and has become its unofficial repository. In the 1990s alone, he annotated nearly 6,000 new pieces, convincing him that more music is being written for saxophone today than for any other instrument.

Over the last twenty years of his career, unhappy with the quality and volume of the "classical" saxophone repertoire, he devoted his efforts to premiering new music, 200 pieces in all, much of which explored extended techniques,* and helped promote the growth of the modern Bordelais school of saxophone composition. For his farewell concert, he premiered *Steady Study on the Boogie*, a highly complex piece by the Bordeaux composer Christian Lauba. Often harshly dissonant, using extreme ranges of dynamics, the piece showed off the saxophone's extraordinary vocabulary—multiphonics, microtones, air noises, timbre trills, grunts, barks, moans, freight-train roars, the muffled drone of the deep sea, the background whine of the cosmos—and was exceedingly difficult to master. Londeix practiced for months, played the piece once, then tucked away his alto, a Selmer Mark VI, in a closet. "The timbre of the saxophone is achieved only with great attention," he explains. "To obtain this it's necessary to have good muscles and practice very much. I refuse now to work three hours every day to achieve the attack, the *sound.* I do another job."

Part of that job is to reconcile the saxophone's many inherent contradictions. Why does this instrument, music's gifted but resentful bastard child, arouse such intense feeling among both fans and detractors? How can it be considered profane by some, and sacred by others? By what acoustical legerdemain is this imperfect cone of

---

*The natural range of the saxophone is two and a half octaves, but by using unconventional fingering and deploying a highly developed embouchure, players can extend that range by as much as another octave, into what's known as the altissimo range. *Extended techniques* also refers to the unconventional sounds, most of them nonmusical, that the saxophone can produce and that characterize modern or avant-garde compositions.

brass, impaled at one end by a sliver of cane, able to speak, like a child possessed by a thousand demons, with so many voices, evoking vixen seductiveness, ethereal calm, wrenching sorrow—all within a single musical passage? Whenever he has an insight, a lead, a new direction, Londeix is U-turned back to the instrument's volatile inventor. "When we understand the personality of Sax, we understand the personality of the saxophone," he muses, sipping his whiskey. "Is very strange, very strange, how this man and his instrument are the same. Even its name . . . the word means the 'voice of Sax.' But what is *that*?"

Like its inventor, the saxophone is ambitious, aggressive, insinuating, and contrarian. It encourages personal expression; because of its revolutionary acoustical design, everyone who puts a saxophone to his lips produces a unique sound—"the one thing," Coleman Hawkins once said, "nobody can take away from you." It's not surprising that within just a few years of its invention, it received a hearty embrace in America.

The two had much in common: like the saxophone, America was an invention with no precedent or history. Upon its arrival, the horn was adopted as the voice of the country's own fiercely independent spirit. It became a big hit in the patriotic wind bands of Patrick Gilmore and John Philip Sousa, a workhorse in vaudeville, the favored instrument in the home music-making movement of the early twentieth century, and a catalyst of the dance-band craze of the teens. In the decade following the Great War nearly a million saxophones were sold in America, a phenomenon then described as the "saxophone craze" and equaled since only by the popularity of the electric guitar in the late sixties. An entire city—Elkhart, Indiana—evolved to support the manufacturing and sale of the saxophone as it went on to become the most innovative instrument in jazz and the go-to instrument in rhythm and blues, rock and roll, Motown, funk, and soul music.

At the same time it was finding its voice in nineteenth-century America, it wafted across the Caribbean, playing a central role in the evolution of merengue—in which it performed timbral, melodic, and rhythmic functions—in the Dominican Republic. Later it would infiltrate spouge, a fusion of Jamaican ska and Trinidadian calypso that originated in Barbados. Meanwhile, in Jamaica aspiring saxophonists made their instruments from bamboo.

Capitalizing on its popularity, it piggybacked on the export of American music to distant corners of the world. A lively jazz scene on Jackson Street in Seattle in the early twentieth century, for instance, was largely responsible for producing a generation of fantastic Filipino saxophonists: the owners of Japanese ocean liners hired Filipino workers for the cruises between Seattle and Asia, and the laborers discovered a special affinity for the instrument, which they studied at Jackson Street speakeasies and practiced on board. The popularity of the instrument in the Philippines hasn't waned since.

In China, a love of the saxophone spread like a highly contagious virus. Russian refugees from the revolution established émigré communities in Shanghai, Harbin, and Beijing, where ten full-time jazz orchestras were firmly established by 1927. When he was seventeen, in the early thirties, Oleg Lundstrem, who grew up in Russia and sought refuge in China with his family, formed a six-piece band that has since become the longest continuously existing jazz orchestra in the history of the music. At the same time, Shanghai, the colonial port known for its cabaret and dance-hall culture, supported a small African-American jazz community and became known as a "Seventh Heaven for the jazz musician." All of this came to a crashing close in 1937, when the escalation of hostilities between Japan and China forced the communities to scatter. (Lundstrem took the trans-Siberian railroad from Harbin to Russia, where he was promptly arrested for playing jazz.) A half century later, in 1984, the Canadian recitalist Paul Brodie, on a tour of China, discovered a clique of saxophonists frozen in time— 100,000 of them, all of whom were eager to demonstrate their skills playing the music of Rudy Wiedoeft, the 1920s American vaudeville virtuoso, and accompanying the tepid arrangements of vintage dance-band leader Guy Lombardo.

In southern China, just before Lundstrem began jazzing the nightclubbers of Harbin, the saxophone penetrated a completely different idiom. In the 1920s it was adopted into the instrumental ensemble of the Cantonese opera community; it is still used extensively, especially in Hong Kong and Chinatowns around the world, to amplify librettos.

Meanwhile, the saxophone was also meandering through South America. In the twenties, the instrument was welcomed into the *orquestas típicas* of the Mantaro Valley in the central Andes of Peru by the mestizo peasantry of the region. A tradition of intense competition among the brass bands of the valley encouraged performers to seek greater volume and more color from their instruments—qualities the saxophone provided immediately. Its adoption was considered so significant that the legend surrounding its first appearance is passed from player to player: a well-known musician from the province of Jauja, Rojas Chucas, was given a saxophone by a "gringo" from the mining center of Cerro de Pasco. Rojas then tried the instrument in his orchestra and found that it "filled the vacuum."

The American military extended the saxophone's reach during World War II, often into seemingly unlikely cultures. The South Pacific island of Tonga, which the American army used as a staging area for battles in the Solomon Islands and New Guinea, is perhaps the most exotic example. The 147th Infantry regiment, stationed in Tongatapu, included a 28-man band, five of whom were saxophonists. In the saxophone, the islanders, who valued a musical quality they described as mellowness (*nqatuvai*), instantly recognized a familiar and much-revered sound, that of the nose flute. The ancient four-holed instrument, made from a joint of bamboo, is played by depressing the right nostril with the thumb and blowing through either end with the left. Historically, the instrument was used to *fanquqanqu*, to "arouse gradually or gently" from sleep a person of high rank. The saxophone perfectly satisfied the Tongan aesthetic of *nqatuvai,* a word first used to describe flowers that have faded but continue to provide a lingering scent and which is now applied to pleasing sounds as well. To provide mellowness to their brass bands, which the Tongans had inherited from European voyagers a century before, they installed saxophones.

The saxophone's ability to insinuate itself into the classical music of cultures whose traditional music predates the instrument by hundreds of years might be the most striking example of its flexibility. In India, Kadri Gopalnath, known as Saxophone Chakravarthy ("Emperor of the Saxophone"), has discovered the instrument's affinity for South Indian classical music. Samir Sourour has introduced the saxophone to Egypt's classical tradition, using it to provide timbral color and solo flourishes to urban orchestras. The demands on instrument and player are considerable, inasmuch as the Arab modal system, or *maqam*, recognizes twenty-four notes per octave, some of them non-Western notes called half-flats. Sourour manages the complex scales on the horn by combining cross-fingerings with changes in his embouchure—biting the reed or lipping up or down.

Virtually everywhere it's been heard, the saxophone sound has found a home—whether in Fela Anikulapo Kuti's West African Afrobeat or in gamelan, the highly percussive ceremonial music of Bali. Like an aural variation on the *Rashomon* story, everyone hears its sound as something different. But to every new convert it's also strangely familiar and personal, and once that sound gets inside their head, nobody, as Hawk says, can take it away from them. Even if they're not sure where it comes from.

"It's the sound of sex," Jean-Marie Londeix concludes as he refills my glass with a fragrant Corbières he has produced for our lunch, which we've been lingering over in his kitchen. "For me, the saxophone, where it comes from, is close to the sex—not the act, but the energy and power. The mistake of the classical saxophone players is not to recognize that. They make it something it isn't . . . *fweet, fweet,*

fweet." He flutters a hand in the air, mimicking the flight of a bird—
a sexless bird that sings only in its highest register.

For the past three hours we've been eating, drinking, laughing,
and somehow, despite my French, which is limited to being able to
ask for directions or order a croissant, and Jean-Marie's considerably
better but heavily accented English, understanding each other well.
Londeix is a natural, unhesitating performer. Exhibiting the genetic
endowment from his gymnast father, he frequently springs from his
chair to animate a point he is making and usually follows the athletic
outburst with a squeal of self-deprecating laughter. And he is a true
sensualist—many of his observations about life and art have eros,
"the sex," as their referent. For instance, at one point I tell him of my
dislike of saxophone "art" music, which just sounds like so much
noise to me. What does he find pleasing in it?

"The pleasure is not necessarily immediate," he explains. "We see
this in everyday life. Sometimes it's afterward that the pleasure is
better. In art and music, for me it is the same. In the act of love, you
have immediate physical pleasure, but it's short. Many times I say I
prefer to play a recital to making love, because two days later the
pleasure is still there, and may be still growing."

The saxophone—"a Dionysian instrument"—can trace its seductive power back to the Greeks, says Londeix. Greek mythology,
which connects nearly eighty characters with music and its effects—
Orpheus produces bewitchment, Amphion attraction, and Dio-
nysus a trance—accurately describes the temperamental nuances
among the aerophones, or wind instruments. "There is great difference between the Apollonian and Dionysiac horns," he says. "The
cylindrical instruments are Apollonian, the conical, like the saxophone, Dionysiac. On the cylindrical instruments, like the flute, the
timbre and emotional content of each note, from high to low, is always the same. Can you imagine a flute ever sounding sexy? Or a
Platonic instrument like the harp? But the saxophone . . ."

The saxophone has a complexity that is almost human, says Londeix, and not just because it has a concentration of harmonics at
around 200 hertz, the same as the human voice. "For me, it's a great

instrument because it's possible to sound very bad," he says. "This is not possible on the piano or flute, where if you hammer a string or blow a note, the quality is always the same. On the saxophone, you make a choice all the time, it's necessary to choose at the beginning of each note—shall I bend it in this direction or that? The characteristic of the human, too, a free and intelligent being, is it's possible to be the demon or the god, to choose between the bad and the good. So the saxophone becomes capable of expressing the most extreme aspects of the human condition. It can be coarse or it can be delicate, it can sound like a prostitute or a virgin. It's a mix of contradictions, just like a human." Only a few instruments are invested with such human qualities, he says, including the oboe (the alto of the family is called the oboe d'amore) and the ancient aulos, a double-chambered reed-blown conical pipe that was the instrument of orgiastic dances and of the Spartan army—an accompaniment to both loving and fighting. Many people would add to that group one of the Platonic instruments, the cello, to which the lower saxophones—the bass, baritone, and tenor—are often compared.

"Is it masculine or is it female?" Londeix muses. "The form, with its beautiful curves, is female. But when viewed from the side, it could also be an erection. Part of its appeal is that it's never clear what it is. Is it brass in front of sweet wood—male—or wood in the middle of brass—female? In the army, it's the more female instrument—wood softening brass. In jazz, it's both male and female. Its ambiguous sexuality is very modern."

The most enduring component of the saxophone's image and reputation—its rebellious, subversive nature—is clearly traceable to its inventor, says Jean-Marie. "Adolphe Sax was an anarchist," he says, "an *anarchiste de droite*, of the right. The right is the institution, and he was a member of it but always refused and contested it." He leaps up to illustrate, points to an imaginary institutional convention before him, then turns his back to it, crosses his arms, and stamps his foot. "No, no!" he says like a defiant child. He laughs, amused by his enactment, and returns to his seat.

An ideal of the true French revolutionary, Sax the anarchist never became a naturalized citizen of France, although at one of the peaks of his success—there were several highs and lows—he owned a large factory, employed hundreds of workers, and built a *maison particulier*, a huge mansion, along the Seine. Neither did he marry the mother of his five children—"Very, very rare for this time," says Londeix. Sax also refused to give his last name to his children, finally capitulating to convention when his oldest daughter planned to marry. "He was a great example of the anti-institutional Romantic. He was in the school of Delacroix, Madame de Staël, Goethe, Byron, and Victor Hugo. He wished to construct an organ in Montmartre so big it could play the music of Meyerbeer for all of Paris—that's typical of the Romantic."

Sax's idealism, though, did not always serve him well. He established a workshop in the Melun prison, near Paris, where he taught criminals how to make brass instruments so they would be able to find a job when they were released. After they were sprung, a couple of the ex-cons he had trained blackmailed Sax and stole instruments and tools from his factory.

Like its parent, the saxophone is filled with roiling contradictions, says Londeix. Somehow, despite worldwide popularity, it is still considered a marginal instrument. "Many, many people, when they hear the instrument, they think it cannot be for serious music," Londeix says. "It is like in the everyday life: immediately you see a beautiful woman, you imagine she cannot be intelligent or serious." At the height of his own career, Londeix encountered this bias repeatedly. In the late 1980s, the composer Olivier Messiaen agreed to write a piece for him. "I wait one year, two years—no composition. I write to him four times, no answer. Then he premieres a six-hour opera, *Saint François d'Assise*. There are over two hundred instruments in the piece from all round the world, but not a single saxophone. So I give up. Messiaen was very religious and believed the saxophone was representative of bad character. So he refuse it." Londeix links Messiaen's reluctance to a decree earlier in the century from the Vatican declaring the playing of the saxophone and other "profane" instruments in church to be "*interdict*."

"Everything we talk about the saxophone," says Londeix, "it's always about being on the margin, working its way in from the outside. It's on the margin of the orchestra, on the edge of polite society, on the fringe of serious music. It's a troublemaker and a nonconformist, which is why it represents opportunity and freedom to so many people and why it is the soul of nontraditional music. It stands opposed to the institution, just like the man who invented it."

True to its inventor's irascible spirit, the saxophone mixed it up in the social and political arenas as well. In addition to the snobbish longhairs who considered it too proletarian to be admitted to the symphonic orchestra, it had a variety of other detractors. Conservative religious leaders, desperately clinging to a besieged Victorian morality, considered it the symbol of all that was low and dirty, and it became an emblem of the genteel and not-so-genteel decadence that defined the Roaring Twenties. Sax himself first suggested the instrument's diabolical lineage: in a letter to his brother shortly before he died, he recounted a dream in which black devils were blowing his horn and summoning all the damned to the infernos of hell.

The Nazis banned the saxophone as a symbol of moral corruption and racial impurity—the sound of "Jew-Nigger music" and a form of *entartete Kunst*, or "degenerate" art. Both czarist and Communist Russian officials frequently banished saxophone players to Siberia. The Japanese, as part of a campaign to cleanse their culture of Western influence before World War II, limited the number of "lascivious" saxophones allowed in dance orchestras. In the 1950s, American censors demanded that the "carnal" sound of the saxophone be excised from some movie scores.

More happily, as a symbol of independence, the saxophone had an early presence in the women's rights movement, when countless all-female saxophone quartets organized in the teens. It also played a central role in the introduction of music education to American schools. It spawned a stylistic cool, beginning with Coleman Hawkins's natty threads, that has never gone out of style. The jazz dot or soul patch, the tuft of hair beneath the lower lip, is so common among "cats" who can play as to almost be considered a part of the saxophone embouchure.

And, of course, as Jean-Marie points out, the instrument provided the sound track for bedroom foreplay. In countless movies and television dramas, a few moaning, lilting bars in the score indicate that a sexual liaison, usually illicit, always hot, is only a seductive move or two away. Adolphe Sax the anarchist may have been surprised that his beloved invention became an instrument of love, and he may have been mystified by players who suggestively stroked their horns or writhed on their backs on stage or flaunted their "sexophone," as Don Byas called it, while walking the bar, which club owners insisted players do—even Hawkins and Parker and Coltrane—to arouse the female customers.

But if somewhere somebody was offended by it, Sax would probably have been pleased.

As our long, vinous afternoon draws to a close, I begin to understand why Jean-Marie Londeix is so passionate about the saxophone: as an advocate of experimental music, he, too, is on the margin. But I wonder: Does he love the saxophone because he is a revolutionary, or is he a revolutionary simply because he plays the saxophone? Is he with the institution or the marginal? "I say for the marginal to exist, there has to be the institution," he says. "If there is no institution, then no marginal. So bravo the institution!"

As he drives me to the train station, Jean-Marie delights in telling me one last story. In the late fifties, he played a concerto with the Strasbourg Philharmonic Orchestra. During the intermission a government minister sought out Londeix to express his admiration for the saxophonist's performance. "He says, 'Oh, bravo, fantastic,'" Jean-Marie remembers. "Then he leans forward and whispers so that no one else can hear and says, 'Me, too, I play the saxophone.'" Jean-Marie giggles, still relishing the absurdity of this confession. "Oh, what a *scandale* had I told the other ministers!"

Every lesson begins the same way. We place our tenors together and blow long tones. It's my favorite part of the evening. Bursts of brilliant color explode from the bells of our horns, painting the room with shimmering overtones, buzzing the pleasure centers in our heads.

Tonight the harmonic convergence is particularly pleasing because Michel Gohler, my teacher, has brought along his baritone saxophone. His forty-year-old Selmer, its brass tarnished a burnt orange, is the sumo of saxes. It's big, wide, and blocky, with a huge bell almost parallel to the neck. As we reach down for the low notes, the bari issues a deep, fertile blast, maybe what the universe sounded like during the first few howling seconds after creation. When Michel fingers the low E-flat, I can almost reach out and grab the lumbering sound waves.

Michel owns several saxophones (all Selmer Mark VIs), a clarinet, a flute, and an oboe—ten instruments in all. Each is of the finest quality, any three of them probably worth more than Michel, who lives in a tiny studio in Queens, New York, earns in a year. Single and in his mid-forties, with a full head of gray hair and dark bushy eyebrows that give him a lovable, raccoonish look, he's a typical New York professional musician— wondrously talented but woefully underemployed. He subs on Broadway shows, plays in a quartet—Sax in the City—that teaches city schoolkids about music, and every once in a while agrees to take on a student. When Michel and I first talked on the phone, I described to him that first ecstatic experience on Ortley's saxophone. He knew immediately what I meant. He had grown up in Montreal and received a formal music education, which required learning solfège, piano, and violin, before he gravitated to the saxophone. All through college he played in a variety of bands, then made it through two years of graduate school studying to be a psychologist before deciding to become a full-time musician. He couldn't put the instrument down.

During that initial conversation, I mentioned that I was interested in learning the instrument casually, just mastering a few licks and tricks so I could play with Dan, Craig, and Ortley, three old friends I've been jamming with (on drums) every Tuesday night for the past thirty-five years. I really didn't want to take the time to learn music theory, which has always intimidated me. The closest I came was when I was thirteen and took six drum lessons from a little old man in the back of a record store in downtown St. Paul. But I was eager to learn how to play rock and roll on a trap set like Ringo and Charlie Watts, not tap out paradiddles in a fusty old military brass band. I quit. I persuaded my parents to put my lesson money toward a drum kit and taught myself. As a result, my drumming is long on strength and endurance, short on technique. And, though I sing a lot on Tuesday nights, I've never learned to read a chart.

"Fine," Michel said.

So now, after our warm-up, he writes out the notes to the B minor scale. It will be the sixth scale he's asked me to memorize—from a chart—during the two months I've been taking lessons. He has simply ignored my half-assed suggestion that I skip the reading business but does give me cheat sheets to make the tutorials easier. Tonight he encourages me to play the scale slowly, quoting from Isidor Philipp, a great piano teacher at the Paris Conservatory: "Too much stress cannot be laid upon the usefulness, the necessity of slow work." He cites another motto, from the nineteenth-century composer Stephen Heller: "Practice very slowly, progress very fast." Saint-Saëns, he says, advised, "One must practice slowly, then more slowly, and finally slowly."

By frustrating my impulse to speed-run through my exercises, by deploying a strategy that emphasizes accuracy and repetition, he's helping me "emboss" one version of each scale in my brain, he says. It's like rubbing a soft piece of metal with a tool until it makes an impression that grows deeper and deeper with each pass. If you practice in such a way that you repeatedly make mistakes, you end up with more than one version, and as hard as it is to learn the scale correctly, it's even harder to unlearn the incorrect versions.

I play the scale repeatedly, fighting the impulse to quicken the tempo and make it musical, until I can traverse the two-octave interval flawlessly. "Terrific," Michel says. "You are my prize student."

My heart swells, even though I know I'm his only student at the moment and, seen another way, I'm also his worst. This infatuation grows deeper every day. I think about the saxophone all the time when I'm not playing. I'm always eager to be fingering it, partly to find out how I'm thinking and feeling. Am I melancholic or manic? Angry or anxious? Do I want to practice mournful minor scales or chest-thumping majors? Even at my beginner level the horn is moody and complicated—like a high-maintenance lover, it's seductive and accommodating one moment, aloof and unknowable the next. I just always want to be at it, taking its emotional temperature. I can't leave it alone.

3. A PARISIAN IN AMERICA

At 6 a.m., four mammoth deluxe coaches detailed in the black and gold of the Purdue University Boilermakers roll out of a shopping mall parking lot in north Indianapolis and head for the Indy Speedway a mile away. Every seat is occupied by a sleepy-eyed young musician, the hold of each bus crammed with tubas, drums, saxophones, batons, and all species of horns. Today is Memorial Day, one of the most patriotic dates on the American calendar, and one of the most enduring symbols of national pride, the fleet-footed Purdue University All-American Marching Band, has reassembled a month after final exams to entertain the pre-race crowd at the Indianapolis 500, one of the most populist of American spectator events. Known for more than a century for its rousing performances before 68,000 fans at home football games on the West Lafayette, Indiana, campus, the Purdue band has also been playing the Indy 500 since 1919, when Howdy Wilcox won the race with an average speed of 88 miles per hour.

The 160 students, about half the band's regular number, and I have been up since four o'clock, when Bill Kisinger, the group's associate director, pierced the halls of the Butler University dorm with a shrieking whistle. We've loaded up on a breakfast of powdered eggs, sausage, and fruit and hydrated ourselves for the march around the track. The groggy students now gaze blankly out the windows or chatter in low voices among themselves. Band members tend to sit among their instrumental siblings—the twenty saxophone players cluster at the back of one bus, the altos with the altos, tenors with fellow tenors. The auxiliary units—the Flag Corps, Solo Twirlers, and Golduster Pom Squad—group together, too. This year's Golden Girl, the Girl in Black, and the Silver Twins casually yank on their tights and adjust their spangled outfits in front of the sax players. ("Need help with that?" one tenorman asks.) The band's two drum majors, their two-foot-high Russian-bear-fur shakos sitting neatly in their laps, have paired up in the front.

The buses, escorted by half a dozen buzzing motorcycle cops, lumber down Georgetown Road, past strip malls and bail-bond offices and auto parts stores and tobacco emporia where, if you're carrying ID and have the time to fill out a couple of papers, you can also walk away with a gun. They slip by Coke Field, a sprawling expanse of lush late-spring green that surrounds a Coca-Cola bottling plant, now a campground for thousands of race fans who have pitched tents or parked their Pace Arrows and Airstreams for the week leading up to the race. Farther down the road, the owners of squat pillbox houses, many with huge Coors Light banners inexplicably concealing most of the front of their homes, sit in lounge chairs on their concrete porches, awaiting the press of cars and pickups they'll park on their front lawns at ten bucks per vehicle. Closer to the Speedway, the proprietors of hundreds of shanty food stands fire up vats of vegetable oil, preparing their all-fried menus for the 400,000 expected spectators, a few of whom have already begun descending upon the stadium toting coolers stocked with beer.

As the bus turns into the Speedway parking lot, Ryan Warner, a senior, offers some advice to Nate Lappin, a freshman. Ryan, a baby-faced tenor player with a buzz cut, is the saxophone section leader. He marches at the extreme right of his ten-person rank, with Nate, a lean, shy, handsome eighteen-year-old with floppy hair and braces, usually to his immediate left, and leads the entire section through the clever footwork its members perform while stepping to the martial cadences of the drum corps between songs. Historically, the saxophone section has been known for its showmanship and dance skills, executing a stylistic mélange of disco moves, spins, and kicks and never failing to land on the four or eight—the marching band equivalent of walking the bar. "Be careful on the track," Ryan, a veteran of four Indy 500 performances, tells his charge, "particularly on the turns, where the slope of the bank is pretty steep. You can blow out a knee."

His advice, though, is really directed toward the one member of today's band most likely to suffer a crippling injury: me. A couple of months ago, I asked the band's directors if I could tag along during one of their performances. To my horror, they said yes. Yesterday, outfitted in the band's heavy woolen uniform, wearing spats and a captain's hat topped with a plume of feathers that made me look like I'd been shot in the forehead with an arrow, I completed the two-mile march through downtown Indianapolis in the annual parade. Although back home in New York I'd committed to memory "Back Home Again in Indiana," on the parade route I couldn't recall a single note. I couldn't see the miniature sheets of music in the flip book mounted on my lyre* without my reading glasses, but would lose my balance and my place in the phalanx of saxophonists when I tried to look beyond the music with the glasses on. (Not that the charts would have helped much; my ability to read is still dependent on the "Every Good Boy Does Fine" mnemonic.) Playing while marching was im-

---

*Just finding a lyre in New York was a challenge, too. A clerk at the fourth music store I tried finally found a used one, designed for a Yamaha, which he sold to me for a dollar. I took it home, heated it up with a blowtorch, and bent it into a shape that fit my tenor.

possible, particularly when trying to execute the band's favorite dance move, the swagger step. Fifteen minutes into the ordeal, the mouthpiece had shredded my lower lip and my reed had turned pink. More concerned with shielding myself and my 200 bandmates, all of whom are at least thirty years younger, from embarrassment, I concentrated on executing an acceptable chair step, occasionally finding a note on the horn that wasn't too far afield. No one seemed to notice the many occasions when I didn't even come close.

Now, as the bus comes to a halt, the students gather their flip books and straighten their uniforms. We step out into the cool, moist early-morning air, quickly pull on our white-and-black captain's hats, each topped with that ridiculous fuzzy white plume, or "bird." Many of the organizational principles and protocols of the band, from its "rank" hierarchy to its uniform codes, are modeled on the military's. A band member is never allowed to appear outdoors without his hat or, for that matter, in any form of partial dress. Hair, for both men and women, must be tucked up under the hat and not allowed to touch the collar of the tunic. No facial hair is allowed, nor, aside from wedding rings, any jewelry. Although each graduation is usually followed by a half dozen or so marriages of band members, PDAs, or public displays of affection, are prohibited.

The band has four uniforms in addition to the woolens, which, according to Ryan, "are too cold if it's below fifty degrees and too hot if it's above." Over the past century, the band's uniform has evolved from basic olive-drab military pants, leggings, and tunic to a flashy European-style ensemble. Forty years ago members wore a kind of sport coat topped with a plastic overlay, which resembled a bib running from front to back. Today's tunic is a continental dandy's version of that look: the overlay is vest-length in the front and extends into tails in the back. Now of one piece, its components are held together by a network of zippers, buttons, hooks, and snaps. Heavy gold coin stitching, which must be done by hand, circles the sleeves of the tunic and the edge of the overlay, forms chevrons at the biceps, and runs down the pants legs in a triple stripe. Thick gold braids, secured beneath epaulets, hang from the shoulders. The uniform costs about $600, the captain's hat about $85. (The drum majors' bear-fur shakos cost $1,500 each.) "We want to emphasize and add flash to the parts of the body that move," says Dave Leppla, the band's director. "It's why we also wear spats and white gloves."

The Purdue band was first formed in 1886 by five student members of the Army's Reserve Officer Training Corps (ROTC), with which the band was affiliated until the mid-twentieth century, when it dropped the military connection so it could concentrate on showmanship. Al Wright, the flamboyant band director who made the move, was also responsible for introducing the Golden Girl, the ensemble's solo twirler, as a counterpart to Len Dawson, the Purdue quarterback then known as the Golden Boy, who went on to a Hall of Fame career with the Kansas City Chiefs. When baton twirlers from across the country began to flock to Purdue to vie for the solo position, Wright created another, the Girl in Black. In 1960, Sharon and Karon Roeske, identical twins, joined the twirling line, and Wright broke them out as the Silver Twins. The coveted auxiliary roles are now determined every spring during fierce competitions.

The band prides itself on its "firsts." In 1907 it became the first marching band to break military ranks to create a formation of any kind—the block letter *P*. It was the first band to carry all the colors of the Big 10 and the first to play the opponent's fight song. In 1921 it created the world's largest bass drum, made of solid maple and mammoth steer hides, which it still wheels around during its performances today. (Only seniors are allowed to strike it.) And it's the first band to have had an astronaut among its ranks—Neil Armstrong, the first man on the moon, who played euphonium.

Two thirds of the university's 37,000 students major in science, engineering, or technology—a proportion that holds true in the band as well. ("One reason we're so good," says Leppla, "is because the kids are so smart.") Ryan majored in computer technology, and Nate is aiming for a chemical engineering degree. This summer Nate joins the university's cooperative program, in which students work one semester in a paid internship and take classes the next. During his working semesters he'll be helping build a new chemical plant in northern Indiana.

Presently, the band assembles for a short tune-up and rehearsal and, as I did yesterday, I glue myself to Ryan, our leader. Standing on a ladder, Leppla delivers some last-minute instructions and warnings, reminding us that our pre-race performance on both the track and the infield will be televised around the world. The only acceptable excuse for falling out of rank, he says, is sickness. "Bathroom breaks are not allowed," he says. "That's why your pants are black." He reviews the music we'll play. On the track, we'll cycle through the regular parade trio of "Hail Purdue," "Back Home Again in Indiana," and "We're an American Band." After we gather on the infield at the VIP circle, we must be ready to play at any moment. We'll be drawing from the band's large repertoire—tunes that include pop standards such as "Bad," "Louie, Louie," and "Tequila" and sentimental favorites such as "On the Banks of the Wabash" and "Auld Lang Syne." If it rains and the race is delayed, we could end up playing everything we—the band, that is—know. In the final pre-race ceremonies, Leppla informs us, we'll be accompanying fellow Indianans Florence Henderson (*The Brady Bunch*) on "God Bless America" and Jim Nabors (*Gomer Pyle*) on "Back Home Again in Indiana." New York City Fire Department captain Daniel Rodriguez will front the band on "The Star-Spangled Banner."

At eight o'clock, we march in twos onto the racetrack and loosely coalesce into ranks of eight. The tuba players, who hoist forty-eight pounds of brass, flex their shoulders while the saxophone hoofers stretch their legs. Many are surprised to find the track laced with hairline cracks. "Isn't that dangerous?" asks Matt Janszen, a sophomore alto player from Cincinnati. A mechanical-engineering major, he notes that at 220 miles per hour, a 1,500-pound race car generates 5,000 pounds of downforce and its tires approach 212 degrees Fahrenheit, the temperature of boiling water. Andy Meyer, a junior tenor player from Fort Wayne, kneels down and traces a finger along the surface of the macadam, which is freshly etched with shallow grooves, the scraped bed of each hollow revealing bits of compacted glassy brown-and-green rock. "I took a course in asphalt," he says, "and I've never seen anything like this."

For the next half hour, the public address system crackles with sponsorship announcements. Finally, at eight-thirty, drum major Erik Brockman issues a series of commands. "Band, fall in!" he cries, and we quickly find our positions in our ranks. "Parade rest!" he announces, and we collectively respond with "One!" as our left feet move horizontally to shoulder width, our heads snap down to a 45-degree angle, and our horns, held in the tucked carry beneath our right arms, drop to the same angle. To "Ten-hut!" we respond with "Chop-ho" and, on two counts, snap our left legs up and stomp them back down. "Instruments up" provokes a smart three-count series of wrist snaps and arm extensions as we bring our instruments into the play position. With each of us perfectly erect and focused, the other drum major, Stephanie Swierczek, blows a whistle and barks out the order of the parade songs, the drum corps issues a standard roll-off, and the band slides forward down the racetrack in a precisely executed swagger—we arc our instruments back and forth in front of us above each raised knee, challenging every important ligament in the body—as we play the rousing fight song "Hail Purdue," once impolitically known as the "Purdue War Song."

As Bill Kisinger tells the applicants and recruits at Purdue's grueling band camp each fall, "There's the right way, the wrong way, and the army way" to march. The right way is the Purdue way, which begins with the chair step, an enervating marching style in which the thigh rises until it's parallel to the ground, the lower leg forms a right angle to the thigh, and the toes are pointed straight down. Because the band's primary purpose is to entertain crowds at football games, the marchers use a $22\frac{1}{2}$-inch step, or eight steps to five yards. The football field's grid, with hash marks every five yards, provides the band with short, visible destinations, and the pacing between each mark corresponds neatly to the four- and eight-beat rhythmic phrases of most tunes. When everyone is marching properly, each member separated by ninety inches, or four steps, spectators should be able to see diagonal lines in the rectangular block band.

On turns, the band uses a multigait step: the players on the inside of the turn take short steps or march in place while those down the line take progressively larger ones, extending as far as the army's thirty-inch step, so they all arrive in formation in the same number of paces. When the band attempts a complex formation, like the letter *P*, each rank executes an "option," whereby the members follow their section leader to get to wherever they need to go. "When thirty ranks are exercising an option to get to a different place," says Kisinger, "it looks like a big plate of worms circling around, then all of a sudden it's in formation. It's like the band goes out of focus, then back in again."

Thankfully, no such elaborate formations are planned for the Speedway track this morning, although the band shows off a nifty polonaise of high kicks and twirls. Between tunes, Ryan leads the saxophone section through a series of moves, done in step, that ends with the horns aimed at the sky, as though in a twenty-one-gun salute. The diversion elicits scattered applause from the sparse crowd. After cycling through the parade tunes three more times, we fall out and assemble to the side of the performers' stage on the infield. Although it's a pleasant 62 degrees, many of the players are dripping with sweat. Ryan examines the beat-up reed on his workhorse horn. "The swagger step is hard on your equipment," he says, "and on your mouth."

Over the next ninety minutes, Leppla, a tall, imposing figure in his mid-fifties with a graying brush cut, leads the band through a number of tunes—"Cantina Band," "The Peppermint Twist," and a Beach Boys medley—as the Dusters and Twirlers bounce and kick on the track. Between songs he scurries around the infield, talking with television producers, track officials, and band personnel through a headset. Leppla, who has a Ph.D. in conducting from Ohio State University, is approaching exhaustion. Known affectionately as Doc to band members, he's looking forward to relaxing during the summer by volunteering to take a couple of runs for the local bus company in West Lafayette. He collects buses as a hobby; in addition to a vast collection of models, he owns a 1970 General Motors city bus he bought from the San Francisco Transit Authority, a coach he bought from the Red and Tan Lines of New Jersey, and a silver-clad fifties-era dinosaur he picked up in Florida. Two days earlier, he had piloted a group of guests and band personnel from the West Lafayette campus sixty miles north to Indianapolis in the immaculately maintained city bus.

As the grandstand continues to fill up, arriving celebrities are introduced. President George H. W. Bush shows off his sport coat lined with the Stars and Stripes. His successor, Bill Clinton, waves to the crowd, evoking a low murmur of boos from the heartland Republicans, although he endeared himself the night before by spending nearly $400 on mementos, including fifteen Hot Wheels model cars. Muhammad Ali, in a wheelchair, performs a few magic tricks, making handkerchiefs disappear in front of a television camera. Former Indianapolis weatherman David Letterman flashes a gap-toothed smile. By ten o'clock, the stands lining the front stretch of the two-and-a-half-mile track are nearly full and plenty noisy, many of the spectators in peak party mood after the previous evening, when thousands gathered outside the stadium to toss Mardi Gras beads at young women willing to lift their blouses, unmoved by the one hundred men from the No Greater Love Ministry in Du Quoin, Illinois, who were there hoping to witness to lost souls.

Leppla, smartly outfitted in a black director's uniform and cap, snaps the band to attention for the ceremonial songs. Florence Henderson sings "God Bless America," Daniel Rodriguez rouses the crowd with "The Star-Spangled Banner," and Jim Nabors, an Indy 500 tradition himself, applies his broad baritone to "Back Home Again in Indiana." A stealth bomber sneaks by overhead, followed by a screaming trio of air force jets. An army colonel takes the microphone to remind the crowd that for more than 200 years American military forces have successfully defended the country's shores "and will never let the American people down." The crowd roars and rises to its feet for an ovation, then abruptly shifts into a solemn mood as the band plays "Taps," the tenor saxophones glissing mournful intervals between low F and middle B-flat.

As the band falls out for the last time, the track announcer issues the proclamation everyone has been awaiting: "Gentlemen, start your engines." The tiny cars, their tumescent, methanol-jacked engines crammed with 675 horsepower and capable of subjecting their drivers to g forces equal to four times the weight of gravity, roar to life. Then, gurgling and sputtering—the high-performance machines are not meant to run at low rpms—they ease out of their pit stations and begin circling the track.

Four hundred thousand spectators again rise to their feet, cheering and clapping as the drivers fishtail playfully among one another, warming their engines and tires. After the third lap, the pace car pulls into the infield, an official waves a green flag, and the race begins. In thirty seconds the cars are around again, this time a blur, a colorful hail of bullets, the whine of their engines like the din of a swarm of hornets amplified a thousandfold. Nate and Ryan, leaning over the infield fence, are beaming and laughing giddily. The raw power, the ear-bleeding noise, the lusty crowd, the uniforms, presidents, nubile young women lifting their blouses, evangelical soul savers—the dancing saxophones!—it's all way over the top, grandly, magnificently American.

Although it began with only six players in 1886, the Purdue marching band was inspired by the popularity of the large nineteenth-century wind band, the strident voice at that time of heartland patriotism and a vital player in first showing off the marvels of the saxophone in America. Wind bands date to the country's formative years, when musical ensembles marched side by side with the Colonial Militia and later the Continental Army, their instrumentation—oboes, clarinets, horns, and bassoons—modeled after the British "Bands of Musick" that came to America in the early eighteenth century. According to John Newsome, head of the Library of Congress's Music Division, the number of bands grew steadily after a 1792 congressional act that required every healthy white male between eighteen and forty-five to join a battalion of his state militia. In 1798, when the U.S. Marine Band was formed, Thomas Jefferson, emulating the Europeans, recommended continuing a chromatic instrumentation for the ensemble, with clarinets and oboes carrying the melody, and natural horns and bassoons providing harmonic support. "The lineup closely resembled the orchestras for which Haydn and Mozart, fulfilling royal commissions, wrote their divertimenti, serenades, and other open-air music," says Newsome.

But with the rise of the brasswinds industry in the early 1800s, conductors began to favor all-brass units consisting of a couple percussionists and two dozen cornets, trombones, and other horns. The availability of instruments, along with a sheet-music industry that had been in high gear since 1790 and new army regulations that subsidized a band of as many as sixteen musicians for each regiment, helped wind bands thrive and multiply. The introduction of the keyed bugle in the 1830s ignited a thirty-year national love affair with all-brass bands; almost every town in the country had one, no matter how inept, and metropolitan areas had several. When they weren't performing at official ceremonies, the ensembles would provide entertainment at hospitals, churches, social functions, and on the bandstand of the town green, mingling patriotic songs such as "Washington's March," "Yankee Doodle," and "Hail Columbia" with parlor favorites such as "Auld Lang Syne" and "Home, Sweet Home" and the odd selection from an Italian opera. When a dance was held, they would provide the music.

The saxophone first penetrated this idiom in 1853, when Louis Jullien, a French-born conductor known for his energetic histrionics with a baton, brought twenty-seven instrumentalists to New York, where he hired another sixty musicians and set out on a two-hundred-performance tour of the United States. Among the group was Henri Wuille, the talented saxophonist who is credited with being the first player to demonstrate the instrument's wonders in America. By the end of that year, the New York Seventh Regiment Infantry Band, led by two bandmasters, Kroll and Reitsel, was reorganized as a mixed woodwind and brass ensemble. For the youthful saxophone, the two events cracked open the brass ensembles' monopoly on band instrumentation.

America's love affair with the brasswinds ended with the Civil War, Newsome says. An influx of German musicians, many of whom had served in the Prussian cavalry bands that included clarinets, saxophones, and tubas, "made it a foregone conclusion that we were going to have every instrument you've ever heard of." The result was a number of hybrid bands, some of them containing saxophones. Although official instrumentation records and music scores of the U.S. Army show no saxophones until the twentieth century, the instrument, in typically stealthy fashion, managed to infiltrate postwar ensembles nonetheless. In a photograph of a ceremony in Promontory, Utah, that celebrated the linking of the Union Pacific and Southern Pacific rail lines in 1869, one of the members of the Twenty-first Infantry Band is holding a saxophone. Photographs of cavalry on the western frontier in the 1880s also show band members with saxophones, some of them on horseback.

Demonstrating a Zelig-like ability to show up anywhere, the saxophone became an important member of the touring ensembles of Patrick Gilmore, "father of the American concert band," and the hugely popular bands of the March King, John Philip Sousa. By the turn of the century, with a firm foundation in concert bands, Adolphe Sax's invention set about conquering the other popular entertainment media of the day, including minstrel shows, circuses, vaudeville, the Chautauqua and lyceum circuits, which delivered tent-show "culture" to the American outback, and, most important, dance orchestras. All of these engines of dispersal, combined with a rapidly evolving recording industry, the marketing savvy of midwestern instrument manufacturers, and the impressive skills of a few homegrown virtuosos, helped the horn's renown reach critical mass by the end of the second decade of the twentieth century, when America found itself in a full-blown love affair with the voice of Adolphe Sax.

Patrick Sarsfield Gilmore, whose weeks-long musical extravaganzas would be duplicated by the organizers of rock festivals a century later, was the first conductor to envision the instrument's grand commercial potential. Gilmore, a twenty-year-old cornetist and aspiring composer with an Irishman's typically keen instinct for the common touch, had arrived in Boston in 1849 and promptly established his reputation by challenging a keyed-bugle virtuoso, Ned Kendall, to a public competition. The duelists blew to a draw, but the cutting session conferred upon the spunky Irishman enough fame to attract top players to his thirty-two-piece Gilmore Band, which played concerts, parades, dances, and other venues and, by 1859, included a couple of rare though underused saxophones. When President Lincoln called for 75,000 volunteer troops in 1861, the War Department tried to encourage enlistment by announcing that well-known bands would be attached to particular regiments. Gilmore and his band, now swollen to sixty-eight pieces with the addition of a few dozen drummers and buglers, were assigned to the Twenty-fourth Massachusetts Volunteer Regiment, where the conductor's feisty nature was allowed full expression. As did other bands during the war, Gilmore's occasionally found itself happily engaged in post-battle skirmishes with musical ensembles from the Confederate Army. When soldiers laid down their rifles at the end of the day, musicians from opposing bands would pick up their instruments and perform "competition concerts." The Southern band would play "Dixie," "Bonnie Blue Flag," and "Maryland, My Maryland" and the Northern band would return the volley with "America," "The Star-Spangled Banner," and "John Brown's Body." The next morning they would be back at regular duty, cheering their troops on with polkas, marches, waltzes, and quicksteps accompanied by the hissing and bursting of shells.

A year into the conflict, there were nearly 30,000 musicians enlisted in the Northern army, half of them bandsmen. The War Department, facing an invasion by General Robert E. Lee, decided to muster out the regimental bands, some of which had become collection pools for slackers and other nonessential personnel. Gilmore and his crew returned to Boston, where they performed concerts featuring, in Gilmore's words, "such music as has revived the drooping spirits of many a weary soldier, or soothed the pain of many a wounded patriot." In 1863 the Gilmore Band debuted "When Johnny Comes Marching Home," which its conductor, despite credits given to the unknown Louis Lambert, is now thought to have written.

Gilmore had a theatrical streak, borrowed from the French conductor Louis Jullien, whose concerts he attended in 1853 and 1854. Jullien was known for dressing in magnificent outfits, used a jeweled baton, and retreated wearily to a golden throne between numbers, much the way James Brown, a century later, would be covered by a cape and led from the stage by his handlers after feigning emotional collapse while singing a steamy ballad. One of Jullien's crowd pleasers, the "Firemen's Quadrille," included a brigade of firemen who flooded the aisles with water, followed by fireworks. In an early expression of his own grandiose streak, Gilmore's band performed a concert in New Orleans in 1864 in which "Hail Columbia," a tune that glorified the Union cause, was "punctuated by thunderous roars from a battery of cannons, one of which boomed on each beat of the drum, reinforced by the pealing of bells in neighborhood churches." The firing of cannons and the pounding of anvils during his concerts were to become his kitschy trademarks, and a primary reason for any turnover in his bands—most of the musicians with any tenure at all went deaf.

Gilmore, a gregarious charmer with a neat goatee, rimless spectacles, and slicked-back hair, handled all of the band's business, from advertising and bookings to the choice of repertory. He drew on all of his talents, from his personal warmth to his ability to drive a hard bargain, when he organized a National Peace Jubilee in Boston in 1869 designed to heal the lingering bitterness between the North and the South. He built a coliseum that held 50,000 people, assembled an orchestra of 500 players, a band of 1,000, and a chorus of 10,000, including all manner of musicians, from European conductors and soloists to entire church choirs, barbershop quartets, and fire department ensembles. The event was a huge success and netted Gilmore $40,000.

Pressing his luck three years later, he staged the International Peace Jubilee, a three-week-long musical celebration, also in Boston, featuring thousands of musicians from around the world. The Europeans sent their noblest ensembles, including the English Grenadier Band, the Kaiser Franz Grenadiers of Berlin, the Irish Band from Dublin, and the magnificent French Garde Republicaine Band, which had been magically transformed by Adolphe Sax's instruments following the inventor's victory in 1845 on the Champ de Mars. The band that arrived in Boston consisted of fifty-three performers, including six saxophone players and sixteen saxhorns.

To Gilmore's disappointment, the jubilee was a flop. Despite a glorious concert of Johann Strauss waltzes led by the composer himself, who had been lured from Austria to preside over an orchestra of 800, the public's interest simply could not be sustained over three weeks. Gilmore and his backers lost all of their money, but the keen-eared bandleader heard the future of his own ensemble and, by extension, the now-classic sax-heavy American wind band. The Garde Republicaine Band, following Adolphe Sax's concept, was organized by families of instruments much like the voices of a choir, each member linked to the other from highest to lowest—the clarinet family, for instance, could pass along a melody from the A-flat sopranino to the E-flat soprano to the B-flat soprano to the E-flat alto to the bass—each able to express its distinct voice while blending beautifully with its siblings. The saxophones in the French band occupied a glorious position in this organization. They were largely responsible for the ensemble's slick performance at the jubilee and for the sold-out concerts that followed in New York and Chicago. Taking his cue from the natty Frenchmen, Gilmore quickly reorganized his New York Twenty-second Regiment National Guard Band, a sixty-six player ensemble, to accommodate a complete family of saxophones. Within a year, he had lured the eminent French player Edward A. Lefebre, the Saxophone King, to join the band, bringing a high degree of professional saxophony to the domestic wind band for the first time. Lefebre also organized a saxophone quartet within the band. After hearing the quartet in 1880, the composer Caryl Florio wrote in the *Art Amateur*, "The effect is charming. The tone resembles that of an organ."

Lefebre's feats were particularly heroic considering the deafness he suffered after a decade with Gilmore. The flamboyant conductor had a fondness for the "Anvil Chorus" in Giuseppi Verdi's *Il Trovatore* and "The Blacksmith in the Woods" by Theodore Michaelis. Both pieces used two dozen anvil beaters, to which Gilmore, in his inimitable fashion, added the firing of artillery guns for extra effect. After hundreds of performances, Lefebre could still obtain his signature sound on the saxophone, but he couldn't hear it.

The Gilmore Band became America's favorite entertainment for the next twenty years. "Gilmore relied upon a considerable amount of bravura, with the cannon volleys and all," says Newsome. "He was a professional businessman and wanted his band to make money. But he also felt his mission was to bring faithful transcriptions of orchestral music by railroad to people all over the United States. And he did." His big-band successor, John Philip Sousa, the former conductor of the U.S. Marine Band, upheld Gilmore's high standards. "The measure of that," says Newsome, "is that most of Richard Strauss's tone poems were given their American premieres not by symphony orchestras but by Sousa's band. When Strauss heard them, he was fascinated by how good they sounded."

By 1892, shortly before his death, Gilmore had increased the number of saxophones in his "Famous One Hundred Men" Band to ten, including three sopranos and the enormous contrabass. The lesson was not lost on Sousa, who started out the same year with a quartet of saxophones in his orchestra, called simply Sousa's Band. Acknowledging his audience's desire for saxophone solos, he later doubled the size of the saxophone section, which performed at each concert by itself for about thirty-five minutes. Sousa's Band featured the best players in the world, including Lefebre, who joined the ensemble after Gilmore's death; the Belgian Jean H. B. Moeremans; Ben Vereecken, who wrote the first American method book; H. Benne Henton, one of the first players to master the altissimo range, the notes above the saxophone's two-and-a-half-octave compass; and Jascha Gurewich, nicknamed the Saxophone Prince (even at the end of his career, the deaf "King" Lefebre was unwilling to vacate his throne).

The spawn of Gilmore's and Sousa's success were numerous. Capitalizing on the national mania for concert band music, Arthur Pryor, Patrick Conway, Victor Herbert (who conducted Gilmore's band for a few years after Gilmore's death), Allen Dodworth, Bohumir Kryl, and Herbert L. Clarke, some of them alumni of Sousa's Band, organized giant ensembles that let their saxophone sections break out mid-concert. Colleges and universities, like Purdue, formed economy-size bands, combining concert music with marching.

Women became some of the saxophone's earliest pioneers, extending the instrument into other idioms and venues. Etta Morgan, a member of the Berger Family's Ladies' Orchestra, lined up a two-week engagement in New York at the Olympia Theatre in 1876, performing as a soloist with her troupe, which billed her as "the only lady saxophone player in the world." Elsie Hoffman, in 1889, is thought to have been the first black American to solo on the instrument, with Will Marion Cook's band. By the turn of the century, Alice Calloway and May and Maydah Yorke were playing saxophones with the Musical Spillers, a rare all-black vaudeville band that became the inspiration for the more popular Six Brown Brothers, a white troupe formed around the same time. Myra Keaton, mother of Buster Keaton, was often referred to as the first white woman to play the saxophone professionally in America, though she was born a year after Etta Morgan's New York concert. In 1892, Bessie Mecklem made the first recordings of the saxophone when she cut twelve wax sides at the Edison factory.

More importantly for the opportunistic saxophone, the number of amateur community bands exploded. By 1890, there were 10,000 such ensembles in America; a decade later the number had doubled. No town worth visiting was without an eight- or twelve-unit band. As American manufacturers, which were now producing saxophones, struggled to keep up with demand, the horn eventually found its way into many of these ensembles and, in its typical hegemonistic style, consumed them. Soon the seductive but aggressive saxophone was established as the core of thousands of amateur bands formed in the name of fellowship, patriotism, education, ethnic heritage, or just fun.

By the late teens, hundreds of those ensembles had reduced their instrumentation exclusively to saxophones, ranging from four to a hundred. Many saxophone bands were affiliated with a business, union, or industry that supplied workers with instruments to boost morale and stifle labor unrest. The ability to play was often a prerequisite of landing a job. Employers even advertised their positions in music journals. "Saxophone players, who are coal miners, tailors, or barbers," read one such advertisement, "please address George J. Pearson, Hillsboro, Ill." The Chicago Health Department Saxophone band was organized to promote the physical and mental well-being of its employees, as was the Denver Gas and Electric Saxophone Band. Lodge bands were ubiquitous—from the Zuriah Shrine Temple Octet of Minneapolis to the Kosair Temple Saxophone Sextet in Louisville. All-female saxophone bands, like the Darling Saxophone Four, the Schuster Sisters, and the Milady Saxo Four, gained prominence in the years just before women's suffrage was achieved in 1920. Even the Joliet, Illinois, prison had an all-sax band.

After the saxophone had mingled with the many voices of

nineteenth-century wind and concert bands, its admirers had discovered it had more than enough wind of its own for just about any occasion in the early twentieth century. Tiny backwaters that could barely support a general store didn't need a twelve-piece band to celebrate the Fourth of July in the town square or the mayor's daughter's wedding or the unveiling of a war memorial. With their lush hybrid sound—evoking strings, brass, woodwinds, and the human voice—and capable of both fiery bombast and pacific calm, a couple of saxophones would do.

4. A VIRTUOSO ON HORSEBACK

At the same time concert bands were expanding the saxophone's reach with a haughty mixture of patriotic marches, overtures from Rossini and Wagner, and selections from the works of Mozart, Mendelssohn, and Meyerbeer, variety entertainment, or vaudeville, and a brand-new recording industry were conspiring to help the instrument conquer light, or popular, music. The pastiche of song styles performed on the turn-of-the-century stage was as diverse as the country's ethnic makeup, and all of them—Victorian parlor tunes, Tin Pan Alley numbers, ragtime, "coon" songs, spirituals, and airs from operettas—were vulnerable to the charms of Adolphe Sax's creation.

Among the burgeoning pool of pop entertainers who traveled by rail and riverboat to cities and towns across America, Tom Brown, the son of a Canadian cornet player, emerged as "the discoverer of the gold mine concealed in a saxophone." His all-saxophone sextet, the Six Brown Brothers, helped make the horn "the most-talked-of instrument in America," according to Bruce Vermazen, who has documented the history of the group.

Vermazen can explain how but not necessarily why he became the keeper of the Brown Brothers' flame. A retired professor of philosophy at the University of California at Berkeley, Vermazen had bought some Brown Brothers recordings at garage sales when he was a teenager in the 1950s but was disappointed to find that they weren't jazz. Later, playing cornet and trumpet in a ragtime orchestra, he learned more about the brothers' music—they played a lot of ragtime, too, although at a languid pace. Then, in one of those chance encounters that turns a sometime hobby into a serious and scholarly pursuit, he met the son of Tom Brown, who played alto in the sextet. Before he knew it, Vermazen was not only in possession of a garage-load of Brown Brothers scrapbooks, photos, and memorabilia but, like every other devotee who has been mugged by the instrument, was learning to play the saxophone.

Over a two-decade run that ended with the Great Depression, says Vermazen, the Brown Brothers worked their way up the popular-entertainment food chain, from circuses and minstrelsy to burlesque, vaudeville, and musical theater. Their recorded tunes—"That Moaning Saxophone Rag," "Dill Pickles Rag," "The Hustler March," "Chicken Walk," "Pussyfoot March," "When Aunt Dinah's Daughter Hannah Bangs on That Piano," and "For Me and My Gal"— were hugely successful. Moreover, they expressed a communicable joy in playing that helped fuel the country's growing infatuation with the saxophone. After attending their Broadway show *Tip Top*, in 1921, one reviewer exclaimed, "No one in whose veins flows the stuff which has made this country what it is today can listen to the Six Brown Brothers and not feel consumed with a desire to throw over whatever work he may be doing in the world and take up the saxophone."

A similar feeling had seized Tom Brown years before. In 1904, working as a clarinetist with the Ringling Brothers Circus, he bought a used saxophone and began playing at the small "concerts" that followed the main show. As his act developed, he bought a pair of outsize shoes from the circus sideshow giant, dressed in a clown costume, covered his face in greasepaint, and "ripped off rag" on the horn. He appeared in blackface for the rest of his career.

During the next few years, Tom brought his brothers into the ensemble, dressing them in military uniforms while keeping his own clown persona. By 1911, the Six Brown Brothers, combining goofy skits and music, had moved on to the burlesque circuit (the *Broadway Gaiety Girls*) and had recorded "The Bullfrog and the Coon (Medley)" and "American Patrol." They toured the Orpheum vaudeville circuit, which owned a string of "big time" theaters between Chicago and San Francisco, then traveled on the Keith and Williams circuits on the eastern seaboard. Their success coincided with the rise of the American entertainment industry and the scrappy agents, producers, bookers, and theater owners who nurtured it. In 1914 they joined the hugely successful show *Chin Chin*, which featured "girls and girls and girls, circus clowns, circus horses, and circus performers," in Philadelphia and traveled with the production to New York, where it played nearly 300 performances. By now the Brown saxophonists—two altos, two tenors, a baritone, and a bass—had settled on their trademark costuming: polka-dot clown getups and cone-shaped hats, with Tom in blackface.

In 1921 the Browns were the highest-paid musical act in the country, earning $1,000 a week. In addition to introducing the saxophone to large audiences, the Brown Brothers were among the first pop musicians to find a harmonic structure for saxophones, a necessary step for it to become an indispensable voice in new, twentieth-century music. "If you listen to their pop tunes, like 'Pretty Baby' and 'For Me and My Gal,'" says Vermazen, "what you're hearing is the saxophone section in a modern dance orchestra, which emerged in the early-to-mid-twenties. That's when the arranging for two altos and a tenor got codified, but the Browns were doing it long before."

Although they did much to demonstrate the saxophone's humorous personality to wide audiences, they also contributed to its reputation as a lowbrow instrument, suited to imitating the braying of donkeys, laughing hyenas, a flatulent dowager, and the roar of an approaching locomotive. In a business in which a family of seals playing "My Country 'Tis of Thee" on batteries of horns was thought to be wildly hilarious, they were advancing a certain ignoble tradition. The Browns' predecessors in vaudeville included such entertainers as the Elliotts and their specialty tour, which featured not only saxophones but a Grand Russian Quadrille on Unicycles and hat spinning; Billy and Lilly Mack, who, in addition to tootling on saxophones, performed on musical bottles, cowbells, funnels, sleigh bells, and Swiss handbells; "The United Twins"—Violet and Daisy Hilton—a saxophone-wielding English duo who were joined at the hip; Arthur H. Rackett, a tenor sax player who rounded out his repertoire with the "Leedle German Band and singing dog finish"; and Lew Wells, whose selections were accompanied by "mechanical birds, the beautiful rose bush, harmonious window blinds and magic flower pots."

The brothers had discovered and exploited a quality of the instrument often credited for the horn's worldwide popularity: its tonal similarity to the human voice. In one routine in which Tom played a jilted bride, "he laughed, cried, entreated, cajoled and threatened thru his instrument in such a way that every listener has no difficulty in ascertaining what is being said by the sad little deserted bride." One reviewer perfectly understood the horn's personable nature and its ability to stoke a listener's emotions: "The performance of the Brown Brothers suggests that if primitive man had had the saxophone, speech might never have been developed, for it would not have been needed."

By the end of the twenties, the Browns had been displaced by other rapidly evolving entertainment media. The number of radios in the country grew from a few thousand experimental sets in 1917 to 7 million a decade later. Twenty to thirty million Americans tuned in every evening. "Somewhere during the evening hours, when millions of people are listening in . . . the friendly jazz bands blare. The saxophones begin at seven," wrote the social commentator Charles Merz in 1928. And those horns were much more likely to be members of a hot jazz ensemble than of a novelty group. The Great Depression delivered a final, fatal blow to vaudeville—and to the Brown Brothers. Tom moved back to Ontario and worked as a waiter and piano tuner, while his brothers went on welfare.

No such fate awaited the saxophone, inheritor of its inventor's indomitable, perhaps immortal, spirit. The most demotic instrument ever invented had found a permanent home in the New World. A million and a half Americans now played the saxophone, which exceeded in number all other musical instruments in the country.

The Chautauqua entertainment and lecture circuit, described by Theodore Roosevelt as "the most American thing in America," also exposed the saxophone to millions of new listeners; more importantly, it helped develop the instrument's reputation for producing sounds more pleasing and musical than laughs, squeals, and catcalls.

Founded in 1874 by a Methodist minister, the circuit began as a summer camp "assembly" on Lake Chautauqua in western New York to train Sunday school teachers and offer visiting families "education and uplift." By the turn of the century, the "Mother Chautauqua" camp had evolved into numerous traveling tent shows that would often follow a spoke of the country's railroad hub from town to town, bivouacking for as long as two weeks. Regular speakers included William Jennings Bryan, advocate of temperance and populism; Maud Ballington Booth, the "Little Mother of the Prisons," who preached reform of the penal system; and Gay MacLaren, "The Girl with the Camera Mind." The program would be rounded out by music performances, plays, poetry readings, and wholesome novelty acts. For many rural Americans, Chautauqua, a sort of morally respectable vaudeville, provided their only exposure to mass culture. At the circuit's peak in the 1920s, Chautauqua entertainers had appeared in more than 10,000 communities in 45 states before 45 million people. Among the entertainers were Clay Smith and G. E. Holmes, who hit pay dirt in the gold mine concealed in the saxophone.

Smith and Holmes were typical of the upright and wholesome entertainers who appeared on the tours. Born in Bainbridge, Indiana, in 1876, Smith learned to play the guitar, mandolin, cornet, and trombone as a child. When he was seventeen, he appeared as a guitar soloist with a mandolin club at the 1893 Chicago World's Fair, then joined minstrel shows, the Barnum and Bailey Circus, and the Buffalo Bill Wild West Show, giving exhibitions as a crack marksman. When times were lean, he boxed professionally. Some time in his teens, after seeing a Patrick Gilmore concert, he picked up the saxophone.

His partner, Holmes, was born in Baraboo, Wisconsin, in 1873 and had a more formal musical background. At an early age, Holmes began playing piccolo with his hometown band, then studied harmony and flute, cornet, and saxophone with various instructors. Before he was eighteen he had composed and published his *La Grande March*, the first of fifty he would write during his career. Holmes first worked as a solo flutist with a concert orchestra and as the director of a number of other bands.

Smith and Holmes met in 1901 and, with a banjo player named Arthur Wells, formed the Three Musical Cowboys after the close of the St. Louis Exposition, in 1905. The trio expanded into the Apollo Concert Company, "strictly high-class musicians and entertainers," which, despite its self-assigned pedigree, found its greatest success on the rowdy vaudeville circuit. The group, whose members also played the other novelty instruments of the day—the marimba, mandolin, and xylophone—toured for ten years before Smith and Holmes left to form a new company. The two musicians had fallen in love with the sisters Coyla May Spring and Lotus Flower Spring, a singer and cellist, respectively. Both couples were married on the same day in 1915. For the next fifteen years they toured almost continuously; when they weren't performing, they lived in the same house in Chicago.

The Smith-Spring-Holmes band, a "company of high-class musical interpreters who play the best in music, and who use no clap-trap methods in order to win applause," featured a variety of instruments in several different configurations, including a popular saxophone duet by Smith and Holmes. The snooty promotional copy was an indirect put-down of their former partner's penchant for the novelty act: after Smith and Holmes left Apollo, Arthur Wells commissioned a saxophone that could be played with one hand, leaving the other free for juggling. It was also an attempt to counter a growing perception that the saxophone, because it was now being played—and played badly—by growing hordes of home music makers, was incapable of answering a higher musical calling.

By 1915, Holmes alone had written more compositions for saxophone quartet than anyone else in the world. The group's supposed sophistication and popularity enabled Smith and Holmes to begin sharing a byline on an instructional column for the *Dominant*, a publication for amateur musicians. Smith, who did most of the writing, used many of his columns to condemn the emergence of jazz music, which he considered an obstacle to the saxophone's acceptance in more serious musical circles. Referring to jazz players as "human hangnails," Smith and Holmes wrote that "the 'Jasser' should be subject to the same quarantine restrictions as if he had the foot and mouth disease."

"Clay Smith was a bit of a blowhard. He was definitely not shy about voicing his opinions, even if they were frequently contradictory," says Tom Smialek, a professor of music at Pennsylvania State University, who has studied the performance techniques of early-twentieth-century saxophonists and wrote his dissertation on Smith and Holmes. "Smith was a Freemason, espousing 'brotherhood' among men, yet like many Americans of his day, he was fairly comfortable with his racism. He was a Baptist, but was sympathetic to those who drank liquor during the years of Prohibition. He and Holmes considered themselves musical progressives in promoting the saxophone to American audiences. But at the same time, Smith would rail against what he called the 'hideous cat-calling' of the saxophone in jazz music."

Despite their moralizing, as two of the horn's earliest missionaries Smith and Holmes helped lay the groundwork for the American "concert" saxophone school, which, with the help of a few special talents who followed—Cecil Leeson, Sigurd Rascher, Marcel Mule, Larry Teal, Vincent Abato, Al Gallodoro, Donald Sinta, and Fred Hemke—developed piecemeal through the century until the 1970s, when the repertoire suddenly exploded with exciting and innovative new music and a generation of formally trained "legit" musicians who could play it. At a time when the popularity of "Chicken Walk" was helping bring the saxophone into just about every living room in America, Smith and Holmes were providing the instrument with a more refined literature, transcribing dozens of classical pieces and writing hundreds of compositions, ranging from marches to duets to tutorials for the school bands that were organizing all across America. Thanks to the extensive repertoire they provided for the instrument, the legions of amateur ensembles that came together in the teens and twenties had something to play that didn't require difficult transposition into another key (a conversion that only players of the hard-to-find soprano saxophone could avoid, as it had the same notation as parts for the B-flat cornet). Toward the end of their run, which concluded with Smith's death in 1930, their performances were often given as college extension courses on the lyceum circuit, which was first organized in 1826 as a series of lectures given at schools and meeting halls during the winter.

Smith and Holmes never recorded; instead, their live performances enabled listeners to appreciate the authentic beauty of the saxophone's sound, which was flattened and dulled by primitive radio transmission and recording techniques. With the formidable talent, charisma, and showmanship of a young virtuoso from Detroit, Rudy Wiedoeft, they helped make the saxophone, by the mid-twenties, the most popular instrument in America.

When he was twelve years old, in 1925, Al Gallodoro's father took him to the Forbes music store in Birmingham, Alabama, to buy a

Perfect Tone C-Melody saxophone, the same instrument played by his idol, Rudy Wiedoeft. Two years later young Al, who had already mastered the clarinet, was playing saxophone every night with Romeo and his Juliets at the Beverly Gardens, a cabaret and gambling house in Birmingham. There he was discovered by a producer named George Evans, who asked Al's father if he could join his traveling band, which included a banjo, two saxophones, a trumpet, a piano, and drums. "'If that's what my son wants,'" Al remembers his father saying. "He knew I was good, and I knew I was good, too." At the age of fourteen, the precocious woodwind doubler began touring on the Orpheum Theatre big-time vaudeville circuit.

By the early thirties, Al was performing for radio broadcasts six days a week in New York and appearing on stage with Bob Hope, the Three Stooges, Milton Berle, and Blackstone the Magician. He would dazzle audiences with passages from such Rudy Wiedoeft compositions as "Saxarella" and "Saxophobia." "Wiedoeft was my idol and everybody else's who wanted to play saxophone back then," says Al, a short, round man in his nineties now, with a fringe of white hair around his head and a full white beard. "If it hadn't been for him, I'd still be playing the clarinet."

He and tens of thousands of others. Wiedoeft, a dazzling technician, had that effect on those who heard him, although one listener, Thomas Alva Edison, wasn't entirely convinced of his talent. In 1917, when he was twenty-four years old, Wiedoeft paid a visit to the crusty, eccentric inventor of the lightbulb, the phonograph, waxed paper, and the movie camera at his studios in West Orange, New Jersey. Wiedoeft, who was then playing in the pit orchestra of a show called *Canary Cottage,** which had just landed in New York,

---

*In typical stealth fashion, the saxophone was sneaking into Broadway musicals as early as 1913, when saxophones were used in the orchestration of *Oh, I Say*, a musical with a score by Jerome Kern that ran at the Casino Theatre. A few years later, saxophones were featured regularly in the enormously successful musical comedies mounted by Kern, Guy Bolton, and P. G. Wodehouse at the Princess Theatre.

had a number of original compositions he hoped to record on Edison's Diamond Discs label. Although the inventor was nearly deaf, he insisted on auditioning all of his recording candidates and made notes about their performances. Wiedoeft, according to notes Edison took, barely passed the audition—most likely because the vibrato he used bothered Edison's ear. "He will do," the inventor wrote, even though "his saxophone don't seem so mellow as others I have heard."

Despite his reservations, Edison recorded Wiedoeft's "Canary Cottage One-Step" and, a month later, "Valse Erica," one of the many waltzes Wiedoeft would go on to record. The sessions launched a career that made Wiedoeft wildly popular and fabulously wealthy in the 1920s but that ended in ignominy and destitution in the thirties. His compositions, with corny titles like "Saxophobia," "Saxarella," and "Sax-O-Phun," straddled vaudeville and the legitimate concert field. His abbreviated transcriptions of works by Massenet, Verdi, and Romberg attempted to present serious literature to audiences that had never heard a minuet (a marketing ploy imitated forty years later by the pianist Liberace, who boasted that by eliminating the "bad" parts, he could play the Minute Waltz in thirty-seven seconds). Wiedoeft performed on every major stage in the country and was heard on the radio almost nightly. Among the popular novelty groups of the teens—some featured only a saxophone and a drummer, or a saxophone and a xylophone—he was king of the virtuosos.

With his bland good looks, Wiedoeft became the icon of the American saxophone craze or, depending on your point of view, one of its chief perpetrators. Some towns blamed Wiedoeft for having to impose music curfews—in Kansas City it was illegal to play a saxophone outside a nightclub between ten-thirty at night and six in the morning. For every one of the millions of saxophone lovers, there appeared to be a corresponding detractor. Saxophone invective was everywhere, most often in the form of jokes: "Home is where the saxophone isn't," "The worst thing about the saxophone is the fellow who plays it," "To silence your next-door neighbor's lawn mower, borrow it; to silence your next-door neighbor's saxophone, shoot him."* But the diatribes could get nasty, particularly those from elitist longhairs. In 1917 the composer and pianist Isadore Berger condemned it repeatedly. "No other musical instrument can be so immoral," he wrote. "The saxophone is guttural, savage, panting, and low in its appeal."

Nonetheless, saxophone-toting amateurs wanted to be just like Wiedoeft. One, a smitten young singer named Hubert Prior Vallee, wrote eight letters to Wiedoeft describing his love of the instrument and his admiration of Wiedoeft's skill. After finally being granted an audience with the virtuoso, Vallee, the first singer to use a microphone and speakers during his live performances and whose career would span much of the remaining century, changed his name to Rudy.

Wiedoeft had grown up in a show-biz family and, unwilling to forsake his vaudeville roots, often appeared on stage in a cowboy outfit, replete with chaps, spurs, studded vest, ten-gallon hat, and boots. During a swing through England in 1926 with the urbane Oscar Levant as his accompanist, Wiedoeft wore his cowboy hat everywhere, to the eternal embarrassment of his pianist. He even rented a horse and toured the city on horseback. Two years later, at the peak of his career, he formed a troupe of gorgeous showgirls, all of whom played the saxophone, and took his Saxophobia Idea on the road. The ensemble toured coast to coast for a year, often playing three or four shows a day, and earned an unprecedented amount of money.

---

*The saxophone's history is filled with inventive diatribes against it, the earliest one probably from Salomon de Rothschild, who, in a letter to his family in Paris from Havana, Cuba, in 1861, wrote, "We were present at a ball at which, at the beginning of the evening, the men wore dominos and masks. Instead of flirting with the ladies, they contented themselves with shouting and making the noises of hell, which seemed to please the young people very much but which produced an exceedingly disagreeable effect on me—all the more so since the msuic is played mainly by pounding a huge drum and blowing imperfect saxophones." From *A Casual View of America: The Home Letters of Salomon de Rothschild, 1859–1861.*

On tunes whose sole purpose seemed to be to show off his extra-ordinary talent, Wiedoeft used staccato, slap-tongue, and other techniques to get the horn to laugh, cry, and emit odd percussive pops that resembled the uncorking of a champagne bottle, a sound the hard-drinking Wiedoeft knew well. But his fingering speed and precision were equally dazzling on classier works, like Beethoven's "Minuet in G," Tchaikovsky's "Melodie," and on his own lush and exotic "Dans l'Orient." The beautiful tone he extracted from his C-Melody on his recordings was impressive. The C tenor, which en-joyed a popular run during the saxophone craze, was a member of Adolphe Sax's proposed second family of saxophones, the "orches-tral" group in C and F that never entered full production. It was closer to the B-flat tenor than to the E-flat alto—a full step above the tenor and a minor third below the alto—and its bore was smaller than that of the alto, which theoretically gave it a warmer sound. American manufacturers had resurrected its design because it used the same notation as the piano, making it easy for amateur converts to read music. But to more sophisticated ears its tone was often sour, uneven, and wimpy, with neither the focus of the alto nor the fierce authority of the B-flat tenor. (When the saxophone craze ended, so did production of the fickle C-Melody.) Ted Hegvik, a retired pro-fessor of saxophone and a Wiedoeft buff, claims the virtuoso rounded and centered the tone by using the smaller, more compact alto mouthpiece. But others have a different explanation. Cecil Lee-son, who did much to promote the "concert" saxophone in the thir-ties, reportedly always admired the rich tone Wiedoeft managed to obtain in the lower register of the instrument—until he heard him play live. He realized then that the primitive recording devices of the time were incapable of capturing the upper partial tones and could only record the fundamental tones, giving Wiedoft's sound a reso-nant, but artificial, bottom.

Befitting his showboat persona, Wiedoeft, who had become one of the most instantly recognizable figures of the Roaring Twenties, flamed out in spectacular fashion in the 1930s. The Depression forced many record companies to cut back production or go out of business altogether, and the extraordinary early bands of Fletcher Henderson, Duke Ellington, and others were nudging musical taste, and the saxophone, in a new direction. Wiedoeft, who by then had a serious drinking problem, reportedly decided to invest most of his money in a Death Valley gold mine. He hired teams of workers to plumb the mine until his money ran out, then worked it by himself whenever he could raise the cash to travel west. By 1937, he was nearly flat broke. During his long descent, his wife, Mary, grew increasingly furious that she could no longer live in the luxurious style to which she had become accustomed, and one day, during a particularly feverish row, she stabbed him with a butcher knife. His recovery was slow, painful and medicated by booze. Still walking with a cane, he made his last radio appearance six months later. In 1940 he died from cirrhosis of the liver.

Although Wiedoeft is often remembered as one of a small cadre of performers, including the Six Brown Brothers and Smith and Holmes, who helped bring the saxophone into almost every home in America, his influence on performance technique may be his most lasting legacy (followed closely by his many demanding compositions). Although the saxophone had been around for about seventy-five years, players were just beginning to explore its dynamic potential and discovering effects ranging from glissandi, or pitch bends, to clean and rapid strings of notes produced by the flutter-tongue technique. Wiedoeft derived his playing style—most notably his use of vibrato, the quavering sustain at the end of a note—from a seemingly remote source: the violin. Like several popular vocalists of his era, Wiedoeft was captivated by the style of the Austrian-American violinist Fritz Kreisler, one of the first great instrumentalists of the recording age, who used a continuous vibrato, an ornamental technique disparaged by European musicians, who felt it should be used only sparingly. Unlike other players and singers, though, Wiedoeft came by the skill naturally: as a child playing in the Wiedoeft Family Orchestra around Los Angeles, young Rudy was himself considered a violin prodigy until he broke his bowing arm when he was ten and switched to clarinet.

His influence on other players was immediate and long-lasting. A recording of an Otto "Toby" Hardwick solo with Duke Ellington's early band in the mid-twenties is pure homage, as is a triple-tongued Jimmy Dorsey chorus in "Oodles of Noodles" a few years later. Charlie Parker was known to practice Wiedoeft tutorials. But Wiedoeft's influence extended far beyond American borders. Early recordings of English bands in the thirties reveal sax sections playing Wiedoeft passages note for note. As a child in Germany, Sigurd Rascher, who became one of the most celebrated teachers and players in America, switched to saxophone from clarinet after hearing a Wiedoeft recording. Even xenophobic China could not resist Wiedoeft's musical charm. When Paul Brodie, the Canadian saxophonist, arrived there in 1984, he met saxophonists eager to play for him a lush solo by the famous "Russian" player "Vidov." The passage, Brodie recognized, was from Wiedoeft's "Dans l'Orient."

5. THE COLLECTORS

And it rose in front of me. A mechanism of strong, silverplated wires, the gears, the levers, like the mechanism of some huge and absolutely nonsensical apparatus, the fantasy of some crazy mixed-up inventor. I had never held one in my hands before; I felt as if I were embracing a mistress . . . I blew into the mouthpiece, running my fingers down the valves; what emerged from the bell like a washbasin was a cruel, beautiful, infinitely sad sound. Maybe that's the way dying brachiosaurs wailed.

JOSEF ŠKVORECKY, *The Bass Saxophone*

Vince Giordano has insisted on washing the mouthpiece of his bass saxophone before I play it. "It probably hasn't been cleaned since before the horn was manufactured," he says. Vince bought the behemoth from Artie Drelinger, who played in the Paul Whiteman and Bunny Berigan bands in the 1920s, the beginning of the golden age of dance-band music. Mounted on a stand in his living room in central Brooklyn, the bulky bass, a 1924 Buescher, debuted with some of the first dance bands to use saxophones as a section—a move that pushed the instrument closer to its apotheosis as the eloquent voice of jazz—although the bass itself was then mostly used as a member of the rhythm section. Wiedoeft, the Browns, Smith and Holmes, and hundreds of novelty groups helped introduce the instrument to millions of amateur players, but the hot-jazz bands and dance orchestras of the early twentieth century were the ensembles that began to develop the instrument's extraordinary lyrical and expressive potential. In penetrating jazz music after being

excluded from its early brass-heavy lineups, the saxophone demonstrated its ability to fit in almost anywhere—a talent it would deploy,
with increasing effectiveness, with every new idiom that came along
in the twentieth century.

Like a space cowboy whose time-travel device has malfunctioned,
Vince has been marooned in the pre– and early–Swing Era since he
was born. As a kid growing up on Long Island, New York, in the
1950s, he began collecting old phonograph records of early jazz and
pop music without really knowing why. In the seventh grade he
learned to play violin, then tuba. At thirteen he was playing banjo, a
staple in his beloved early orchestral and cabaret dance bands, in local Fire Department ensembles and working in an antique store on
weekends, trading his time for old recordings and other musical
"junk." A year later, after a lengthy search, Vince bought a bass saxophone, tarnished black, for $95 from an elder at the Long Island
Banjo Society. As his high school grades began to sink, he faced a
draft call and a certain tour in the Vietnam War. He joined the navy
and, after boot camp, passed an audition for the Navy Show Band,
for which he played tuba, electric bass, and banjo as it toured
throughout the United States and South America. Following his discharge, he formed his first band in the seventies with musicians who
were several decades his senior—veterans of the California Ramblers, the Goldkette Orchestra, and the much-revered ensembles of
Paul Whiteman, Fletcher Henderson, and Duke Ellington. Cats
who hadn't received a call in thirty years suddenly heard from Vince,
who persuaded them to get their chops together and join his ten-
piece Colony Club Orchestra. Most were happy to show up for gigs
at the Carlyle Hotel in Manhattan but wouldn't travel, so the less ro-
bust players alternated with the spryer members of the group, which
included men whose names were once legend: Bernie Privin, Jimmy
Maxwell, Spiegle Willcox, Chauncey Morehouse, Artie Baker, Al
Pace, and Clarence Hutchenrider. They delivered a nostalgic mix of
hot jazz and light music, tunes like "The Charleston," "Sugarfoot
Stomp," "Ain't She Sweet," "The Breakaway," and "The Payoff."

The producer Ahmet Ertegun heard them and opened some doors, finding them gigs at the first President Bush's inaugural ball and Steven Spielberg's wedding, which even the most rickety pensioners on Vince's roster were willing to attend. Today, with more contemporary (that is, living) players, he and his latest band, the Nighthawks, entertain dinner crowds at a Manhattan restaurant a couple of nights a week with the same twenties-era tunes.

"The future for me is what I can find in the past," says Vince, a tall, handsome man with a blade of a nose and a full head of reddish-brown hair that he waxes back like a Roaring Twenties crooner on gig nights. He's standing in the center of what most people would consider a living room but by Vince's design, an aesthetic ruled by benign neglect, is more like a shrine to the instrument manufacturers of, say, 1929. In the center of the room is the old Buescher bass saxophone, with a stool in front of it. Occupying nearly as prominent a position is a straight baritone saxophone, its tangle of switchbacks at the neck stretched out to fully eight feet or so. Vince bought the instrument, the only one ever made, from Benny Meroff, a 1920s Chicago sax man. Other giants in the room include a massive harp; a helicon, the forerunner of the tuba; and a bass fiddle.

As we pick through the artifacts and clutter, Vince shows off his favorite oddities and period pieces. There's a sock cymbal, also known as an alligator cymbal, a precursor of the high hat; a gramophone-like machine with a conical brass horn that can play old wax and acetate cylinders; a recorder-like instrument made by Couesnon, called a goofus, with a fake curved bell attached to make it look like a saxophone; a collapsible bass drum from Duke Ellington's band; a fiddle with a projecting horn attached, presumably for recording purposes; and a vintage player piano, a baby grand, that's capable of converting any of the thousand-plus rolls stacked on a nearby wall of shelves into three minutes of aural nostalgia. Yellowed and fading pictures line the walls—there's Jimmy Dorsey and Don Murray, circa 1924, each with two saxophones in his mouth, and Ross Gorman, the "celebrity" reedman in Paul Whiteman's band who improvised the opening glissando on George Gershwin's *Rhapsody in Blue*. Gorman is surrounded by about twenty reed instruments, including an octavon, which Vince describes as a "sawed-off bassoon." Just about every available surface is covered with old sheet music, books, vintage catalogues, period magazines, compact discs, and cannibalized instrument parts.

Most of the printed matter will eventually find its way to the basement, which is cramped because of rows of metal filing cabinets, dozens of them, every drawer filled with the issue of the music-publishing industry of the 1920s, which never saw a chart it was unwilling to print and sell. Vince owns about 30,000 orchestrations, each one of them catalogued on a computer and arranged alphabetically for easy cross-referencing. He also owns a house next door, which he rents. Its basement is filled with about 10,000 queues to silent films.

The music of the twenties often defies categorization, Vince says, one reason it's overlooked by musicologists. "In the twenties, pop and jazz music were the same thing," he says. "A lot of people put down the dance orchestras of Paul Whiteman and Ted Lewis for not being jazz. But they didn't pretend to be. They were just great showmen making music for people who wanted to have a good time."

To a modern musician like Vince, who has to beg and whine just to be considered for a recording contract, the sheer volume of recorded music from the dance-band era is astonishing. "Edison, Pathé, Victor, Columbia—they didn't have any idea about how many records a band would sell, they just recorded everything. Art Hickman recorded thirty-six sides in two weeks—and he was playing two shows a night at the Biltmore Hotel. There was a lot of stuff recorded then that we'd call avant-garde today."

Vince's model is the saxophonist Adrian Rollini, who played the bass in the California Ramblers, the quintessential college dance band of the flapper era. "'Schnoz' was the first guy to play melodically on the bass," he says as he affixes a now-sanitized mouthpiece to Artie Drelinger's old warhorse. He motions for me to sit astride the instrument and try it out. After my fingers find the right positions on the keys, I blow. Ridiculously low blasts of sound escape from the horn. Despite its size, the bass speaks more readily than my tenor. What's truly remarkable, though, is the transforming power of the instrument—of all saxophones, really. The tenor imparts to the player a lean but muscular power and confidence, the baritone a kind of blustering machismo, and the bass . . . as your breath is organized into sound waves, you're suddenly capable of noises that are superhuman. Or perhaps subhuman—Škvorecky's "dying brachiosaur" is not far from the mark.

"Before Adrian, the bass saxophone was a member of the rhythm section, bumping along the bass line," Vince says as he puts a roll in the player piano. "But Adrian played it in the higher register." He mounts the bass as the piano unfurls a ragtime tune and joins in, first oompahing the bass part to demonstrate its use as a timekeeper and then playing a countermelody. "Adrian is still the best to have ever played this instrument," he says after the tune ends. "He had a great sound." Vince once took a lesson from Adrian's brother, Art, a tenor saxophonist in Benny Goodman's band, who revealed the secret of Adrian's mellifluous sound: "He used a baritone mouthpiece," says Vince.

Soon the doorbell rings, signaling the arrival of Chinese food. Vince sweeps a stack of old *Variety*s and *Metronome*s from a low surface, revealing a coffee table. "I'm way behind; there's so much to do," he says with a frown. "All of this stuff has to be indexed and filed. But when someone calls me with an old photograph or catalogue or sheet music, I can't resist acquiring it."

Vince, a man living out of his own time, surveys his living room, a capsule of a golden moment in the nation's, and the saxophone's, musical history that he desperately wishes he could beam himself back to.

"I just felt this was an era nobody cared about."

Nobody, that is, except a small cadre of fellow fanatics Vince introduces me to. One of them is James T. Maher, who has invited me into his study on the Upper West Side of Manhattan to discuss the evolution of the saxophone in dance bands, beginning with its introduction as a lone voice that often doubled violin parts—although some historians think it was first added simply because it looked cool—and continuing through its use as a harmonizing section that grew from two to as many as eight players and gave Duke Ellington's and Count Basie's bands their rich, ribald sound.

Maher, born in 1917, personifies the noblest definition of *amateur*. As the French word implies, he has pursued his interest in music scholarship out of pure love. He spent half his career working as a public relations executive for oil companies, often composing secret reports on oil and water reserves in the Middle East. After leaving Texaco in 1958, he pursued a full-time freelance writing career, augmenting regular assignments on the oil industry ("The Recycling of Petrodollars in World Economies") with magazine articles on the cultural history of American palace architecture, concert reviews, and scripts for a variety of television shows and documentary films. In writing liner notes for more than 200 long-playing albums, including legendary recordings of Harry James, Coleman Hawkins, Benny Goodman, and Gene Krupa, he met and became friendly with many jazz icons from the thirties, forties, and fifties who passed on to him an oral history of the music that didn't always jibe with what was being written about it by so-called experts. "When I was younger I was in awe of the people who wrote about jazz," he says, "until I realized that many were just repeating the canonical bullshit that had somehow become enshrined as authentic jazz history. There's a lot of the story that has yet to be told, and the parts that have been left out have nothing to do with New Orleans."

A college dropout—"My first semester at Ohio State I had four withdrawal slips, which, if you put them together, were about the same size as a diploma"—Jim was working as the public relations director for the Big 10 in Chicago, writing and mailing weekly statistics on the universities' football and basketball teams, when he began composing his first "contemplations" about music. His office was in the Sherman Hotel, home to a legendary nightclub, and one night, while grabbing a bite to eat in the hotel restaurant, he met the saxophonist Bud Freeman, who was playing with a pickup band. The encounter kicked off a lifelong friendship and led to introductions to other musicians, including Benny Goodman, with whom Jim became particularly close. In 1948 he attended a New York University lecture course in jazz taught by the producers George Avakian and John Hammond; a year later he attended a course given by the historian Marshall Stearns. A medieval scholar (his specialty was Chaucer) who would go on to write histories of jazz and dance in America, Stearns had a huge archive of records and print material that became the start-up collection of the Institute of Jazz Studies, which he, Jim, Rudi Blesh, and Dan Morgenstern dreamed up one night and incorporated the next day with four $100 checks. (The highly respected institute, headed by Morgenstern, is now at Rutgers University in Newark.)

"After I took that course with Marshall, he became the focal point of my life," Jim says. "I met everybody of any consequence through him. I must have met Duke Ellington a dozen times, and Duke, who I didn't really expect to remember me, understandably always acted like we were meeting for the first time. Finally, Marshall said to Duke, 'I probably introduce you to Jim four times a year.' And Duke, who was enormously charming—and quick—said, 'And it's a greater pleasure every time.'"

Jim's filing cabinets, which line his study along with shelves of scholarly books, phonograph records, and compact discs, are frequently raided, with his blessing, by music scholars. "For fifty years, I've been writing notes to myself," he says. "But there's a lot of historical fact, too—or, rather, documentation of historical corrections."*

Much of his most entertaining material has not been archived, except between his ears—like the sidebar he has slipped into now about the night he and Stearns spent with Charlie Parker.

---

*Jim is a little too modest about his writing credentials. He is the coauthor, with songwriter-composer Alec Wilder, of *American Popular Song*, which evaluates about 800 of the 300,000 popular songs copyrighted in America between 1900 and 1950.

"He was an absolute angel of a human being," Jim says. "He was with his girlfriend, Chan, and her daughter, Kim. He sat in this big throne of a chair and the little girl snuggled up to him all evening. Marshall recorded everything about how he began playing.* It was a very warm and friendly evening, and as I was going out the door, I said to him, 'Charlie, I've got to make a confession. Sometimes I find your music very difficult.' He broke into this huge grin and said, 'So do I!'"

Jim erupts in a staccato laugh, a hearty, youthful laugh that hints at the energy and joy with which this man, now frail, gaunt, and palsied, stalked the jazz dives and their players in New York and Chicago for sixty years. He is tall and birdlike, with large ears, bright blue eyes, and a hairless head. A couple of years ago he underwent a triple bypass operation, and his wife, Barbara, looks in on us occasionally, warning Jim to wear a mask if he goes out in the sharp cold and not to talk too much, lest he lose his voice. He nods reassuringly after each visit and then, with a conspiratorial wink at me, rises and closes the door. We would talk for another three hours before stepping around the corner for a hamburger. Dan Morgenstern, head of the Institute of Jazz Studies in Newark, of which he and Jim are the last living founders, told me that Jim's health is not too good but that "his noodle is just fine."

A few minutes into our conversation, Jim produces evidence of his noodle's dexterity—a thirty-two-page single-spaced manuscript titled "Sax Notes—Mike Segell" that he has compiled for me. In this "first installment," he has meticulously combed through many of his files looking for references to the saxophone, with a particular eye for its earliest uses in dance bands. Each item is dated and its source fully documented and is followed, in many cases, by a "comment."

The citations reach back to the nineteenth century—to 1853, when the Dodworth brothers, who formed theater pit orchestras,

---

*The interview, part of a series titled "Miles Ahead: Charlie Parker Interviews," is available on CD.

chamber music ensembles, and dancing academies and were among the founding members of the New York Philharmonic, introduced reed instruments to their marching band. "Saxophones?" Jim asks. "Probably." Another entry notes the engagement by Etta Morgan, a member of the Berger Family's Ladies' Orchestra, who played for two weeks at the Olympia Theatre in New York in 1876. Another draws my attention to that first saxophone solo presented by a black American in an orchestra—Elsie Hoffman, with Will Marion Cook's orchestra in Washington, D.C.'s Grand Army Hall on September 26, 1889. "There's a story to be told about women and the saxophone," he says. He dates the saxophone's breakthrough in the pit bands of Broadway musicals—"thirteen and a piano"—to 1913, when the instrument was used in Jerome Kern's second complete score, *Oh, I Say.*

Jim's citations are culled from eighty-year-old trade magazines, transcriptions of radio addresses, catalogues, discographies, billboards, theater advertisements, essays, dissertations, biographies, letters, photographs, and obscure pamphlets—"Mimeographed Hand-Out for a Meeting of the Record Research Society," for instance. His "comments" often digress down odd paths. He writes of an evening with Coleman Hawkins, whom he got to know well sometime in the fifties. During the course of small talk with Hawk as he assembled his horn for a recording session at Webster Hall, Jim mentioned that he really enjoyed Hawk's playing for Fletcher Henderson's stomp band in 1925. After a long silence, Hawk turned to him slowly and said, "What do you want to listen to that shit for?" A few pages later, commenting on a 1927 piece in *Variety* on the saxophone craze, he tells of a lunch he had in Paris with some French clarinetists years later who told him that the American demand for reeds, which came almost exclusively from the Var region of southern France, did more to damage the cane fields there than the German bombers in World War I.

Interspersed throughout his "Sax Notes," and in no particular order, are several references to early uses of the instrument in dance bands. He quotes from *Black Manhattan* by James Weldon Johnson, one of the leading figures of the Harlem Renaissance, who wrote in 1930 that "the first modern jazz band ever heard on a New York stage, and probably on any other stage, was organized at the Marshall [Hotel] and made its debut at Proctor's Twenty-third Street Theatre in the early spring of 1905. It was a playing-singing-dancing orchestra, making dominant use of banjos, mandolins, guitars, saxophones, and drums in combination, and was called the Memphis Students—a very good name, overlooking the fact that the performers were not students and were not from Memphis."

A stickler for the well-established fact, Jim is not convinced that Johnson's memory served him well in this instance, as other, more contemporary accounts of the band's instrumentation on that gig don't support the claim. "But it could have happened," he says, "and maybe for only one engagement. The biggest problem in those years was finding a professional saxophone player who was available at the given time and date."

Jim also questions the claim by W. C. Handy, "the father of the blues," that in 1909 he was first to feature saxophones in an orchestra. And he reserves judgment on James Reese Europe's boast that the saxophone made its dance-orchestra premier in his band in 1914 when the band backed up the society dancers Vernon and Irene Castle on their tour. "You always have to be wary of 'first' claims," Jim says, "because sooner or later, someone will come along and predate you. The exact date doesn't matter. The important thing to realize is that around this time the dance craze is beginning in America, and that's what really propelled the saxophone into mainstream music."

Or perhaps it's the other way around. Whatever the case, the addition of the saxophone to the dance band and the simultaneous passion for dancing that began to sweep through America's cabarets, ballrooms, and roof-garden parties around 1910 appear to be no coincidence. This was an era of sweeping social change, and Americans were eagerly exploring new notions about sex and the role of women. Not surprisingly, it took only a few years for Adolphe Sax's subversive creation to become, in its inimitable attention-grabbing style, the most widely recognized symbol of the racy modern lifestyle and of the emerging music, jazz, that epitomized it. Its enshrinement in the exciting new nightlife was guaranteed in 1914 when the Vatican condemned both the turkey trot, the most popular dance then, and the saxophone.

Americans have always loved to dance. In the nineteenth century, polite society readily embraced European imports such as the waltz (considered scandalous on its introduction in 1814 because partners faced each other), the galop, the polka, the mazurka, the quadrille, and the schottische. With their frequent partner exchanges, the dances stressed formality, self-control, and above all, social interaction. Allen Dodworth, who provided dance classes for the elite, told his students that all dancing pleasure "depends entirely upon the kindly cooperation of others" and that when a group of steppers is properly attentive, "the pleasure is augmented in proportion to the number engaged."

"But by the turn of the century," Jim says, "young people in the fancy families and Mrs. Astor's Four Hundred were getting fed up with the cotillions. They hired new musicians and began to have afternoon dances called kettledrums, modeled after those at a club in London. Finally, the patriarchs abandoned the winter cotillion."

Meanwhile, at the other end of the social spectrum, "dirty" dancing was in full swing. In major cities, the "sporting" districts were rife with prostitution, drugs, gambling, and violent crime. In numerous exposés of low-life culture, the spotlight was trained on the barbaric behavior that went on in the seedy bars and clubs. When the doors of demimonde joints like the Squeeze In Club, the Zaza Café, and the Cave were kicked down by vice squads and the goings-on reported by newspapers, the findings both shocked and titillated: men and women were dancing in sexually explicit fashion to ragtime music with wildly syncopated melodies. Like contemporary stylistic trends that began on the "streeet"—rap music, say, or graffiti art— the dance styles were quickly absorbed by the mainstream.

And so in came the "animal dances"—the turkey trot, the bunny hop, the chicken scratch, the kangaroo kant, the possum trot, the snake, the crab step, the lobster trot, the chicken glide, and walks and trots that eventually coalesced into the fox trot. Accompanying them were the shimmy, or shimmeshawobble, and the Texas tommy (*tommy* meant whore), otherwise known as the Dance That Made the Whole World Stare. Almost all of them originated on the Barbary Coast, the phantasmagoric underworld of seedy dance halls, brothels, opium dens, and gambling parlors that came to life after the sun went down in the San Francisco neighborhood bounded by Broadway and Montgomery, Stockton, and Washington streets. The term *jazz*, some historians think, was first used to describe these dances—as early as 1910. Although the origin of the word has been the subject of endless research (in New Orleans it referred to sexual intercourse), its application to a style of dance is supported by its linkage to the French word *chassé*, a dance step, which is also the source of the word *sashay.* It was only later, this line of thinking goes, that musicians on the Barbary Coast appropriated the term to describe their music.

The grizzly bear was the lewdest of the new dances. Crouching slightly and locked in a grinding bear hug, a couple would rock from side to side as though almost too drunk or opiated to stand but sexually inflamed nonetheless—the conditions that no doubt prevailed for the barroom originators of the dance. It's not difficult to imagine how effective a moaning saxophone would be in the mix.

In short order, the animal dances were sped up, sanitized, and eventually subsumed in the one-step, made famous by Vernon and Irene Castle. In the early teens, the tango, born of the precoital negotiations of prostitutes and visiting gauchos in Buenos Aires, provided another stimulus to the dancehall mania. It, too, was considered outrageously sensuous, even though it had spent a decade in Europe getting cleaned up.

Naturally, the saxophone became the center of attention—and the scapegoat for all the evils attached to jazz dancing. An article in

1922 in *Jacob's Orchestra Monthly* declared "something has got to give. There is a wave of protest against the immoralities, the indecencies, the suggestiveness, the savage wrigglings which evil-minded or merely ignorant dancers interpolate in their dancing and this wave is being surely directed—not directly against the dances themselves or the dancers themselves, but against the MUSIC FOR this sort of dancing, against the MUSICIANS who produce it and against the INSTRUMENTS from which it is produced, with the saxophone heading the list as the worst offender of them all."

The Dionysian call of the saxophone, to believe the crusading moralists, was leading its followers deep into a behavioral sink. In a 1917 newspaper editorial titled "The Saxophone—Siren of Satan," Isadore Berger, the San Francisco composer, wrote that the saxophone "preys upon the passions and emotions. It becomes patently suggestive, instinctively animal-like" and "possesses some strange psychologic power over the young dance devotees of America." Too often, he implied, it simulated orgasmic release, "breathing hurriedly, calling short and fast over and over again."

The self-styled moral arbiters of the day appeared to experience some sort of release themselves simply by writing about the decadent saxophone-centric jazz culture. In an article in the *Ladies' Home Journal* in 1921, Anne Shaw Faulkner worked herself into a lather lamenting the introduction of the corset checkroom, where young ladies could shed their suspension garments so that they could quiver and wriggle freely on the floors of municipal dancehalls. Her screed, titled "Does Jazz Put the Sin in Syncopation?" cites scientific research, conducted in insane asylums, that showed that "the effect of jazz on the normal brain produces an atrophied condition on the brain cells of conception, until very frequently those under the demoralizing influence of the persistent use of syncopation, combined with inharmonic partial tones, are actually incapable of distinguishing between good and evil, between right and wrong." She concludes that jazz is "the accompaniment of the voodoo dancer, stimulating the half-crazed barbarian to the vilest deeds," and that "it is not music at all. It is merely an irritation of the nerves of hearing, a sensual teasing of the strings of physical passion."

With American libertines simulating sex on their feet every night as their brains atrophied, there was an ever-increasing demand for dance bands (the standard size was six or seven members) and, accordingly, a growing demand for saxophonists. Jim's notes contain numerous entries documenting, often by photograph, the inclusion of the saxophone in dance orchestras, many from California, of the early teens. By 1916, Jim says, stock arrangements—common scores to which conductors could add their own flourishes—began to include parts for alto or tenor saxophones, a sign that the instrument was now considered standard in dance bands. And that laid the foundation for the saxophone section, which was key to the horn's own evolution, as well as that of jazz.

Exactly when the saxophone section was born is anybody's guess. "And everybody will," Jim says, "even though it's sort of like looking for the origin of life."

Jim defers on that line of inquiry to Lawrence Gushee, who, although he doesn't know Vince Giordano personally, would certainly qualify for membership in his Meticulous Archivists' Society. A professor of music nearing retirement at the University of Illinois at Urbana-Champaign, Gushee built a reputation earlier in his career as one of the world's preeminent scholars of medieval music. His interests took a sharp turn as he began to explore the early jazz music he loved to play so much as a clarinetist. He began to train his sights on the Creole Band, an ensemble of New Orleans musicians who organized themselves in Los Angeles in 1914 and were part of the great wave of Crescent City musicians who exposed the rest of the country to ragtime music, planting seeds everywhere—but most notably in Kansas City and Chicago—that sprouted into jazz. Twenty years after his research began—not long before we talked, in fact—Gushee finished writing *The Creole Band*. He is widely known as a music scholar who has unearthed new and unusual sources of documentation, primarily the long-forgotten trade press of the demimonde—boxing journals such as the *Referee* and the *Announcer*, cabaret broadsheets such as *Jacob's Orchestra Monthly*, and crime logs such as the *Police Gazette*. His research places the saxophone in cabaret bands in San Francisco, Oakland, and Los Angeles as early as 1908. He's particularly interested in the creation of the saxophone section, which is thought to have begun with Art Hickman's Orchestra in San Francisco in 1919.

As the story of jazz's origins has broadened beyond New Orleans to include other parts of the country, California has emerged as one of the new music's important tributaries—and, not incidentally, as a place where the saxophone obtained a strong foothold in the evolving idiom. In the first decade of the century, San Francisco, the breeding ground of the grizzly bear dance and a whole phylum of animal trots, was a particularly hip city, flush with reconstruction money following the great earthquake and fire of 1906, its appetite for excitement and thrills shared by sailors and other riffraff who washed up in the port city. In 1915 it absorbed another wave of novelty seekers, including many Eastern musicians, who arrived for the Panama-Pacific International Exposition, at which the linking of the transcontinental phone lines was officially inaugurated.

In researching *The Creole Band*, Gushee came across numerous references to the use of the saxophone in California cabaret bands. "I have a theory that the saxophone, used in a quartet with a banjo, was an early California thing," he says. In 1914, when Hickman organized his first band, which ranged between four and six players, according to Gushee, it's unclear whether the lineup included a saxophone. But there's some indirect evidence that Hickman was doing the California thing from the start. A banjo player, Bert Kelley, often sat in with the group at tea dances until he left later that year for Chicago to form his own group, Bert Kelley's Jazz Band. Kelley, says Gushee, later wrote an unpublished book with the modest title *I Invented Jazz*, in which he claimed that the only real jazz is a quartet sound consisting of piano, banjo, saxophone, and drums, the sound he knew in San Francisco—most likely while playing with Hickman. "If you accept Kelley's premise, then you'd have to conclude that jazz was born in California," says Gushee.

Although it was a dance band that played for the tea and dinner sets at the Sherman Hotel in San Francisco, Hickman's ensemble imported much of the Barbary Coast's saucy flavor and swagger. Hickman, whose father was a saloonkeeper in Oakland, worked for Western Union as a teenager and often delivered telegrams to clubs in the notorious neighborhood. In 1928 he told the *San Francisco Examiner* that he used to "greet with joy the chance to deliver a message to some hop joint or honky-tonk in the Barbary Coast. There was music. Negroes playing it. Eye shades, sleeves up, cigars in mouth. Gin and liquor and smoke and filth. But music! There is where all jazz originated." In 1916 he met a kindred spirit in Ferdinand Rudolph von Grofé, a pianist whose musical instincts were shaped by the "medley of folk songs, Negro dance tunes, and sailors' shanties" he had played in Barbary Coast nightspots. Ferde Grofé helped Hickman with his arrangements; his orchestrations show that he was writing saxophone parts not long after he joined the band. An accomplished composer, he later became the arranger for the Paul Whiteman Orchestra, and orchestrated *Rhapsody in Blue* for a young George Gershwin.

Hickman wasn't the first bandleader to think of adding a second saxophone to his dance band—there's evidence that bands led by Wilbur Sweatman, Earl Fuller, W. C. Handy, Isham Jones, and others were using more than one saxophone in 1917, and a tune, "Jazzarimba," was recorded with three saxophones by the Yerkes Jazzarimba Orchestra in 1919—but he was the first to use players, Clyde Doerr and Bert Ralton, whose talent and personality on the instrument helped shape and drive the music. Almost immediately, hundreds of other bands added another saxophone to their lineup, a change in instrumentation that forever altered the sound of the dance band, not to mention employment prospects for saxophonists.

While Hickman had long been playing for overflow dance crowds at the Sherman Hotel, his decision to add a second saxophone changed his fortunes forever. Word of the band's popularity reached the Columbia Gramophone Company, which equipped a private Pullman car with a piano and, in 1919, brought the Art Hickman Orchestra to New York, where the band recorded thirty-six tunes over two weeks. "Those recordings are amazing," Gushee says. "The dance band saxophone begins with Hickman." The group also played every evening at the Biltmore Hotel. Hickman refused to play on the gallery stage, arguing, "We've got to be down on the floor where we can feel the dancers' feet!"

Gushee thinks Hickman may have added the extra horn simply as a novelty. Whatever his motivation, the move paid off handsomely. New York, which had been enthralled by a lengthy engagement of the Original Dixieland Jazz Band, the first jazz band to be recorded (in 1917), at Reisenweber's Café in Manhattan, was ready for something new. The improvisational talent of Doerr and Ralton brought the saxophone's voice to the front of the band, subduing the formerly unassailable primacy of the brasses, and audiences loved the new mix. The band played around town for about a month, but when Broadway impresario Florenz Ziegfeld offered them $2,500 a week to play for after-show dance crowds on the roof of the New Amsterdam Theatre, Hickman turned him down. The band was homesick and wanted to get back to San Francisco.

Hickman came back the next year to play twenty weeks in the *Ziegfeld Follies of 1920*, but again spurned lucrative offers after the show's run and returned to his hometown. Into the void stepped another San Franciscan, Paul Whiteman, who had once played violin in Hickman's band, then formed his own band in a skating rink in 1916, relocated it to Los Angeles, and by 1919 had virtually the same instrumentation, including two saxophones, as his former boss. Whiteman and his band also came east, and performed at the Ambassador Hotel in Atlantic City, New Jersey, while Hickman was playing the *Follies*. When Hickman returned to San Francisco the second time, Whiteman took up residence at the Palais Royal in Times Square, recorded several sides, and watched his orchestra's popularity soar to the point at which he considered it appropriate to anoint himself the King of Jazz, even though the music he played was, by contemporary definitions, a far cry from it. By the mid-twenties he had begun franchising his ensembles, eventually establishing fifty-two Paul Whiteman Orchestras around the world.

Much of the credit for Whiteman's early success is due to the arranging of Ferde Grofé, Gushee says. "In 1919 they were still operating by what Grofé called the huddle system," Gushee says, "where the band gets together and decides who plays the head, who takes a solo, who does a duet, and so on. Grofé began to organize those arrangements into interesting cumulative riffs without losing any of the improvisational quality. It was kind of a nice sound—two brass, two reeds, a strong rhythm section—the first dance band sound. Grofé showed how to take a small band and make a lot of it."

By 1921, many bands, including those of Isham Jones, Ray Miller, Gene Rodemich, and the California Ramblers, had added a third saxophone. In the same year, Arthur Lange, the premier dance-band orchestrator of the era, sent out a letter with his charts for "Stolen Kisses," announcing that he would routinely include saxophone arrangements in his scoring. "Dear Friends and Fellow Musicians," he wrote in the note. "During the evolution of dance music in the past few years it has become a necessity for saxophone players to read from the cello parts . . . In order to give more value to the arrangement, I am now arranging cello parts which are strictly intended for the cello, and saxophone parts which are intended for the sax. You will find these parts more effective and melodious than the cello parts."

The inclusion of a saxophone trio in popular dance bands had an interesting impact on music publishing. When the violin players in thousands of nonprofessional bands around the country abandoned their bows and began taking saxophone lessons, the publishers, acknowledging the likely lack of proficiency among the newly converted alto players, decided to include alto parts that had no more than a couple of sharps—preferably none—in the stock arrangements that were distributed to amateur players. That was the reason most of the songs of Kern, Berlin, and Gershwin were in F, B-flat, or E-flat.*

By the end of the decade, the saxophone section in Duke Ellington's band featured a quartet. "It's an interesting question why the extra instruments were added," Gushee says. "Certainly no club owner wanted to pay for another musician. Maybe it was just fashionable. Or maybe it had to do with the larger dance halls. In Chicago, the Aragon and Trianon had 2,000 couples on the floor, and the band had no amplification."

Whatever the reason, saxophones now made up a section in dance bands, ready to take advantage of the kind of sophisticated arrangements that could reveal their harmonic potential.

Which is the final step in the dance-band story. Although Hickman's arrangements brought saxophones to the front of the band, Doerr and Ralton obeyed their own separate musical instincts while playing. "As good as they were, it didn't occur to them to play the same rhythmic figure in harmony," says Tony Hagert, a friend of Vince Giordano's, referring to the classic choral voicing of saxophone sections that was about to become standard in dance bands. "There was no concept of a blend, no idea that they should be anything but separate voices."

Tony has spent many hours poring over orchestrations of the teens and twenties, tracing the evolution of the concerted saxophone section. It's an important development, because out of that harmonious blend the soloists would eventually break free, establishing the instrument's primacy in jazz music, with a royal lineage extending

---

*This observation came by way of James T. Maher from a reader of his book *American Popular Song*, which he coauthored with Alec Wilder.

back to Hawk and Johnny Hodges and up through Prez, Bird, Trane, Rollins, and modern masters like Joe Lovano and Michael Brecker.

Tony is another avid collector who can't quite explain why he needs to own every piece of historical material he comes across. Now in his mid-sixties, he's worked most of his life as a small-loan administrator while using a modest inheritance to develop a one-man organization called Vernacular Music Research, which never managed to push its bottom line out of the red zone but did enable him to avoid the tax consequences of his insatiably acquisitive streak. Standing in the living room of his townhouse in south Philadelphia, Tony assures me that it would look a lot like Vince's had he not just moved from the eastern shore of Maryland. At the insistence of his wife, his collection is neatly packed away in boxes and stored a few blocks away.

So off we go to root around in it. After a short walk, Tony, a small, bearded fellow in khakis and a flannel shirt, stops in front of a two-story former carriage house, releases the various security devices, and throws open the door. The second story is his daughter's painting studio, the ground floor, what used to be the stable, his collection's new home. The periphery of the large room is lined with metal filing cabinets that support columns of books and catalogues rising precariously like paper stalagmites. Stacks of shelving with just enough room between them to accommodate a lithe librarian criss-cross the stable, reaching all the way to the sixteen-foot-high ceiling. The shelves sag under the weight of hundreds of cardboard boxes, each one neatly labeled. The cartons contain old copyrights, sheet music, catalogues of phonograph records, orchestrations for theatrical and dance bands, method books, the bookkeeping data of pre- and post-Depression record companies, and anything else that might offer a window into early-twentieth-century American musical history. He has 15,000 78 rpm recordings from Victor, Emerson, Pathé, and a number of dime-store labels and about 5,000 long plays. An entire stack is devoted to books on deviant culture—smuggling, gambling, prostitution, "the cultures that supported the music," Tony says. Other stacks have sections on African-American life, film, and theater. Strategically positioned amid the shelving are a couple of small tables and chairs—workstations outfitted with pencil and paper, a couple of packs of Camel cigarettes and a few Twix bars to sustain the attention and energy of a compulsive archivist who can't be bothered with the time-consuming rituals of daily life, like eating.

As we make our way to the rear of the stable, Tony shows me a few pamphlets he thought I'd enjoy. One is a method book called "Sax-Acrobatix" by Henri Weber, published in 1926. The booklet promises that even the novice saxophone player can easily learn "the roar, talk, auto-horn, moan, bark, yelp, cry, laugh, gliss, sneeze, meow and caw." Another is titled "Jazz Breaks," a 1926 alto tutorial by Miff Mole, who is caricatured on the cover with devil horns, wild eyes, and a tongue pocked by quarter notes that stretches all the way across the page. A third offers instruction on tonguing techniques— slap-tongue, flutter-tongue, triple-tongue—which, read aloud and out of context, could easily be mistaken for a passage from a sex manual.

At the back of the room, on top of a long section of oak card-catalogue drawers that he got from a public library, Tony has laid out the labors of the previous evening's explorations, performed in anticipation of my visit. On thick sheets of yellowed twelve-stave music paper, he's written out the charts to "Beale Street Mama," a 1923 tune played by the Arthur Lange Orchestra, and "My Blackbirds Are Blue" and "Sweet Ella May," both 1928 songs arranged by Frank Skinner. All three contain parts for a saxophone section of two altos and a tenor.

"You can see that the 1923 tune is scored in an all-purpose fashion, with five different ways the saxophones can play," Tony says, tracing a tobacco-stained finger along the notation. "The section is not standardized yet. The second alto and tenor play a counterpart rather than harmony. The arrangers still thought the alto and tenor saxophones were as different from each other as, say, a trumpet and trombone."

He turns to the arrangement of "My Blackbirds." "In 1928, you can see the arranger trying to get the fullest sound by writing open harmony for the section." He points to four bars written for lead tenor, and those directly below, for the two supporting horns. Even my untrained eye can see that the notations for each instrument, which Tony has stacked on three staves, all move together at the same rhythm. "This is the concerted saxophone section we now know so well."

Tony has combed through hundreds of orchestrations, looking for the "Aha" moment when small bands first began using saxophones in concert. "The arranging is all over the place," he says. "The important thing is that it happened." In 1925, Arthur Lange published a series of articles gathered in one volume as *Arranging for the Modern Orchestra*, which codified scoring practices and declared that a saxophone trio was now the "backbone" of the modern dance orchestra. "Officially," says Tony, "I guess you could say the concerted section began then."

By then Fletcher Henderson, "the father of the big band," or alternatively, "the black Paul Whiteman," had organized his first orchestra, teaming a brilliant young cornet player, Louis Armstrong, with Coleman Hawkins.

And the saxophone, after a seventy-five-year adolescence, was about to find its true voice.

"PLEASE . . . CLOSE . . . THE . . . WINDOW!!"

Mortified, I creep over to the open window, out of view of my clearly perturbed neighbors, pull down the shade, then lower the sash. On this uncommonly warm late-winter afternoon, I wanted to air out my office and get in a little practice time. I hadn't thought about the aural consequences for the innocents in immediate range of my horn. My fifth-floor office, which doubles as my kids' gaming parlor, looks out onto the rear courtyards of the surrounding apartment buildings, most of which rise a few stories above ours. I really don't wish to find out who among my few hundred or so closest neighbors I've so thoroughly ticked off with the ungodly noise I've been making. Neither do I want them to know who is the author of that sound. On the street, venturing around the corner to get a newspaper, my life could be in danger.

I've been practicing long tones on my Armstrong tenor, starting with the lowest note, the B-flat, ranging up to the F, then the next B-flat, all by using the same fingering. According to Michel Gohler, my teacher, the amount of pressure I have to exert on the reed to hit the middle F by fingering the B-flat is exactly what I want to bring to the middle F when fingering it properly. For this exercise, Joe Allard, the late master teacher of some of today's greatest players, says it helps to try to "hear" the tone before playing—to try "pre-hearing" it. Easy for him. I'd say it's more like "pre-contortion." Not only do I have to tighten my lips around the mouthpiece like a boa constrictor squeezing the life out of its prey (which is the wrong way to do it but the only way I know how at the moment), paralyzing tiny muscles in my jaw and cranium that prevent me from chewing properly for an hour afterward, but my diaphragm must slowly contract to force air from my inflated lungs like a powerful but finely calibrated bellows. There are also a thousand other things going on involving distant outposts of my body's wiring grid and network of soft tissues, none of which have had much to do with just about any other activity I've ever been engaged in. Much of my nervous system, consequently, is in a state of anarchy.

The three-note slide up the horn is not nearly as hard on those who simply have to listen to it. This is the Upper West Side of Manhattan, after all, where the density of musicians, both professional and aspiring, is probably greater than that of any other neighborhood in the world. We like to hear people practicing. But in fact, as so often happens when I work on scales, long tones, or fingering exercises, I've ventured into exploratory territory. I've discovered to my great pleasure an extraordinary sound produced by two notes, along with a mix of partial tones, speaking at once—what modern "art" saxophonists call a multiphonic. It's lush, gorgeous, and incredibly dense—the low notes on the tenor set into vibratory motion anything not glued or bolted down—like the signal blast of an ocean liner. It undulates gracefully from the bell of the horn, the sound waves magically gathering themselves into a sympathetic rhythm around me. As the two sound waves intersect at different frequencies, they add and subtract from each other, creating beats, or the impression that someone is repeatedly raising and lowering a volume button on the horn. For the past hour or so, I've repeatedly tried to find that complex tone, locating it about every fourth try. When I do, I just wail and listen, ecstatic. It comes from deep within me and it feels so good. I'm producing the acoustic phenomenon, I am the sound, and as it stretches out before me I can hop aboard and take a ride. I've never felt or heard anything like it. I'm flush with joy and think of the saxophonist Wessell Anderson—"Warmdaddy," to the cats who play with him in Wynton Marsalis's ensemble. If Warmdaddy were a noise, this is what it would sound like.

But only if you're playing. If you're within listening distance—trying, say, to read, nap, or make love—apparently it feels like you're trapped in sonic hell. There's an old joke about a gentleman being someone who knows how to play the saxophone but doesn't. My vocal neighbor, desperately issuing his plea from a nearby window, obviously wishes he lived next to such a man. So, once again, it looks like I'm going to have to exile myself to the one room in my home where I bother those within range the least—the bathroom. It's actually a great place to practice. The acoustics are terrific, particularly for notes in the lower register. There's a mirror, in front of which Michel advises practicing so I can create a mental grid of where my fingers should be on the horn. And there's room for a music stand, so that if anyone bursts in on me I can at least look like I'm trying to read the charts.

I suspect I'm just the latest in a long line of saxophonists who have been banished to the nearest rest room. Stan Getz, I know, often took to the toilet for his practice sessions when he was a kid. He grew up in a tenement in the Bronx surrounded by other tenements, and in the summer he practiced in the bathroom with the windows open. "It was all tiles and echo," he once told an interviewer. "Then somebody would say, 'Shut that kid up!' And my mother would say, 'Play louder, Stanley.'"

Which is exactly what I feel like doing. But I'm no Stan Getz. So I close the window and slink off to the bathroom.

6. IT'S ALL ABOUT RELATIONSHIPS

The saxophone, particularly the tenor, has such a rich history," says Joe Lovano as he sips a drink between sets at the Jazz Standard in New York, where he's playing a weeklong gig with his Street Band. "The players whose personalities and tones and sounds and imaginations have come through that horn have been amazing. It wasn't *what* they were playing but *how* they were playing. When you really study the lineage of your instrument and realize how each of the players listened to the cats before him and then found his own way, they inspire you to keep going in new directions."

Lovano's personal tour through tenor history, and his assimilation of its most distinctive voices in his own playing, has been as comprehensive as that of any player alive. Born in 1952, the son of tenor saxophonist Tony "Big T" Lovano, he was tutored by legendary innovators such as Sonny Stitt, Lester Young, and Rahsaan Roland Kirk when they landed in his hometown, Cleveland, to play with his dad. As a feisty teenager, he instigated raucous Texas-tenor-style cutting sessions, jammed in organ trios, and deconstructed the abstruse free-jazz experimentations of Ornette Coleman, John Coltrane, and Jimmy Giuffre. After attending the Berklee School of Music in Boston, Lovano earned a chair in the Woody Herman Thundering Herd in the late seventies, a three-year gig that crescendoed in a fortieth anniversary concert with Stan Getz, Zoot Sims, Flip Phillips, and Al Cohn, and in the Mel Lewis Orchestra a few years later. He worked extensively with the legendary drummers Elvin Jones and Paul Motian and has played in just about every small-ensemble configuration, from trio (Motian, guitarist Bill Frisell, and Joe have regrouped every few months for the past twenty years) to his ongoing nonet. He has surrounded his sound with string quartets, woodwind quartets, and the ethereal, wordless vocalese of his wife, Judi Silvano. His eagerness to introduce his instrument to new company has led to extensive collaborations with the renowned composer and conductor Gunther Schuller, most impressively on the Third Stream masterpiece *Rush Hour*, which was voted Album of the Year in 1995 by *Downbeat* readers. A mentor to the generation just behind him, he generously invites "young lions" such as Joshua Redman and Greg Osby to contribute to his recordings.

"It's all about relationships," says Joe, a large, warm, round man with a lush Vandyke. "All that history, all those sounds the people before you have discovered on the horn, dovetails in what you play now. All those great cats' personalities—you draw from all their feelings and moods. You have this obligation to the past, not just to follow or imitate the cats who came before you but to absorb and decipher what they were doing and try to put it together in your own way. No matter what you do, you're connected to that first guy who discovered a different way to blow the horn, and all the guys who came after him."

In the liner notes to *Tenor Legacy*, an album he recorded in 1994 with Joshua Redman, Lovano listed more than sixty saxophonists whose music he has studied. In interviews and comments, he has mentioned countless other influences. "He's a living repository of the horn," his wife, Judi, told me during one of the breaks at his show, affirming, as T. S. Eliot once declared, the importance of the past to the creative process. "Tradition is a matter of much wider significance," Eliot wrote in "Tradition and the Individual Talent." "It cannot be inherited, and if you want it you must obtain it by great labour." In honoring the saxophone's jazz tradition, Joe's labor has been truly great.

For Joe, the historical boundaries of the solo saxophone in jazz, which most people believe begins with Coleman Hawkins, occasionally become blurred. Recently, the many voices of his predecessors have dovetailed in the music of . . . Enrico Caruso. For a historian of the tenor who is also recognized as one of a handful of great contemporary jazz saxophonists, Caruso is an inspired choice as a role model. The smoldering Italian opera great, himself a tenor, whose legend was fully established by the time he died at thirty-eight, was roiling the world of opera just a few years before the saxophone began to find its solo voice.

"I studied his sound, his projection, and learned a lot," Joe says. "The quality of those recordings around 1920 was poor, so you don't catch the subtleties. But even so, the dynamics are so intense, you can hear him just vibrating. You can imagine the tone, from superpianissimo to really forte. In every piece of music, he was a different personality. It was amazing how he could use his voice to create moods and constantly be changing the color of the music. It made me realize that that's what Ben Webster did. When he played a blues, it was one way; on a swing tune he had another kind of growl. On a fast tune he had a brute, aggressive thing. A lot of cats play the way they play no matter what the tune is. Some great players play the same solo on every tune. But not Ben. And not Caruso."

And not Joe Lovano. I had been listening a lot to *Rush Hour* when Joe sent me *Viva Caruso*, a soulful, atmospheric, genre-busting opus that underscores the remarkable versatility of the saxophone and the breadth of Joe's tastes. Joe and the arranger Byron Olson transcribed and restructured Caruso arias and folk songs, and then, immersed in the singer's world, Joe wrote a couple of tunes of his own—the tan-golike "Streets of Naples," which evokes the early-jazz sounds Caruso heard before he died in 1921, and a four-part suite, *Il Carnivale di Pulcinella*, which captures the wild, orgiastic mood of the annual Neapolitan event, named after a commedia dell'arte clown. For Joe, the band was the thing, the nexus of the relationship to the past—to Caruso's and his own. After a string of high-profile efforts that won him numerous honors, he was back jamming with a group of guys he first began playing with thirty years before, some during his school days in Cleveland, others during the seventies when they played for free during multimedia "happenings" at Judson Memorial Church on Greenwich Village's Washington Square.

Now the band migrates toward the small stage at the Jazz Standard for its second set of the evening, some of its members remaining in the shadows offstage. The instrumentation is peculiar—two drummers, two bass fiddle players, a guitarist, an accordion player, a vocalist, a soprano saxophonist, and, of course, Joe, on his custom-made Borgani tenor, which, even with its outsized bell, seems like a toy instrument in his huge hands. The bodies of many saxophone players match their instruments—little guys tend to play soprano, big guys the tenor or baritone—but Joe's looks like it could easily accommodate a contrabass. Without introduction, he begins running rhythmic figures on his horn, and gradually the quartet of rhythm section players joins in. Their separate parts eventually resolve into "O Sole Mio," one of the most widely recognized songs ever written.

"I call this my street band," Joe tells the audience when the song ends, "because you just never know who's going to show up." He looks offstage, feigns surprise, and points to a short, blond man in a shiny green suit who's holding a soprano saxophone. "Awww, man," says Joe. "Look at this. See what I mean? It's Billy Drewes."

Counting silently, Joe launches the band into "For You Alone," one of the few songs Caruso recorded in English. Over the next forty-five minutes, the group, adding a player or two per song, explores a complex mix of emotions and moods, evoking the happy-but-sad aura of a New Orleans funeral march in one song and a Neapolitan carny-funhouse atmosphere in the next. As Gil Goldstein's fingers fly across the accordion keyboard, you half expect to see an organ-grinder standing in the shadows with a tiny monkey on a leash, or harlequin figures dancing in the silvery shadows of moonglow. Guitarist Michael Bocian, whom Joe first met in high school, joins him for a duet on "Streets of Naples," followed by a sweet homage, "Ballad for T," which Michael wrote when Joe's father died in 1986. Demonstrating his ongoing commitment to his tenor ancestors, Joe plays John Coltrane's "Countdown" and uses a calypso tone on "Santa Lucia" that is pure Sonny Rollins. Judi Silvano, in a flowing peasant dress, emerges from backstage and offers scat improvisations and a keening Middle Eastern cry to the already polyglot sound. "I didn't know these people would show up," Joe jokes at one point with a shrug. "This was supposed to be a trio."

Toward the end of the show, which on this night is attended by Lee Konitz, Gunther Schuller (whose son Ed plays bass in the band), and Bruce Lundvall, head of CBS Records, the band plays a rousing, stomping version of *Il Carnivale*. The third and fourth movements of the suite, titled "The Bite" and "Tarantella Sincera," explore the folkloric origins of the tarantella, the medieval dance-frenzy thought to cure the victims of a deadly spider bite. The piece allows for long statements by each player; after working through her parts, Judi leaves the stage and settles at a table with friends who have come to the show. Joe then plays his solo and departs to join Judi. The couple, now married for nearly two decades, smile with satisfaction as they listen to the ensemble they've assembled from among their friends from the "street." Nearing the end of his solo on soprano saxophone, Billy Drewes wedges his upper body beneath the lid of the grand piano, now played by accordionist Gil Goldstein, the bell of his horn nearly touching the strings. ("I just like to get close to a person's sound," he says later.) Joe and Judi laugh and Joe's hand fumbles in the dark until it finds hers. He sits silently, beaming, admiring his creation, surrounded by the echoes of Hawk, Prez,

Rollins, Trane, and a handful of other great innovators whose spirits he has summoned in his playing.

As Joe says, it's all about relationships.

The first relationship most studious solo saxophonists develop is with Coleman Hawkins, George Avakian's late friend. Dressed in a white nylon jacket and white pants and sporting a pointy beard, George, at eighty-four, still looks the part of the urbane jazz impresario. He began earning his creds, which have won him just about every award in the recording industry, in his teens, long before he produced the records of some of the music's mightiest innovators, including Hawk, the man who is considered the primogenitor of the solo saxophone. As a student at Yale in the late 1930s, George became friendly with the pioneering jazz scholar and collector Marshall Stearns, who was then working on his doctorate in English literature. Stearns, the first critical analyst of jazz, gave his friend all-night tutorials in the music, and, before he graduated, Avakian had lined up a deal with Columbia Records to unearth forgotten jazz gems from the twenties and thirties and launch the Hot Jazz Classics line for the label. His choices rescued out-of-print sides from Bix Beiderbecke, Bessie Smith, Louis Armstrong's Hot Fives and Sevens, and the bands of Fletcher Henderson and Duke Ellington.

He went on to organize recording sessions that celebrated the distinctive styles of New York, New Orleans, and other hotbeds of early jazz. In 1940, for instance, he reunited guitarist Eddie Condon and clarinetist Pee Wee Russell to re-create the late 1920s sounds of Chicago. In the fifties, while still at Columbia, he pushed the label into the field of live pop and jazz recording, which led to the spectacular four-album collection that chronicled the storied 1956 Newport Jazz Festival, at which Duke Ellington's saxophonist Paul Gonsalves played twenty-seven riotous choruses on "Diminuendo and Crescendo in Blue."

Of course, Avakian also produced records for Louis Armstrong,

John Coltrane, Paul Desmond, Miles Davis, Sonny Rollins, and Hawk, among many others. Like Joe Lovano, when he listens to contemporary saxophonists he hears the cumulative history of the horn's great artists—plus one great trumpet player. "Most people feel the solo saxophone starts with Hawkins," he says, sipping tea in the solarium of his bright, airy home overlooking the Hudson River in Riverdale, New York. "But where it really begins is with Louis Armstrong."

Almost single-handedly, George says, "Pops," who became a close personal friend of George's, established jazz's rhythmic phrasing. "The trumpets swung first," he says. "As Dizzy Gillespie said later, 'No Pops, no me.' Miles Davis said you can't play anything that hasn't been played by Armstrong. The singers were the same way—Bing Crosby, Frank Sinatra, Billie Holiday. The phrasing, the improvisational quality—they all learned it from Louis. Hawk was special, though, because as a young man he had the advantage of playing along right next to him."

In the mid-twenties, Hawk and Armstrong were playing in the Fletcher Henderson band—a gig that, for Hawkins, would last a decade, with long engagements at the Roseland Ballroom in New York. Hawk, born in 1904, had traveled east from his hometown of St. Joseph, Missouri, in 1921 with a blues singer, Mamie Smith, and her band, the Jazz Hounds. A year later he was in the Henderson band, the "colored" counterpart to the slick Paul Whiteman ensembles. Hawk had a big, big sound and often spoke proudly about his ability to be heard above the brasses.

Armstrong joined Henderson in 1924.* During the couple of years Louis was in the band, he and Hawk would regularly retreat to Hawk's apartment in Harlem after Roseland gigs for all-night jam-

---

*This was also the year Louis recorded a session with Sidney Bechet, whom many consider the first jazz saxophonist of any note, when both were members of a swinging pickup band called the Red Onion Jazz Babies. Bechet was a prodigiously talented clarinet player from New Orleans who picked up the soprano saxophone while on tour in Europe with Will Marion Cook's Southern Syncopated Orchestra in 1919. Bechet left behind a curious legacy: his pioneering work is often ignored by the most meticulous scholars of jazz history,

and-bullshit sessions. It's probably not too much of an exaggeration to say that some of the most innovative music of that era was being played in Hawk's living room.

Although the saxophone was gaining prominence as a section instrument, it was still incarcerated stylistically by the slap-tongued, herky-jerky dotted-note playing apotheosized by Rudy Wiedoeft and other virtuosos of the era, who played in a buttoned-up classical European style. When Hawkins, who had studied piano and cello and had a keen grasp of music theory, first heard Armstrong's rhythmic bluesy gait, he heard the future of the American saxophone. With his extraordinary wind ("Hawk was so strong he used a reed that was like a two-by-four," says Dan Morgenstern), he had the power and technique to follow Louis's swinging lead. Two years later, on a Henderson recording of "Stampede," Hawkins revealed the shimmering results of his sessions with Louis: a thrusting, slurred, harmonically complex solo on which, like Armstrong, he ignored the beat and allowed his phrases to flow past the bar lines. "It was a total revolution," George says. "He changed the sound and rhythmic basis of the playing, and his followers, like Chu Berry and Ben Webster, took it from there."

Hawk's suddenly swinging tenor, which, like Armstrong's cornet, had its roots in the highly vocal tradition of African music, sprang saxophonists from the prison of overarticulation. In 1929 he fairly patented the idea of the flowing saxophone solo when he recorded what many musicologists consider his first masterpiece, "One Hour." On the tune, based on James P. Johnson's popular song "If I

---

probably for reasons that have to do with geography and temperament. He moved to London in 1919, but was deported back to the States after some unfortunate business with a prostitute. By 1925, he was back in Europe, but was deported again after he got into an argument with a banjoist in Paris—a woman was at the center of the fight—and the two began shooting at each other outside a café. Even by the generous standards of a profession that tolerated a lot of outrageous behavior, he was considered difficult to work with.

The Sidney Bechet Society, of which George Avakian is a founding member, has worked to correct the neglect without much success.

Could Be With You (One Hour Tonight)," Hawkins never actually played the melody, instead delivering richly romantic phrasing that only obliquely referred to it. On that one song, the rhapsodic qualities and harmonic flexibility of the tenor were unveiled. There was now a new way to play the saxophone and its future was wide open.

In 1934, Hawkins decamped for Europe, where, like many black jazz musicians who followed, he was treated like a king. He returned to the States in 1939 to record "Body and Soul," perhaps the most famous tenor solo of all time, around the time that George Avakian, a junior at Yale, began cutting classes to catch his performances in New York.

"He was one of the gods," George says. "He was playing at Kelly's Stables on Fifty-second Street. When he was playing you got the feeling nothing was going to take this man away from what he was doing. His tone was fantastic and he had this focused strength, this discipline. You could see that on the bandstand. When he stood up to take a solo everything changed. He was a master of each performance."

In breaching the single-note limits of the saxophone that had been so clearly observed by his predecessors, Hawkins conveyed a sense of multiple sounds—an idea later perfected by Charlie Parker, whose fingering speed allowed impressionistic chords to resonate long after he'd gone on to the next passage, and John Coltrane, who covered listeners with "sheets of sound." When playing the tenor, Hawk sometimes said, he strove for the sound of the cello. Although he had little else in common with Rudy Wiedoeft, the two virtuosos did share a fascination with stringed instruments. Whereas Wiedoeft imitated the vibrato of the violinist Fritz Kreisler, Hawkins's hero was the cellist Pablo Casals.

The tenor has often been compared to the cello—a likeness that may first have become apparent in Hawk's full, opaque, masculine sound and that has been affirmed by modern masters like Joe Lovano. Known for his sophisticated tastes—Hawk had a fondness for expensive cars and fine liquor and was always immaculately turned out, usually in a mohair suit, with perfectly conked hair and a neat sliver of a mustache—he also loved classical music, an appreciation he acquired from his mother, who made him study piano and cello before he took up the saxophone. He was always eager to share this interest with his friends. During his first stay in Europe, Hawk rented an apartment in Amsterdam, where he often entertained American guests. One night he met up with Harry Lim, the producer who later recorded Hawk and a few other jazz greats for the short-lived Keynote Records before it went bankrupt after the war. Hawk asked Lim to hang in the club until after his gig; there was a record he really wanted him to hear back in his apartment. Jazz was just beginning to flourish in Europe. Lim wondered, Was there some new European talent Hawk had discovered? Back in his flat, with great fanfare, Hawk spun the record for his guest. It was the Schubert Trio in B-flat played by Casals, with Jacques Thibaut on violin and Alfred Cortot on piano. As he grew older, Hawk's tastes apparently didn't change. When he died, his friends discovered that his extensive record collection consisted solely of classical music.

As the king of the tenor, Hawk wore his crown uneasily. He was constantly fending off young comers who wanted to carve him onstage (although as a young man he was usually the instigator of such cutting contests); invariably, when blood was spilled it belonged to the challenger. His brilliant sea-parting solo on "Body and Soul," a divinely inspired exercise in improvisation, became a leaden cross he had to bear everywhere: audiences demanded that he play it note for note wherever he went. George Avakian, who once paired Sonny Rollins and Hawk on stage at Newport—"A mistake," he says. "They were too deferential to each other"—noticed that toward the end of his life Hawk, who uncharacteristically grew an unruly beard and often appeared disheveled, had an air of sadness about him. "There was this sense of disappointment," he says. "Other musicians were very respectful, but despite a long and distinguished career, he felt he never really got the acclaim he deserved.

"But he was a person of great influence at a time when it was desperately needed. Without him, nobody would have played the way they played later."

Not a single seat is empty in the 92nd Street Y's auditorium, a wonderful place to hear live music, on the Upper East Side of Manhattan. Tonight the cultural center is featuring the music of Bix Beiderbecke, the "hot-sweet" cornet player of the twenties whose collaborator, Frank Trumbauer, had a strong influence on Lester Young, the next great soloist to emerge after Hawk. It's a check-your-cane-at-the-door kind of crowd: the average age of audience members seems to be somewhere between eighty and ninety. On stage, Dick Hyman, a pianist, composer, and encyclopedic archivist of early jazz music, has been introducing each tune with a saucy mix of historical detail and gossip. "Let's see," he says at one point, trying to remember the writer of one of the few tunes not written by Beiderbecke. "Was it Ory and Gilbert?" A low murmur from the audience indicates it was not. "I don't think it was Hoagy Carmichael." "No," a few in the audience can be heard to say. "Zez Confrey!" The crowd erupts in laughter and affirmative applause. This is a knowledgeable group.

Vince Giordano and his Nighthawks, who specialize in this era, are the mediums and channelers for tonight's romp down memory lane. Toward the end of the concert, reed player Dan Levinson rises from his chair to take a solo on "Cryin' All Day." He places his saxophone to his lips and a sweet, keening, almost whimsical sound emerges from its bell. The center of the tone is elusive and seems to float like smoke above the supporting instruments. The horn itself is a peculiar shape, skinny and a little tall, like a gangly adolescent after a growth spurt. It's a C tenor, or C-Melody, the ubiquitous, much-maligned amateur favorite of the 1920s that never found a voice in jazz.

Which is not to say that it yielded no influence on the evolving idiom. Hot music had one brilliant C-Melody exponent in the form of Trumbauer, a straitlaced, conscientious, and responsible family man whose four-year collaboration with Bix, his hard-partying foil whose thirst for alcohol killed him before he was thirty, produced some of the most searing popular music of the twenties. It's difficult to know how either musician would have developed without the other, but the interplay yielded real magic and, for the solo saxophone, charted the first steps in a key stylistic alternative, adopted and perfected a few years later by Lester Young, to the path outlined by Coleman Hawkins. "Frank Trumbauer greatly influenced Lester," says Dan after the show. "Like Dizzy Gillespie said of Louis Armstrong: No Tram, no Prez."

Tram and Bix established a conversational rapport on their duets, or "chase choruses," that set an early standard for saxophone-cornet partnerships. Bix was the hothead, tearing through the full spectrum of human emotion like a borderline personality yet playing with a tone, Eddie Condon once said, that was "like a girl saying yes." Trumbauer seemed to hover above all the mercurial affect, coolly keeping his distance, reshaping and enfolding the melody with elegant, sophisticated phrases as he constructed his own narrative. Bix swung; Tram respected the conventions of meter. His approach was too mannered for him to step out of the rhythmic box that Hawk had crashed through. But his restrained, debonair style was also partly a reflection of the weaknesses of his chosen instrument, infamously known for its inconsistent pitch. He avoided the sour notes on the horn and glissed others, smoothly easing into a passage like a gentleman into his hand-tailored tuxedo. Lester Young, who was given a Trumbauer record by saxophonist Eddie Barefield, the star of Chick Webb's band, and never gave it back, always acknowledged his debt to the C-Melody maestro. In his way, Prez said, Tram "told a little story." Prez told stories, too, often while playing behind Billie Holiday, who told some poignant ones of her own.

"In 1936, on his first recording with Count Basie's small band, Lester's sound and solo on 'Lady Be Good' is unlike anything else then on record," says Dan. "It's smooth, all the jagged edges have been shaved off. It's a lot like Trumbauer's sound. Prez was the first one to have that smooth sound on the tenor. He always sounded like he was lying back in his easy chair and relaxing. It didn't matter what the tempo was, it never seemed like he was playing fast. And he wasn't laying back on the beat. It was just easy and effortless. Suddenly, soloing saxophonists had two major stylists they could emulate. Lester's approach not only influenced Charlie Parker and the whole bebop thing to come, but it helped launched its antithesis, the whole cool-jazz movement of the forties and fifties with Stan Getz, Dexter Gordon, Gerry Mulligan, Gene Ammons, Zoot Sims, Al Cohn, and a host of others."

The "Lady Be Good" solo, along with another on "Shoe Shine Boy," presented the first significant challenge to Hawk's reign as king of the tenor. Everything about their contrasting styles could be summed up by a physical comparison of the two innovators. Hawk, though not tall, had a big, earthy presence; Prez was lean and airy. Hawk exuded a virile masculinity, Lester a slightly fey carnality. Hawk was forceful, direct, a determined extrovert. Prez was sensitive, remote, and not a little cunning. Hawk was well spoken and articulate, while Lester, the original jazz hipster, kept his distance by inventing a language no one could understand.*

For all his reserve and desire to play just offstage, outside the spotlight, Lester was the embodiment of a shift in popular music, particularly among its lyricists, that explored more mature and realistic thematic material, especially concerning romantic love. Before World War I, popular songs tended to reflect commonly shared values and beliefs about the importance of home, family, and work; being in love was considered to be a "general condition on a par with grieving or feeling patriotic." As twentieth-century developments—suffrage, prosperity, social mobility, among others—allowed for

---

*Johnny Otis, who played drums and vibes with Charlie Parker, Count Basie, and Lester Young, recalled in *Upside Your Head: Rhythm and Blues on Central Avenue*, that Prez prefaced everybody's name with the moniker "Lady." Otis, whose nickname was Hawk (because of his beaked nose) was "Lady Hawk." After Otis discovered a singer named "Little" Esther Phillips, he and Prez had an exchange that went like this:

LESTER: "So, the Little Estherennie kittie was a good lick o'reenie for you, huh?"

OTIS: "Yeah, the little chick was a blessing for us. She's raisin' sand all over the country."

LESTER: "Y'all eatin' regular now . . . dig."

OTIS: "Yeah, and payin' the rent too, sometimes."

LESTER: "They'll be tryin' to copy her soon, evonce—that's the stuff you gotta watch, dig."

Evonce, says Otis, was one of many Lester Young words nobody knew the meaning of.

greater personal autonomy, songs about romantic love began to encompass its most self-absorbing affects, from ecstasy and longing to loneliness and despair.

Prez was supremely gifted at evoking these moods, particularly the blue ones. Touring with his family's orchestra as a boy, he had skipped childhood altogether, and at seventeen he ran away to escape his domineering father. Later, when he joined the army, he spent a year in detention barracks for admitting that he smoked marijuana; although he never discussed the particulars, he apparently suffered the cruel indignities and violations that typify prison life. When he returned to performing, he found a kindred spirit in the soul-wracked Billie Holiday. Their collaborative excavations of the blues were as moving as anything recorded since. Although the two melancholics were never linked romantically, musically they could finish each other's sentences.

Even on upbeat tunes, Prez managed to convey his isolation. As a soloist, he was always slightly askant of the original tune, hovering just outside its melodic conventions, dipping in occasionally to signify a keynote or phrase for reference, then embarking again on some lonely exposition. In his early years, with the solid support of Basie's rhythm section, Young was free to develop his unique style of asymmetrical improvising, stepping outside the rhythmic structure of a tune— playing a five-bar phrase while the rest of the band played four, for instance, or subversively advancing an eight-bar phrase by one bar. Prez, the loner, and the saxophone, an outsider's instrument, were a perfect match. Together they declared that, in jazz music, conventions are meant to be breached, that there is always a new way of looking at and playing a particular composition. That attitude has been passed down, almost like genetic material, to every important soloist who followed. Among the first to embrace it: Charlie "Yardbird" Parker.

Charles McPherson has just finished his late set at the Iridium, a tony jazz joint just north of Times Square, where he's been appearing all week with Tom Harrell, a brilliant cornet player who has courageously managed to sustain a productive career as a composer and player while suffering from schizophrenia. It's a warm late-summer night halfway through a week devoted to celebrating the genius of Charlie Parker, and Charles and Tom have been re-creating the sound and spirit, if not the actual tunes, of Bird and Dizzy Gillespie, who introduced bebop to the jazz lexicon. Around town, clubs are filled with ensembles of all sizes, billing legendary players with young lions summoning the muse of Parker, who, like Hawk and Prez, discovered a brash new way to play the saxophone. On a sunny afternoon in Harlem the day before, I heard and watched the legendary saxophonists Gary Bartz and Sonny Fortune duel with the smart young stylists Wessell Anderson, Vincent Herring, and Marcus Strickland while the wise old percussionist Roy Haynes battled with Jeff "Tain" Watts, perhaps the most dynamic drummer around. And that was just an opening act. The popularity of jazz music may be in decline, but this week in New York you'd be hard pressed to find evidence of it.

Charles McPherson, born in 1939, one of post-bop's great alto players, spent a good portion of his career playing alongside Charles Mingus before going on to lead his own groups. Handsome, gregarious, thoughtful, he has long been considered one of the few contemporary players whose sound and skill has come close to Bird's.

"Stylistically, everything we do comes from Bird and Diz," he says. "They're the forefathers. But they didn't come out of nowhere. Bird liked Lester Young, Buster 'Prof' Smith; he liked many people. Diz liked Roy Eldridge, and Roy liked Louis Armstrong before him. They were the younger guys playing at the end of the Swing Era, just playing their version of it. It became known as bebop, which sounds esoteric, but it was really just an offshoot of swing music."

That offshoot, however, almost instantly changed jazz music's identity, advancing it from a danceable idiom played with the audience's casual listening pleasure in mind to a more personal and cerebral modern music. The saxophone enabled Bird's bebop to become virtuoso music, with constantly shifting rhythmic and harmonic currents that were difficult for the listener to follow but that brought him into greater communion with the music if he could stay with it. The inventions added up to a whole new language for jazz—or rather, a syntactical foundation for the music, sort of like Latin, from which other dialects could develop. In keeping with the saxophone's rebel spirit, the bebop revolution announced by Bird and Diz (along with pianists Bud Powell and Thelonious Monk) met a lot of resistance. After Bird recorded two magnificent tunes, "Anthropology" and "Koko," a *Downbeat* reviewer called them "the sort of stuff that has thrown innumerable impressionable young musicians out of stride, that has harmed them irreparably."* Not surprisingly, the new music, difficult to understand and follow, inspired a reaction movement: so-called revivalist jazz, which lured out of retirement older players who managed to give the less demanding swing tradition a few extra years of life.

"Bird's accents and rhythmic phrasing were more syncopated for the time," Charles explains. "But when you listen to other players around him, like Benny Carter, you realize the differences are not that great, just an accumulation of small things. Bird's tone was a bit more strident, there was more edge. He played long musical sentences, there was a long time between breaths. Several Kansas City alto players sounded a lot like him. But I've heard from many musicians who were circling the same ideas that they remember where they were and what they were doing when they first heard Bird, and they all said, 'That's it!' It was like the collective unconscious, an idea being floated around the planet by different mentalities, several people with the same idea. But the point is that Bird nailed it."

Within bebop's frenetic rhythmic framework—Bird claimed to have learned double time, or phrasing at twice the stated tempo, from "Prof" Smith—Parker inserted deeply emotional melodic

*Parker apparently took this criticism seriously. He repeated similar sentiments to Jimmy Abato while they were having a drink one day at a bar called Jim and Andy's in Manhattan. (See Chapter 13.)

ideas. In executing them, he ignored sentimental vibrato for a harder, yet more sensuous, tone. The almost insanely upbeat tempo of his most challenging tunes, usually provided by drummer Kenny Clarke, prevented many jazz fans from appreciating the beauty in the music: they simply couldn't hear fast enough. For his part, Bird said simply, "It's playing clean and looking for the pretty notes."

The pretty notes he found while playing at a lightning tempo can continue to astound even the most learned archivist of the Bird songbook. Repeated listening reveals new moments of genius. Despite killer addictions to heroin and alcohol, Bird practiced obsessively. The horn became a fifth appendage. "To me, he looks like the saxophone," Charles says. "He's perfectly built for it. I saw footage of Bird playing 'Hot House' with Dizzy on a television show, and the camera was right up in his face. His embouchure is just perfect. You could see the muscles around his eyes were involved; his whole face was involved in the sound. His fingers are just beautiful. There's no movement—all these notes are coming out and you can't see his fingers moving. You could tell he wasn't working hard.

"But again, there were a lot of people capable of wonderful feats of virtuosity," says Charles. "When I listen to Bird, what sticks out is that it seems like he's playing the best note for the moment, almost like Bach. You couldn't get a better note if you mused over it for ten years. It's like listening to someone who speaks perfect English. What he's saying is important—Bird had wonderful, sophisticated deep thoughts in his playing—but the way he's saying it is amazing.

"Musically, he was totally eclectic. There used to be a place called Charlie's Tavern in Midtown where all the musicians hung out in the daytime. The jukebox had jazz for the most part, but also a little country-and-western music. Parker would come in, put a nickel in, and play a country-and-western tune and piss everybody off, but nobody would say anything because it's him. One day somebody said, 'Why do you play this crap?' He says, 'Just listen, listen to the stories.'

"So he could sing on the instrument and fly on the instrument. He had so much dimension as an artist: he was a ballad master, a blues master; he could swing and he could rip and run.

"And what was really amazing was that the saxophone was able to take dictation from a guy like Parker. The instrument had never been tested to that degree, it was like an engine being pushed beyond the red line. Whenever anything new comes along, the saxophone says, I'm ready. Whatever you want, I can do it. Nobody proved that better than Bird."

Charlie Parker was thirteen when Charles Davis was born in 1933. By the time Davis was thirteen, he was sneaking into Chicago's Persian Ballroom and the Regal Theatre to hear Bird, Stan Getz, Lester Young, Sonny Stitt, and every other saxophonist who was passing through town. If he brought a girlfriend, invariably he would lose her. "When Bird or Prez did a solo, I'd rush up to the bandstand just to see their fingers move," says Davis as he stretches his legs in the living room of his apartment in Manhattan. "By the time I got back, I'd learn she'd gone home with someone else."

Davis, whose family had moved to Chicago from Mississippi, was then learning to play alto saxophone in high school. But as he continued to haunt the clubs, where Gene Ammons, Clifford Jordan, Von Freeman, and Johnny Thompson were developing what would come to be known as the Chicago sound, he found himself increasingly enamored of a baritone player, Leo Parker, whom he'd first heard on a recording of a Charles Greenleaf composition, "Elcino," with Gene Ammons.

"I just loved his sound," says Davis, whose voice was then dropping into the booming baritone range he speaks in today. "I didn't like the way the other baritones played. But I really liked Leo Parker."

Leo, no relation to Charlie, was doing something unusual for the time, playing bebop on the bari, and the jazz police—the emerging legion of writers who were beginning to write critically about the music—didn't much care for it. The swinging lyricism of Harry Carney, whose resonant bari backed up Duke Ellington's orchestra for forty-seven years, had defined the stylistic boundaries of the bulky instrument; other great baritone players, such as Serge Chaloff and

Gerry Mulligan, were proponents of the more laid-back "cool" style. The baritone was thought to be a harmonizing instrument, a section player, and when it broke out on its own for a chorus or two, its low, dusky voice was not to be displayed too prominently or for too long. It was like asking a walrus to sing.

Davis, who had memorized Charlie Parker solos on the alto, switched to the bigger saxophone, an easy transition since, like the alto, it was pitched in E-flat. "It was closer to Nat Cole's voice, one of the sounds I like on the baritone." Like Leo Parker, he wanted to play nothing but bebop on the bari. "It was considered heretical at the time, but I didn't care," says Davis, whose heretical chops earned him a spot in the Solar Arkestra of Sun Ra, who was "painting pictures of infinity" with his music.* "It became my religion. It's the only avenue into jazz, as far as I'm concerned. It's ironic: I wanted to play bebop like Charlie Parker, but to do that I had to give up the alto. How could I compete with him? How could anybody?"

Parker had that effect on a lot of people. The better they'd get on the alto, the more they realized how impossibly high Bird had raised the bar for the instrument. Bird had a number of acolytes, including Sonny Stitt, Sonny Criss, and Jackie McLean, who imitated his tone and phrasing. In the fifties, Cannonball Adderley carried Bird's torch with some furious playing. But many players, like Lee Konitz, Art Pepper, and Paul Desmond, headed off in a different direction, developing a lighter, airier sound. Describing his tone, Desmond once said, "I try to sound like a dry martini."

In addition to all the other wonderful things Charlie Parker did for the saxophone and jazz music, he inadvertently steered the next generation of players toward the tenor. And in the nimble hands of Sonny Rollins, Ornette Coleman, and John Coltrane, whose big

*Sun Ra's Arkestra was variously known as Band From Outer Space, Solar-Nature, Space, Myth-Science, and Astro-Intergalactic-Infinity Arkestra.

earthy sounds could be traced directly back to Hawk, as well as Cool School adherents—Stan Getz, Zoot Sims, Al Cohn, Wardell Gray, and many others—the tenor became the favorite son of the saxophone family and the dominant voice in jazz music.

Jimmy Heath and his good friend, John Coltrane, were two of those tenor converts. Both were born in 1926—Jimmy in Philadelphia and Trane in Hamlet, North Carolina. After Coltrane moved to Philly in 1943, they began to practice together and formed a big band in which they both played alto saxophone. Before he was twenty, Jimmy became known in Philadelphia as Little Bird, a reference to both his physical stature—in shoes with a sizable heel, he may top five feet—and his skill: he was a precocious, prodigious bebopper. In 1947, when Charlie Parker was playing at the Downbeat in Philly, he borrowed Jimmy's horn for a week and, to pay him back, played a benefit with Jimmy and Trane's big band. As good as they were, being onstage with Bird was a humbling experience for the young tyros. Both soon switched to tenor.

"I had also started listening to Dexter Gordon," says Jimmy, settling into a couch in my living room, where he's dropped by on a Saturday morning for a quick chat. Light and lean, with tinted glasses, a neatly trimmed mustache, and a soul patch of whiskers beneath his lower lip, he appears defiant of age in his pressed khakis and dark green jacket, betraying little evidence of slowing down as he approaches his ninth decade. Although he retired recently from his job as head of the Queens College Jazz Masters program, he continues to write and arrange, plays regularly in David Ostwald's Gully Low Jazz Band, a Louis Armstrong tribute ensemble, and frequently tours Europe with his brothers, bassist Percy and drummer Albert, in the Heath Brothers band. Having played with Coleman Hawkins, Lester Young, Miles Davis, and virtually every other titanic pioneer of jazz music, he is a living reminder of how young the saxophone is and how recently it developed a mature and sophisticated voice.

"If you were studying bebop on the tenor today, Dexter is still where you'd start," he says. "It's a continuum. Dexter and Sonny Stitt were the first to take Parker's bebop language to the tenor. When you think of Don Byas, he was so harmonically astute, he moved right into bebop from the Basie band. And when you hear people like Paul Gonsalves and Benny Golson, they're straight out of Byas. Sonny Rollins and Trane became the two stalwarts of the time, and everybody got some of that in their playing. Each generation comes along with this outstanding person and when people hear him they say, 'Damn, why couldn't I think of that?' But they borrow it, anyway."

Although Jimmy and Coltrane played together in Dizzy Gillespie's band in the late forties, their paths soon diverged. Jimmy displayed a talent for composing and arranging; his most durable tunes include "For Minors Only," "Gingerbread Boy," and "CTA," which he recorded with Miles Davis in 1953. Although Coltrane was a gifted composer as well, he had no patience for arranging, particularly for others.

"He worked harder on getting his direction perfected," Jimmy says. "He practiced all day, every day. His wife, Juanita, who later called herself Naima, said that in their marriage Trane was ninety percent saxophone. But I remember one time he brought me an arrangement of 'Lover Man' that was so beautiful that the idea still permeates my mind every time I play that song. I said, 'Trane, why don't you write some more?' And he says, 'I ain't got no time to write big-band music.' He didn't want to be divided in his devotion."

Jimmy lifts his glasses from his face to clean them, his eyes bright and clear as they focus on some middle distance half a century ago. "Trane had a desire to catch up to people he thought were better than him," he says. "He had spent all that time on the alto. And of course he did catch up. He took the tenor to a whole new level. But unlike Charlie Parker on the alto, Trane didn't scare anyone away from the tenor. Everybody wanted to play it."

Coltrane changed Michael Brecker's life and Brecker can remember the exact moment it happened: at a Trane concert he attended in the 1960s when he was in high school. Right now, fiddling with a bank of computers in his basement studio in Hastings, a leafy village north of New York City, where he lives with his wife and two children, he's trying to locate a recording of it.

Born in 1949 in Philadelphia, Mike began playing the clarinet in fifth grade. Even as a frustrated clarinetist, he was experimenting with the kind of sounds that would propel him and his brother Randy, the trumpeter, to worldwide fame as jazz-rock fusion artists in the eighties. "I used to practice in a trash can," he says. "It was a way of getting some reverb."

He switched to alto saxophone three years after hearing Cannonball Adderley's *Jazz Workshop Revisited*, and then graduated to tenor in high school. "I was listening to Coltrane, George Coleman, Sonny Rollins, Wayne Shorter, Stanley Turrentine, Joe Henderson, and many more," he says. "By then, I was six foot three and the tenor fit in my hands well."

Every night, the Brecker brothers would jam with their dad, a lawyer and accomplished pianist, each circulating among horns, drums, and the classic Hammond B-3 organ his father owned. "When Randy went to college," Mike says, "my dad and I had free rein of the house—and the equipment."

After attending Indiana University, Mike moved to New York in 1969, where he joined a collective of a couple dozen musicians who put on free concerts in one another's lofts. The music was wide open and respected no boundaries. "I grew up listening to jazz, funk, pop, and gospel," he says. "It was very exciting to take rhythmic elements from R&B and apply a jazz aesthetic and harmony. I found it exhilarating to play over a funk rhythm."

A few years later, he and Randy teamed up as the enormously successful Brecker Brothers, fusion cowboys with power chops that rivaled those of rock-guitar superheroes. Soon, Mike became the most in-demand session player in the world, making more than 500 sideman appearances with artists such as Paul Simon, James Taylor, and Chaka Khan. He became known for his highly conceptual improvisations, his conversational style, and his blinding technique, all of it overlaid by a warm, fat sound.

Less visibly, though, he was also playing a lot of acoustic jazz. Although he had internalized the sounds and styles of many of his idols, one voice could always be heard louder than the others, beckoning and challenging him to reach for something higher: that of John Coltrane, who not only had an extraordinary sound but demonstrated that the saxophone, like the piano and the violin, was capable of executing and translating the commands of musical genius.

After nearly dying of a drug overdose in San Francisco in 1957, Coltrane found God, cleaned up, and for the next decade produced a body of work that continuously pushed the saxophone, and jazz music, to dazzling new heights. Everything he did, it seemed, was a daring experiment, devoted to exploring newness for its own sake. He had a tone, instantly recognizable, that was hard, aggressive, free of affectation and sentimentality, yet somehow warm and ethereal. He practiced constantly, before and between sets, before and after recording sessions, in his quest to ride the saxophone as far into outer, and inner, space as possible. He reached for every note in a chord, played endless thirty-second notes, sprinted through furious cycles of arpeggios, perfected harmonics, double notes, and overtones, and issued manic shrieks and wails. Just as often, though, his music was stunningly peaceful, soulful, and reverential. His audiences were never allowed to get comfortable but were kept in a state of perpetual apprehension as they lined up behind Coltrane on his voyage toward total expressiveness. Trane said a musician's mission was simply to "give a picture to the listener of the many wonderful things he knows of and senses in the universe." In his case, that was a lot.

To Mike Brecker fans, it should come as no surprise that he feels such a powerful link to the brilliant Coltrane. Mike is considered one of the brainiest musicians around, capable of weaving extraordinary narratives with depth, emotion and personality. As guitarist Pat Metheny says, "Following a Mike Brecker solo is like nothing else that I have ever experienced, and very few musicians on any instrument can do it." His colleagues said the same thing of Trane.

So many of modern jazz's ideas originated with Coltrane, Mike says—or at least the ones that appealed to him. "He was one of the first jazz musicians to play extended solos, taking the listener on a journey unlike any previously experienced," he says, as he continues to search for the Trane concert recording. "Coltrane had an individual approach to playing lines and a singular methodology toward chord changes. In addition to incorporating exploratory scales and intervallic motifs in a modal setting—and he was one of the first jazz musicians to explore such a setting—Coltrane was somehow able to superimpose harmonic devices, like his 'Giant Steps' chord changes, which were used as improvisational pivot points, creating tension and release. That was brilliant."

Much of Coltrane's most brilliant work, culminating in one of the best-selling jazz recordings of all time, *A Love Supreme*, was done with his supergroup: pianist McCoy Tyner, bassist Jimmy Garrison, and drummer Elvin Jones. The communication between Jones and Trane was particularly heavenly, explained thus by Jones: "He left me absolutely alone. He must have felt the way I played, understood the validity of it. There were never any rhythmic or melodic or harmonic conflicts . . . I was never conscious of the length of Coltrane's solos, which sometimes lasted forty minutes. I was in the position of being able to follow his melodic line through all the modes he would weave in and out of, through all the patterns and the endless variations on variations. It was like listening to a concerto. The only thing that mattered was the completion of the cycle that he was in. I'd get so excited listening to him that I had all I could do to contain myself. There was a basic life force in Coltrane's solos, and when he came out of them you suddenly discovered you had learned a great deal."

As a high school student in Philadelphia, Mike Brecker found the music as outrageous as Jones did. The only thing that could have seemed more outrageous at the time was the prospect of his being able to play one day with Elvin Jones, which he did several times before Jones's death in 2004. He has also played with McCoy Tyner. Like Charlie Parker, who credited drummer Kenny Clarke with inspiring some of his more imaginative solo excursions, and Coltrane, who praised Jones for creating a wide-open rhythmic environment, Mike feels there's a special connection between drummers and saxophonists.

"There's some kind of umbilical cord," he says. "Playing saxophone is an intensely time-oriented experience—*time* meaning rhythm—and the rhythmic possibilities in any solo context are enormous. A lot of that is tied into the drums. Generally, I think most sax players listen to drums first. That's true of me. Most sax players I know play the drums. I can't explain that. I've played the drums for years and now I play every day."

Mike vividly recalls the Coltrane concert at Temple University in 1965 that "literally propelled me into choosing music as a life's endeavor." Midway through the concert, he remembers, Coltrane was beating his chest and screaming. "The whole concert was incredible," he recalls. "It was at a time when there was a lot of searching going on, people looking for ways to be free. There was a lot of urgent crying out, and unfortunately that was mischaracterized in Coltrane as anger. Years later I was talking to his son, Ravi, who had a tape of the concert. He said [Coltrane] wasn't screaming, he wasn't angry, he was just singing. The PA just wasn't meant for a vocalist and you couldn't hear him very well."

Finally, Mike locates the computer file that contains a digitally stored recording of the concert, given to him by Ravi. "Listen to this," he says. He fast-forwards to the end of the concert. Elvin Jones can be heard thrashing his kit furiously, creating the percussive equivalent of Trane's sheets of sound, while Trane vocalizes. He sounds alternately like an Alpine yodeler and a possessed shaman, his notes often reaching across long intervals, as they did when he played the saxophone. The crazy duet goes on for about a minute before Trane picks up his horn and begins blowing again.

Mike laughs and shakes his head. "His playing was highly emotional; it had a large spiritual, mystical quality to it and a gorgeous sound," he says. "His tone was unique—mysterious, dark, hard, yet lushly beautiful. It took some getting used to. To the uninitiated listener it sounded harsh, but for me, with continued listening, it began to sound just incredibly beautiful. Every note of a Coltrane tune had weight and meaning. From a technical viewpoint it was outrageous; from an intellectual view it was deep, full of exciting, innovative ideas that hadn't been done before. He was also a very curious musician. He had a passion for all kinds of music, from African to Indian and Spanish, and all of it filtered into his repertoire. For me, as a high school musician, it was just outrageous and compelling.

"Through the music of Coltrane I had found a calling. And I remember feeling so grateful that I was playing the tenor saxophone."

In the late 1950s, Steve Lacy found himself working in the same club as John Coltrane. One night, Coltrane explored Steve's thoughts about the soprano saxophone, a somewhat peevish instrument that nobody, aside from Lacy and Bob Wilber, a protégé of Sidney Bechet's, was playing at the time. "We talked about pitch control," Steve remembers,* "and how difficult it is to make it swing. I told him it was a beast that had to be tamed, that you had to teach it to crawl and then walk before you could get it to run. Within a couple of years, he got it to swing."

In 1960, Coltrane released the fourteen-minute-long "My Favorite Things," which became a huge and improbable hit, applying his typical robustness to the soprano saxophone and extracting from it a kind of Middle Eastern wail that became the model tone for a whole generation of soprano players to come. Most serious saxophonists now double on the instrument. By sugarcoating its sound, light jazz artists have made it hugely popular. The soprano player Kenny G is now the best-selling instrumentalist of all time.

To Lacy, Coltrane's embrace of the soprano was perfectly natural. "John was beginning to breathe a kind of distant ether," he says. "For him, the soprano, a full octave above the tenor, helped him along his upward path."

*Steve and I met about six months before he died.

The soprano led Lacy on some far-out excursions as well. Born in 1934 in New York, he played in Dixieland bands as a teenager, then spent his next decade collaborating with or playing the music of three pianists who would shape his music for the rest of his career: Cecil Taylor, Thelonious Monk, and Gil Evans. In the 1960s he moved to Europe, which was more accepting of the free jazz he was interested in, and over the next three decades he recorded more than 150 albums, many with his wife, Swiss singer Irene Aebi. His compositions drew upon such disparate sources as texts from Guillaume Apollinaire and Herman Melville, the paintings of Arshile Gorky and Keith Haring, and the poetry of Bangladeshi feminist Taslima Nasrin. His bold and visionary work earned him a MacArthur Foundation "genius" award in 1992.

Tonight, at the Iridium jazz club, Steve, a small, balding man in a soft-shouldered gray suit, and Irene are performing selections from their latest collaboration, *Beat Suites*, on which she sings ten settings from the beat writers Allen Ginsberg and William Burroughs, backed by trombone and a rhythm section. It's challenging atonal music—an acquired taste, perhaps—but Lacy's playing, even in a musical environment that pays little respect to melodic convention, soars above the cacophony and beatnik prattle to reveal what single-minded devotion to the soprano can yield: a pure, unadorned sound, crisp as a dry wine, delivered with perfect intonation.

"It's taken until now to get anywhere on the soprano," says Steve modestly, as he fiddles with a box of reeds between sets. "When I started, nobody could teach it to me or tell me what or how to play on it because almost no one was playing it. I spent years experimenting, even played the mouthpiece upside down for a few weeks. Now many players double on the soprano, but I've always felt there were enough interesting problems on it alone to keep me interested for a lifetime. After four decades of working on it, I still find the possibilities to be astounding—and daunting."

The soprano is the most difficult of the saxophones to master (the tinier sopranino is even more incorrigible, but virtually no one plays it). The bore expands very quickly over a short distance from the width of a pinky finger to the size of a fist, and tone holes are piled up next to each other, creating a fickle acoustic chamber that requires a player to adjust his embouchure almost for each note. The upper-register keys are so close together they can cause cramping in the left hand. Many players, including Coltrane, dealt with its notorious intonation problems by using it to invoke an Eastern flavor in their music, with droning phrases that allowed pitches to undulate above and below their true centers. Lacy, however, took a different approach. He plays short, declarative figures, revealing, by virtue of his pure tone, that the beast can in fact be tamed.

Even so, its best use is in nontraditional music, says Lacy, whether in the mixed media he explores with his wife or in Paul Winter's hypnotic soundscapes. "The soprano has all the other instruments in it," says Steve. "It's got the intensity of the baritone, the song voice of the alto, the goosey sound of the tenor. Yet when you're playing it, it can feel as unrelated to those instruments as, say, a flügelhorn. You feel like you want to take it where music hasn't been before. You don't have much choice, really, for it will take you there whether you want to go or not."

The young saxophonist Marcus Strickland is holding his cell phone above his head, hoping to transmit to his twin brother in their apartment in Brooklyn a sense of the musical madness filling the room at the Blue Note in Greenwich Village, where Pharoah Sanders, backed by a sizzling quartet and accompanied by the rabbit-fingered alto player Kenny Garrett, has been torturing his tenor. Marcus, who, courtesy of my credit card, has quickly downed a couple of apple martinis, can barely contain his glee as he shakes his dreads in recognition of Pharoah's wild inventiveness. Before the show, the drummer Jeff "Tain" Watts had paused at our table to forewarn us of the sonic madness he'd be helping create. "You're not going to believe this," he said, beaming almost maniacally. "You're just not going to believe this."

A throwback to the "free" jazz era of the sixties, Pharoah Sanders gained his entry into the sax soloists' pantheon as the man who found an acceptably creative use of the freak note. Working at the Playhouse, a nightclub in Greenwich Village, as a short-order chef, he was discovered by the space cadet Sun Ra (a visitor from the planet Saturn, he claimed), who abducted him into his Arkestra for a brief stint; Sanders was then recruited by John Coltrane to join his group in 1965 for his post–*A Love Supreme* recordings. In 1969, two years after Coltrane died, Sanders recorded what may have been the only hit of the avant-garde jazz movement, the thirty-two-minute "The Creator Has a Master Plan." He later worked with Coltrane's second wife, Alice, and, after experimenting with West African musicians in the eighties, returned to otherwordly explorations with his "Nubian space jazz" ensemble in the nineties. Although he is a capable straight-ahead improviser, he is best known for being able to coax unearthly, cataclysmic, and, alternatively, eerily human sounds from his saxophone. Jazz legend has it that he can make a saxophone continue to sing for minutes after removing it from his mouth.

The core group of "free" players—who included Coltrane, Ornette Coleman, Albert Ayler, and, to a lesser extent, Pharoah Sanders and Dewey Redman—announced an insurgency against the "ultrasophisticated art form"* jazz had become. Musically, *free* meant liberation from the restrictions of harmony, melody, and rhythm, from having to play in a single key or use a prescribed pattern of chords as a foundation for improvisation. Ornette Coleman's first album in 1959, *Something Else*, announced the paradigm shift; his ideas eventually coalesced into a concept he calls harmolodics, which no one I've talked to pretends to understand. Coltrane's experiments during the few years he was alive following the release of *A Love Supreme* gave free-jazz soloists further legitimacy, although his last recordings are considered his weakest. Albert Ayler and Pharoah, who was hired

---

*A phrase borrowed from *As Serious As Your Life: John Coltrane and Beyond*, by Valerie Wilmer.

by Coltrane to provide a mystical sonic backdrop to his spiritual explorations, worked the genre by rethinking concepts of pitch, sonority, and, generally, sounds that are considered pleasing to the ear.

Now, as Pharoah rises again from a chair onstage, he prepares to wring a new batch of freak notes from his horn. A short, stout man in his early sixties, Pharoah's dressed in a loud silk shirt with a cubist print, retro wraparound sunglasses shielding his eyes. Millard Fillmore–style muttonchop sideburns reach to his chin; the frizzy gray tangle of hair atop his head is sculpted into a rectangular topiary. The evening is devoted to Coltrane's music, and, as if to evoke the spirit of the American action painters, whose work on canvas mimicked the athleticism of the arty hard bop that gave way to the free style, a man sketches furiously on the floor to the left of the stage, producing a busy likeness of Pharoah's zany profile.

What emerges from Pharoah's horn is equally frenzied, and occasionally terrifying. Lush, rich long tones morph into gurgling screams and hoarse wails, which in turn coalesce into terse runs of harmonic improvisation. His vocabulary is unique: somehow he manages to play high and low notes simultaneously. Occasionally he speaks through the horn. Although the freak notes seem randomly produced—the kind of noise inadvertently obtained by a beginner—the furrows lining his forehead and the rivulets around his eyes indicate he's working hard. As he issues a banshee scream, a filament of saliva escapes his mouth and stretches to the floor, producing a howl of glee from Marcus. At one point, Pharoah disassembles the horn, playing just the mouthpiece and neck, blowing into the top of the tube, or singing into the bell. He's as much theater as music, and his performance, though outrageously entertaining, shows why the avant-garde jazz movement was mercifully short.

Like many players who came into Coltrane's orbit, Pharoah was permanently imprinted by the experience. "I met John at a jazz workshop in San Francisco in 1959," he says after the set ends, looking over a dozen mouthpieces for sale in his dressing room. "I was just a kid, nineteen, and he asked me to take him around to pawnshops in Oakland so he could look for mouthpieces. We did that for a week. So whenever I go to a new town, that's what I do, too, just like I'm doing now.

"What I do all the time is experiment and look for new things. I'm trying to do something no one else can do or has heard. I like to be different. A lot of things I do take a lot of pressure—I have to overblow the horn to get those things out. But trying to get me to write on paper what I'm doing is difficult. When I get into the energy, I find I'm not playing music. I'm playing me.

"John and I used to talk a lot about sound and expression. He often said the saxophone is not completed. He heard something else in it; he thought there was more there but it hadn't been heard yet. So that's my mission, that's what I've been looking for the past forty years. I think he would be pleased with all the new sounds I've discovered.

"Except, of course, they're not new sounds. They're very old sounds."

Dewey Redman was a year behind Ornette Coleman in their Fort Worth, Texas, high school, but because they both played in the school concert band, they got to be friends. Ornette, who played in a Louis Jordan–style jump band, graduated in 1947 and immediately headed for Los Angeles to find his fortune as a musician. Dewey graduated a year later, enrolled at Prairie View A&M, and joined the army after getting a master's degree in education. After his discharge, he taught fifth grade for a few years, then in 1959 moved to San Francisco, where he drove a cab during the day and scuffled at night, occasionally playing with Pharoah Sanders or Wes Montgomery or leading his own band. In 1967, while waiting in line at the airport for a fare, he spotted Ornette Coleman, who had arrived for a weeklong engagement. He jumped the line to pick up his old schoolmate. "He says, 'Dewey, are you still playing? Come down and play with us,'" Dewey remembers. "The next thing I know I'm in New York recording *New York Is Now!* with Elvin Jones and Jimmy Garrison."

The move to New York was part of his make-or-break five-year plan. "One of the first things I did was rent this apartment," says Dewey, looking around the ramshackle five-room fifth-floor flat in the Bedford-Stuyvesant section of Brooklyn. He's rented it for nearly forty years. "The rent's about the same as it was in the beginning—$240 a month. It's one of the secrets of my survival."

In 1989, Dewey released an album titled *Living on the Edge* that aptly characterizes his uncompromising approach to life and music. When his name is mentioned, it is often preceded by the adjective *underrated*. This oversight has something to do with his late start (he was thirty-six when he reconnected with Coleman), and the much-higher-profile success of his Harvard Phi Beta Kappa son, Joshua (whose autograph Dewey is often asked to forge), and even more to do with the cerebral musical company he has kept for the past four decades. In the seventies alone, he played and traveled with Coleman's band, Charlie Haden's Liberation Music Orchestra, Keith Jarrett's progressive ensemble, and, later, a group made up of Ornette's former bandmates Don Cherry, Ed Blackwell, and Haden. The music was intense, groundbreaking, and required repeated listening. But there wasn't much money in it.

And sometimes, even respect was hard to come by. Dewey remembers that Ornette was roundly criticized for being perpetually "outside"—that is, playing without reference to the fixed harmonic structure of a tune. Whereas other players might use the device of playing a half step above the key for a phrase or two to add bite, Ornette would step outside and stay there, challenging everyone's tolerance of dissonance. Dewey says Ornette was routinely dismissed by the generation of players before him, who felt his experimentation was a cover-up for his lack of talent—until they realized he was capable of playing their way, too.

"In 1971, we did a tour called Newport in Europe," Dewey says, pointing to a poster on the wall behind me advertising the event.

"Everyone was on board—Duke's orchestra, Sonny Stitt, Dexter Gordon, Miles. Ornette's and my dressing room was next to Sonny's. So one night I hear all this laughing, talking, and drinking and decide to go next door. Dexter's showing Sonny something and they're having a good time, and all of a sudden I hear Charlie Parker playing somewhere out in the hallway. This was Bird, man. All of a sudden it was very quiet in there. I knew right away who it was. It was Ornette. But I mean this was not Ornette Parker, this was *Charlie* Parker. Ornette could play closer to Charlie Parker than anybody I ever heard. And he was playing alto. Jaws dropped, it was real quiet, you could hear a rat piss on cotton, right? This went on for five minutes. I mean, this was *Bird*, man! I was going to bust out laughing, so I eased next door. Ornette had stopped and had this little shitty grin on his face. Two minutes later, in comes Dexter. He hadn't said a damned word to Ornette all that time. 'How you doin', Ornette?' In comes Sonny Stitt. 'Yeah, man, you sound good.' He'd had no respect from these guys."

Among the younger generation of players, though, the free players were gods. "Dewey's my hero," says Joe Lovano later that evening before he goes onstage at Birdland with his guest—Dewey Redman. "When I was a teenager I was listening to him and inspired by the company he was in—Ornette, Don Cherry, Elvin Jones, Jimmy Garrison, Ed Blackwell, Billy Higgins. It wasn't just a rhythm section and soloist, there was a lot of trading, counterpoint, and free improvisation—playing *free-ly*. I thought, How can I get it together to be that loose and open in my conceptions about harmony and rhythm? Dewey was a guiding light."

The first time Joe heard Dewey live was with Keith Jarrett, Charlie Haden, and Paul Motian. Ten years later Joe was playing with Motian in Haden's Liberation Music Orchestra, which included Dewey Redman.

"Dewey's the truth," Joe says. "In this music, it's really about who you are, not about chops and who cut this guy. It's all about your sound, your feeling, your inspiration, and how you use your personal technique to say something. The music he was playing, the music that evolved out of bebop from Ornette and Sonny Rollins and Coltrane, it was real honest music. You had the sense that it was played because it just had to be played somehow. It certainly wasn't commercial. It wasn't safe. They weren't falling back on something that they knew worked. They weren't thinking about their next gig. They were trying to find the beauty in the music, and to do that they had to communicate and they had to play collectively. They had to be *intimate*."

As Joe says, it's all about relationships.

7. THAT SOUL THING

You have to forgive Steve Wilson when he gets a little excited talking about the rhythm-and-blues saxophonists he listened to in his youth. Known for his ability to play artfully in any idiom, whether bebop, funk, or modern jazz (most notably with Chick Corea), the young saxophonist has just released a record, *Soulful Song*, that he says was inspired by the black radio programming he heard as a kid growing up in Virginia. "On the same station you could hear R&B, jazz, blues, and funk," he says. "So you might hear King Curtis, then a Charlie Parker tune, Hank Crawford, or something by Kool & the Gang, with Ronald Bell's fabulous saxophone. My father had James Brown's *Cold Sweat*, so I listened a lot to Maceo Parker. Along came the Memphis sound with Stax Records, and all the sax solos, particularly baritone, on Motown. And you can't talk about Motown without talking about Junior Walker. In fifteen minutes, you could hear how the saxophone migrated into all this great American music and how it just took over. Listening to all these guys—there was something about the raw emotion and power of the instrument, this sort of human wail sound, that they all had in common. And that traced back to a single voice, the father of R&B, or at least R&B saxophone: Illinois Jacquet."

Nearly disappearing into an overstuffed chair in his home in the St. Albans section of Queens, New York—a neighborhood that has been home to his friends Count Basie, Lena Horne, and Ella Fitzgerald, as well as Fats Waller and Babe Ruth—Illinois Jacquet* belies the notion that it takes a big man to make a big sound on the tenor saxophone. Like his friend Jimmy Heath, another man dwarfed but not intimidated by the mighty tenor, Illinois tops out at only a few inches above five feet. But evidence of his exalted status in twentieth-century music surrounds him here in his living room. The walls are covered with plaques, honorary degrees, gold records, and a collector's trove of priceless memorabilia; the lid of his piano is cluttered with old photographs of Illinois with many of his contemporaries: the man he considers his mentor and a model for his own sound, Lester Young, along with Charlie Parker, Count Basie, Cab Calloway, and Ben Webster, who, when dropping by for a visit, used to cut right to his refrigerator and say, "What ya got, kid?" There's a portrait of Illinois with Lionel Hampton, whose band backed him on "Flying Home," the 1942 hit that catapulted the saxophone to the forefront of a raucous, dance-inducing, party-time music, a happy subversion of swing and bebop, that would later be called rhythm and blues. More recently, he's pictured with his big band at high-profile gigs—the Clinton inaugural ball, for instance.

Jean Baptiste Illinois Jacquet, born in Louisiana in 1922 and raised in Houston, Texas, grew up in a musical family. His father, a sharecropper who put himself through college, played tuba; his mother was a Native American who passed on to her son her limpid

*Our interview took place two months before Illinois Jacquet died.

green eyes. One of six children, Illinois played drums and tap-danced in a family band, then picked up the soprano saxophone when he entered high school. "I played in the marching band," says Illinois, whose full head of bouffantish hair and smooth, dark skin make him look two decades younger than he is. "It was a curved soprano. I don't like nothing straight in a saxophone. It don't sound right, it's too sticky. It needs to wind its way through something."

Illinois graduated to the alto and would occasionally pick up his older brother's tenor. "I'd play it and people would be stunned," he says. "All of a sudden I'd have a crowd. 'You sound like Prez,' they'd say. "I'd say, 'Do I?' They'd say, 'How does a little guy get such a big sound?' Well, your sound doesn't come from your size. It comes from your heart. Lester wasn't a big man, either. But to me, he was the biggest man who ever played. He had a tone like velvet. It all started with him."

After finishing high school, Illinois joined his brothers in Los Angeles, playing in a number of bands. At a jam session on the South Side one evening, he met the pianist and singer Nat Cole, who took a liking to him and let him sit in with his trio. A few weeks later, "King" Cole, standing on a stage in the musicians' union hall—all the members had marched in the Labor Day parade and gathered at the hall for an extended jam session—stood up and asked for everyone's attention. "All the musicians were waiting around for their chance, and Nat said, 'You just want to hear this little guy, Illinois Jacquet,'" Illinois remembers. "There was Jimmy Blanton on bass, Nat on piano, Charlie Christian on guitar, and Sid Catlett on drums. This was like being in heaven. They just carry you along, all you got to do is blow. After that, the word was out: pay attention to the little guy with the alto.

"So Benny Goodman comes into town with his sextet, which includes Lionel Hampton. Benny and Hamp used to jam with Nat, and one night I sat in. Hamp got so carried away his vibes started rolling across the floor. He was about to form his own band and he said, 'If you can do that on the tenor, you got a job.' I was happy to join any band. I was eighteen years old. So I got a tenor."

Hamp's new band included Dexter Gordon, a few months younger than Illinois, who became one of his best friends. "He was the size of Joe Louis, with huge feet, and he couldn't play in time," Illinois says. "When he was playing, his foot was hitting anywhere. He didn't have rhythm. He was sitting right next to me and I'd cuss him out. I said, 'You got to get your foot together, you're throwing me off.' I got him straight. He was a beautiful person."

After touring the South, the Lionel Hampton Orchestra traveled to New York for the "Flying Home" recording session for Decca Records. The tune, credited to Goodman, Hampton, and Sid Rabin, is thought by some to have been written by Charlie Christian, one of the first guitarists to play with electric amplification. In 1939, Christian had contributed a thirty-two-bar solo to a recording of the song by the Benny Goodman Sextet, with Hamp on vibes. Then, three years later (just a few months after Christian died of pneumonia, at the age of twenty-three), Hamp decided to assign solo duties to his diminutive tenor sensation. (A couple of decades later, the electric guitar would deliver its payback, displacing the saxophone as pop music's solo instrument of choice.)

During the southern tour, Illinois had noticed that "at some point every night I'd break up the crowd. Those notes I'd hit became like a score in my head. As you keep playing night after night, it gets riper. The night before we recorded, I knew I wanted to condense everything I'd learned into that solo. So me and God had a prayer meeting. I just asked him to let me be original. I didn't want to make my first record and sound like someone else. When people heard it, I wanted them to say, 'That's him!' That's what I wanted and that's what I got."

Encouraged by saxophonist Marshall Royal to "Go for yourself," and standing on a platform the studio had built so that the bell of his horn could reach the microphone, Illinois delivered a brash, barbaric, buzzing solo that, while owing a little something to his idol and future friend, Lester Young, signaled a stylistic departure for the saxophone. "It was like an anthem," he says. "When people heard it, they'd turn around and look for somebody to dance with. It made you feel happy, like you'd found some money or something."

Illinois was in a "jim crow" hotel in Jacksonville, Florida, when he first heard the release, which became a huge hit for Hamp. "It was hot and I had the windows open," he remembers. "I heard a truck coming down the street playing 'Flying Home,' and I heard my solo. It was the first time I heard it. Man, I jumped up, forgot to put on my clothes, and followed that truck, running after it for at least four blocks. And I wasn't the only one. That was the reaction people had to it."

By the standards that would emerge among the generation of saxophonists who borrowed Illinois's "honking" style, the sixty-four-bar "Flying Home" solo was relatively civil. Two years later, Illinois's wailing, paroxysmal freak-note-filled two-and-one-half-minute solo on "Blues, Part 2," one of the many extraordinary moments on Los Angeles producer Norman Granz's live recordings of the "Jazz at the Philharmonic" series, again raised the bar for saxophonists who wanted to compete in this raucous new idiom, which would prove to be the incubator for rock and roll. But it was the "Flying Home" solo that first infused rhythm and blues with a furious energy.

"It changed my whole life," says Illinois. "And after that, saxophonists went berserk."

By the early forties, the kind of sixteen-piece band that Hamp had put together to record "Flying Home" had become a rarity. Swing bands, declining in popularity, could no longer support a large ensemble; the ranks of capable musicians were also depleted by the war. Blowsy dance orchestras downsized into sextets and octets—rhythm guitar and light instruments, such as the clarinet (which, some jazz fans lamented, had taken a "vow of chastity"), were the first to go—that retained one component of the larger bands: a hefty horn section. The tight little "race music" groups, known as jump bands, played up-tempo blues and simple riff tunes that had been adapted from more complicated big-band swing arrangements. Among the most successful of these mainstream ensembles was Louis Jordan and the Tympany [sic] Five. The band had a string of hits in the forties—including "GI Jive," "Ain't Nobody Here But Us

Chickens," and "Choo Choo Ch'Boogie"—that featured the saxophone at the front of the shuffling dance music, which was crossing over into the white mainstream.* The lighter, leaner sound in these bands fitted nicely with the saxophone's aspirations. Having survived the cut, the instrument was able to vanquish its remaining competition for the leading instrumental role.

Assured of its survival, the saxophone was free to express another side of the character it had inherited from its inventor: its rebellious, anarchical spirit. In bebop it had found a kindred soul in Charlie Parker and his acolytes, whose brash deconstruction of swing music assured their legacy as anti-institutional outsiders—and that of the saxophone as a key accessory for any bebopping *anarchiste de droite*.† At the same time, Adolphe Sax's versatile invention, thanks to Illinois Jacquet, was attracting legions of "berserk" saxophonists who were also bent on defying musical conventions in more mainstream music. Although they, too, positioned themselves as outsiders, they found that their unmelodic honking proved wildly popular among live audiences.

Over the next decade, Jacquet-inspired honking dominated "race music," which was finding ever-greater appeal among white audiences. Tunes like Big Jim Wynn's "Rock Woogie," Arnett Cobb's "Go Red Go," Dick Davis's "Screaming Boogie," Hal Singer's "Blow Your Brains Out," and Earl Bostic's "Earl Blows a Fuse" added a raucous, febrile edge to the music that Jerry Wexler, a producer for Atlantic Records, christened "rhythm and blues" in 1947. That year, Paul Williams had a jukebox hit with "The Hucklebuck,"‡ a shuffle-blues instrumental led by the furious wailing of only a handful of notes

---

*Jordan's "Is You Is or Is You Ain't My Baby" was heard in four Hollywood movies.

†The art and jazz critic Rudi Blesh once wrote of bebop, "Far from a culmination of jazz, bebop is not jazz at all, but an ultimately degenerated form of Swing, exploiting the most fantastic rhythms and unrelated harmonies that it would seem possible to conceive."

‡Inspired by Charlie Parker's bebop original "Now's the Time," which Parker recorded with Miles Davis, Dizzy Gillespie, and Max Roach four years earlier.

from his baritone saxophone. The greatest showman among this cadre was Cecil J. "Big Jay" McNeely, who would often perform a forty-five-minute solo consisting of a single trance-inspiring note while lying on his back in a Day-Glo suit surrounded by a ring of fire—theatrics that would be borrowed by the up-and-coming rock and roll generation. According to his biographers, Harry Shapiro and Caesar Glebbeek, in *Jimi Hendrix: Electric Gypsy*, a young and impressionable Hendrix caught several of Big Jay's shows in Seattle in 1957, years after McNeely's popularity had peaked, and emulated not only his pyrotechnics—Hendrix famously lit his electric guitar on fire at the Monterey Pop Festival in 1967—but also his sound, which he created with the help of shrieking feedback from his amplifier. He also shared Big Jay's erotic appeal. McNeely, his big phallic horn dangling between his legs as he walked the bar or the edge of the stage, would play "Dirty Boogie," Chris Strachwitz, owner of Arhoolie Records, once said, "and the kids would be unzipping their flies."*

To some observers, the flouting of all artistic conventions was more than just showmanship. In *Honkers and Shouters: The Golden Years of Rhythm and Blues*, former producer Arnold Shaw declared the music to be "a conscious or unconscious projection of the postwar segregation of black people, an abysmal expression of the separateness of the black ghettos." He saw the honkers' destructive wailing as an expression of the rage black America felt after World War II, when, despite having contributed their share to ensure victory, they returned home to the same old discrimination, prejudice, and violence. "After all the white promises and black sacrifices made during the war, the musician was not playing music. In the monotonous honking and catlike screeching, he was mocking the audience and destroying the music. And what irritation, anger, desperation, frustration, despair and petulance could be read in the gesture of playing while lying on one's back!"

---

*The phallic theme continued to develop in rock and roll, most notoriously with the Plaster Casters, a groupie duet who made plaster casts of the erect penises of rock stars, including Hendrix's and that of the Doors' Jim Morrison, who was arrested after he exposed himself before an audience. If only he'd had a saxophone, he might have managed to stay out of jail.

In *Blues People*, writer LeRoi Jones (now Amiri Baraka) said the point of the repetitive riffing was "to make the instrument sound as unmusical, or as non-Western, as possible. It was almost as if the blues people were reacting against the softness and 'legitimacy' that had crept into black instrumental music with swing."

But Jones also saw the honkers as "ethnic historians" engaged in a primal "Black scream." The honking represented "hatred and frustration, secrecy and despair." In his autobiographical *Tales*, Jones writes of a concert by saxophonist Lynn Hope, a black Muslim convert who appeared onstage in a bejeweled turban and whose band members wore red fezzes. Near the end of that concert in Newark, New Jersey,

> Lynn got his riff, that rhythmic figure we knew he would repeat, the honked note that would be his personal evaluation of the world.

Screaming "one scary note," Hope descended into the audience but found little room in the crowd.

So Lynn thought further, and made to destroy the ghetto.

Still playing his one scary note, the honking Piper led "five or six hundred hopped-up woogies" out into the street, where they created a traffic jam and a near riot.

> We screamed and screamed at the clear image of ourselves as we should always be. Ecstatic, completed, involved in a secret communal expression. It would be the form of the sweetest revolution, to hucklebuck into the fallen capital, and let the oppressors lindy hop out.

Soon, police with paddy wagons and billy clubs arrived and fire hoses were turned on the honk-crazed marchers. But the crowd, led by Hope, pushed on, under the spell of that one scary note on the saxophone.

———

In 1953, as the exhibitionism of the honkers was beginning to grow tiresome, Bill Haley found himself in the happy position of having to accommodate the unexpected success of his first hit tune, "Crazy, Man, Crazy," whose lyrics were essentially a glossary of adolescent jive. A rube from Michigan with a cartoonish curlicue of hair flopping onto his forehead, Haley faced the challenge of living up to his newly hip aura—no small assignment for a musician whose previous band, the buckskinned Saddlemen, had been cantering along the western-swing-band circuit and who not long before that had been billed as Silver Yodeling Bill Haley. Sensing that he was at the forefront of a new music, Haley began searching for ways to update his new band, the Comets. Taking his cue from Bob Wills and His Texas Playboys, which had evolved from a guitar- and fiddle-based "hillbilly" orchestra into a tight swing band that mixed jazz and blues (however "white") and was dominated by the lead playing of saxophonist Zeb McNally, he added a baritone saxophone to his lineup. The bottom-heavy horn was a poor fit with his Comets, basically a string band, although it did help produce a hit, "Farewell, So Long, Goodbye." Near the end of 1953, on the recommendation of a Philadelphia bar owner, Haley auditioned an eighteen-year-old tenor player named Joey D'Ambrosio.

Although classically trained and enamored of bebop, D'Ambrosio had been playing in strip clubs in North Philly since he was sixteen— "Every night, fifty choruses of 'Night Train,'" he remembers, laughing, "just drums, piano and saxophone." He was familiar with the honkers' mood-elevating tricks and frequently strutted across the bar while playing in his own band. "I was one of those guys," he says. "I had no choice. The other instruments were either plugged in or too big."

Still ambivalent after the audition, Haley agreed to let D'Ambrosio play a few gigs on a tryout basis. "Bill never wrote anything out," Joey says, "so you had to go for yourself. He was also about ten years older than the rest of us, like a member of another generation. We were up in Baltimore one day, playing an afternoon teen dance in a ballroom for Buddy Dean, a disc jockey there. On one of my solos, the girls started screaming, so I jumped down into the audience and they went crazy. I was the same age they were, the girls were screaming, and that was all the motivation I needed. After that, we did it in our movies."

The Baltimore gig cemented Joey's place in the band. In April 1954 the Comets went into the studio to record "Rock Around the Clock," featuring D'Ambrosio's fiery tenor at the heart of the tune. The song is widely considered to mark the beginning of rock and roll—a musical era that, like rhythm and blues a decade earlier, had been jump-started by a blazing saxophone.

"The key to that was turning up the saxophone and turning down Bill's guitar," Joey says. "He was a country guy, he played that strumming guitar type of thing. He'd drive me crazy with that—I didn't think it fit. So when we did records, they'd just cut him out of the mix so you didn't have to hear that. He never noticed."

The almost instantaneous success of the new popular music presented saxophonists with a new world to conquer. Some, such as Plas Johnson, who had been raised on arty bebop, set out to do just that.

At the moment, Plas is recalling the weekend he's just spent playing at a stripper's convention, Tease-O-Rama, in Los Angeles, his home for the past forty years. He's still chuckling. Over and over he was asked to play the theme songs from *Peter Gunn*, the hard-boiled detective show from the fifties that opened with Plas's noirish wail, and *The Pink Panther*, whose theme, thanks to Henry Mancini's clever charts and Plas's slinky, stealthy lead tenor ("Two takes at eight o'clock on a winter morning in '63"), is one of the most widely recognized movie-soundtrack riffs ever. "The pole dancers still love them," he says of the two theme songs, which became striptease favorites. But that's not why he's amused. "The convention featured strippers from seventeen to seventy," he says. "They all had costumes, and I must say, some of the seventy-year-olds are still interesting. Although maybe not if you're seventeen."

I asked Plas to describe for me the role the saxophone played in the popular music of the fifties, after all the honking died down. He responded by sending me a two-disc compilation of some of the better-known tunes he has played on. A first listening gives the impression that you're hearing a comprehensive history of rhythm and blues vocal groups and early rock and roll. Some of the iconic fifties songs are "Rockin' Robin" by Bobby Day, "The Great Pretender" by the Platters, "Margie" by Fats Domino, "Bony Maronie" by Larry Williams, "Young Blood" by the Coasters, and "Primrose Lane" by Jerry Wallace. There's "Foot Stompin'" by the Flares, "My Way" by Eddie Cochran, "I'm Walkin'" by Ricky Nelson, "Ramrod" by Duane Eddy, and the silly "Kookie, Kookie, Lend Me Your Comb" by Edd Byrnes and Connie Stevens. All of this predates his recordings with Marvin Gaye ("Let's Get It On"), B.B. King, Frank Sinatra, Ella Fitzgerald, Ray Charles, Nat King Cole, and dozens of other artists.

Like a lot of young players growing up in the forties, Plas was captivated by the pyrotechnics of bebop and seduced by the rollicking syncopations of R&B. "My father was an alto player and loved Johnny Hodges," he says. "So for me, the saxophone had that great jazz image. But I had idols who did different things, too. I loved the way Earl Bostic did his real raucous growl through a melody. I loved blues players like Louis Jordan and Eddie 'Cleanhead' Vinson. They just made you feel good and played music you wanted to dance to."

As teenagers in New Orleans, Plas and his brother had a pop band that covered jukebox hits by Joe Turner, Dinah Washington, and his heroes Jordan and Bostic. At home they played the art music of the era: bebop. When it was time to choose a career path, the decision was easy: you could at least make a living playing rhythm and blues.

Plas left New Orleans with Charles Brown, a popular blues vocalist and pianist. "It was 1951, and we had three tenor players and guitar in the front line, a rock 'em sock 'em authentic rhythm and blues band. It was the same lineup that Ray Charles had later in the fifties.

The tenor often had a mocking voice, like a second-line singer. You'd trade melodies back and forth like the statement and answer in a church. But it was always improvised."

Although his more memorable work would occur in the studio, Plas says it's hard to have more fun than playing saxophone in a rhythm and blues band. "When I wasn't playing a solo, I was doubling the bass guitar lines, doing fills and riffs behind the vocal," he says. "Basically, you're playing something all the time. You're part of the intro, you do the solo, and then the shout chorus at the end. You're right at the heart of the music.

"No one is busier in an R&B band than the saxophone player."

Some of the credit for the saxophone's role in early rock must be given to the era's most gifted tunesmiths, Jerry Leiber and Mike Stoller. When he was seventeen, the same year he began writing lyrics for his buddy Mike's tunes, Jerry bought a C-Melody saxophone in a hockshop in Los Angeles. "Mike had this '39 Plymouth that was a real mess," Jerry says. "The only thing that looked worse than his Plymouth was my saxophone. I would lie on the backseat, stick my feet out the window, and play 'Deacon's Hop' by Big Jay McNeely, which was the big hit of that year, 1949. I'd play it over and over until Mike would get so distraught he'd stop the car and say, 'If you don't stop playing, you'll have to walk home.' I was terrible. I ended up hocking it for thirty dollars."

Ditching the C-Melody, as it turned out, was a boon for the saxophone, for a friendship and professional partnership was saved that produced some of pop music's greatest songs—and the saxophone, true to form, was prominently featured in most of them. Two years later, Leiber and Stoller had their first number one hit on the R&B charts— "Hard Times," a song they wrote for Charles Brown, who had just recruited Plas Johnson into his band. Over the next decade, they wrote hit songs for the Coasters (a later incarnation of the Robins), the Searchers, the Drifters, Elvis Presley, and Ray Charles—iconic tunes such as "Kansas City," "Hound Dog," "Searchin'," "Spanish Harlem," "Stand by Me," "Jailhouse Rock," "Love Potion #9," "Ruby Baby," "On Broadway," "In the Still of the Night," and "There Goes My Baby." "All the solos were either the piano or saxophone," says Jerry. "Mostly the saxophone."

Gil Bernal, who began playing tenor saxophone in Lionel Hampton's band after graduating high school, provided the fills and solos on a lot of those early songs. He had met Mike Stoller at Los Angeles City College. In 1954, when Leiber and Stoller started Spark Records, he became the label's bandleader and went on to record fifteen tunes the songwriters produced for the Robins and Coasters, including "Searchin'," "Smokey Joe's Cafe," and "Riot in Cell Block #9." "In those sessions," says Gil, "the saxophone was the commentator. The singers would sing a line and I'd mock them. When it came to solos, I'd play simplified jazz, but in that emphatic, aggressive, raucous Texas-tenor style. At one point, I was called the fifth voice of the Robins, because I always had my say between choruses."

In the late fifties, Leiber and Stoller moved to New York as producers for Atlantic Records. One day, while waiting to enter a rehearsal studio, they heard a saxophonist running some rhythmic figures while other musicians packed up their instruments. "It was basically a saxophone's imitation of a bluegrass fiddle," says Mike. "It was fascinating and we loved it." The player was Curtis Ousley, who came to be known as King Curtis.

"We hired him to do the same thing on 'Yakety Yak,'" says Mike. "'Take out the papers and the trash/Or you don't get no spending cash'—it was a rhythmic country fiddle style he had invented that we called chicken scratch. After that, everybody imitated him, including Boots Randolph, who recorded 'Yakety Sax.'"

King Curtis's chicken scratch enlivened several other Leiber and Stoller hits, including "Charlie Brown" and "Along Came Jones." "I wrote out all of his little fills between phrases, but the solos were basically improvised," says Mike. For a talented player like Curtis, who had also spent time in Lionel Hampton's band, the work was less than challenging. "King Curtis was a very fine jazz musician who thought the R&B stuff was child's play," says Mike. "But it amused him." In the sixties, as rhythm and blues became more soulful and funkier, King Curtis backed up Aretha Franklin, Sam Cooke, Wilson Pickett, and the Isley Brothers and jammed with rockers as diverse as the Beatles and Eric Clapton. In 1967, working with his own band, he had a hit with the instrumental "Memphis Soul Stew." In 1971, at the age of thirty-seven, he was stabbed to death outside his Manhattan apartment.

By then, even though the electric guitar was ascendant in pop music, the saxophone was still managing to find ways to contribute to new music. Tenor player Steve Douglas formed the center of Phil Spector's Wrecking Crew, which provided a backup "wall of sound" to the Crystals, the Ronettes, the Righteous Brothers, and Ike and Tina Turner, as well as the Beach Boys, most notably on "Good Vibrations" and the album *Pet Sounds*. The Memphis Horns were a key contributor to soulmaster Otis Redding's success, Jerry Martini to Sly & the Family Stone's, Steve Mackay to Iggy Pop's Stooges', Chris Wood to Traffic's, Dick Parry to Pink Floyd's and, of course, more recently, Clarence Clemons to Bruce Springsteen's.

If they could, Leiber and Stoller, whose music helped push the saxophone into mainstream pop music, would send regular checks to Adolphe Sax. "The saxophone is not the first thing most people think of when they remember the great R&B vocal music of the fifties," says Jerry. "But if you were to remove the saxophone—the great playing of Gil Bernal, Plas Johnson, and King Curtis—it just wouldn't be the same. And it definitely wouldn't have been as popular."

When Tim Ries, who had spent the previous ten years playing acoustic jazz in a variety of ensembles, and "legit" music with a classical saxophone quartet, was asked to join the Rolling Stones' fifteen-month worldwide tour, he found himself the newest executor of a noble tradition within the band. Sonny Rollins and Wayne Shorter, two jazz icons, had recorded with the world's most famous rock band, and Sonny had even toured with the group for a while. "The fact that Wayne and Sonny had done it . . . well, I didn't have to think long about the offer," he says.

Tim began preparing for the assignment by listening to about a hundred of the band's songs. "Then I listened a lot to Maceo Parker, King Curtis, and Fathead Newman," Tim says. "Growing up in Detroit, I was enamored of the Motown sound, which came out of gospel and blues but also jazz. The Stones are very jazz-friendly. And then, of course, I listened to Bobby Keys."

Thanks to one recording session in 1971, Keys had single-handedly ensured that the saxophone would become a permanent fixture in the Stones' supporting instrumentation—and hence a model for other rock bands. The way Keys sees it, the *Sticky Fingers* recording sessions, at which Bobby laid out a now-legendary improvisational vamp on "Can't You Hear Me Knocking," were simply meant to be, the culmination of a string of serendipitous encounters.

Bobby grew up in Lubbock, Texas, where he began playing with his school marching band in the eighth grade. In high school, he played for Arthur Murray dance clubs and a rockabilly band, Buddy Knox and the Rhythm Orchids. His Lubbock neighbor was Buddy Holly, who had had some success playing the Apollo Theater in New York, where the house band included King Curtis and Big Al Sears, two of Bobby's idols. "Buddy flew King back to Texas to play on a couple of tracks," Bobby remembers. "I had the choice of going to a high school football game or picking up Curtis at the airport and driving him to a recording studio in New Mexico. He was very inspirational to me and gave me a lot of confidence. When you first start to play the saxophone, you don't get a whole lot of support from the people around you, your grandparents and friends, because you don't get any music out of the horn for a while."

Not much later, Bobby found himself in Holly's band. After Holly died in a plane crash in 1959, Bobby joined up with the singer Bobby Vee. At a concert produced by Dick Clark in San Antonio in

1965 that included Vee, George Jones, and the Rolling Stones, he became friendly with Brian Jones, Keith Richards, and Mick Jagger, who were staying next door to him at a Ramada Inn. "I was kind of intrigued with them because they had recorded 'Not Fade Away,' which was a Buddy Holly song. When they found out I was from Lubbock, they said, 'Did you know Buddy Holly?' I said, 'Yeah, of course, I played with him.' It turned out Keith and I were born on the same day within minutes of each other. There was a vibe and a bond there that seems to still sustain itself."

A few years later, while working with Delaney and Bonnie Bramlett's band, Bobby and the trumpet player Jim Price were asked by Eric Clapton to join him in the recording studio in England. "En route," says Bobby, "Eric decided he didn't need horns, but his friend George Harrison was also in the studio, so were subcontracted off to him. In the process we ran into Mick in London, who said the Stones might have a couple of tracks they could use horns on for the album they were recording. We did 'Brown Sugar' the first night and 'Can't You Hear Me Knocking' the next. The jam on that tune was the first take—we just let the tape roll and kept playing. The whole second part was strictly ad lib on everyone's part. It just happened to work out real good. Every day I thank my lucky stars that it did."

So does Tim Ries. "That solo pretty much guaranteed that [the Stones] would have a horn section for the next three decades," he says. Curiously, it's also resulted in the Stones' music going "legit." In preparing for the tour and then playing with and observing the band for fifteen months, Tim found himself filtering their music through a classical sensibility, altering harmonies and time signatures on pensive songs such as "Wild Horses" and "As Tears Go By." He enlisted other classical musicians for his *Stones Project*, and eventually Charlie Watts, Keith Richards, and Ron Wood came on as guest soloists for renditions of songs, now fronted by Tim's soprano and tenor saxophones, that they wrote.

Says Tim, "Who ever thought you could take Rolling Stones songs and make them into chamber music?"

———

On the drive to Woodstock, New York, where I'm to meet David "Fathead" Newman, I've been listening to his two-CD anthology, *House of Newman*. The compilation spans his most prolific years, from the early fifties, when he established himself as Ray Charles's tenor soloist, through the eighties, when he backed up Aretha Franklin, Dr. John, and Aaron Neville. One of the Ray Charles tunes, "Let the Good Times Roll," recorded in 1959, condenses a big chunk of pop-music history into a blistering four minutes. You can hear the western swing bands of the thirties, the jump blues bands of the forties, and the primitive rock and roll sound of the fifties—all in a song that anticipates the soul and funk music of the sixties and seventies. The saxophone, of course, contributes much to this musical time capsule. Its value is underscored by the inclusion of an all-star septet: backing up David's solo are Paul Gonsalves and Zoot Sims on tenor, Marshall Royal and Frank Wess on alto, and Hank Crawford and Charlie Fowlkes on baritone.

Born in 1933, David, a man of wide musical tastes, effectively negotiated the swirl of intersecting musical genres that evolved in mid-twentieth-century American music. An early bebop player, he ended up taking a long tour through rhythm and blues and played his share of soul, funk, and rock before settling into his current straight-ahead-jazz modality.* "Because of my association with Ray, I've always been known as a soul-jazz musician," he says, turning down the volume of the big-band music blasting through the speakers in his living room. "But lately, I've become a jazz musician again."

———

*It's a circuitous route now taken by many younger players. While older players who were involved in the early days of jazz and rhythm and blues moved seamlessly between the two idioms—John Coltrane played on Earl Bostic's "Flamingo" in 1951—many younger players have found themselves discovering jazz through R&B. For Steve Wilson, who often gives master classes and lectures about the role of the saxophone in American music, R&B, funk, and soul music opened a back door into the more serious acoustic jazz that now consumes most of his interest. "Believe it or not, I got to Coltrane through Ronald Bell of Kool & the Gang," he says, laughing. "He was the guy I was listening to most in the seventies. Nobody talks about him, but he brought a great deal of sophistication to the R&B funk

Inventor of the saxophone, Adolphe Sax was a Romantic visionary who had big plans for the saxophone. Its success, achieved long after he died, exceeded even his most grandiose dreams.

The saxophone section in the Gilmore Band, which Patrick Sarsfield Gilmore wisely introduced to his sixty-six-instrument ensemble in 1872, became so popular that it would stage separate concerts after the main performances.
(New York Public Library)

The Fletcher Henderson Orchestra in New York around 1924, in which Coleman Hawkins was first exposed to Louis Armstrong's rhythmic bluesy gait. The band featured Henderson (seated at piano), Armstrong on trumpet (center, back), and saxophonists (left to right) Hawkins, Buster Baily, and Don Redman.
(Frank Driggs Collection/Getty Images)

In 1938, the Nazis could think of no better way to illustrate Entartete (degenerate) Musik than with this crude exaggeration of the original poster for the opera *Johnny spielt auf.*
(With kind permission of the Hindemith-Institut, Frankfurt/Main)

Charlie Parker's blinding technique and invention aroused intense feelings among his listeners. Some found his playing totally mystifying, others heavenly. Although stalked and eventually overcome by personal demons, Parker was considered a sweetheart of a man. He was always looking after younger players—his "brood," says Phil Woods. "He wanted to know if you'd eaten that day."

(AP/Wide World Photos)

Lester Young's sweet sound on the tenor has been revered and emulated by generations of saxophonists. When playing and recording together, "Prez" and Billie Holiday often finished each other's musical sentences.

(Charles Peterson/Getty Images)

Benny Carter, shown here during a concert at Tompkins Square Park in New York, countered the saxophone's bawdy reputation by playing with style and sophistication. Playing the saxophone, he said, was a daily "religious experience." (Michael Schmelling / AP/Wide World Photos)

Stan Getz (here circa 1965) had a sound "you'd want to go home to," although with his bad-boy reputation you'd prefer that he not be there when you arrived. (Hulton Archive/Getty Images)

Curtis Ousley—"King Curtis"—shown here wielding his tenor at a 1968 "Soul Together" concert at Madison Square Garden in New York, enlivened hundreds of R&B and soul records with what songwriters Jerry Lieber and Mike Stoller called his "chicken scratch" sound. (Jack Robinson / Hulton Archive / Getty Images)

John Coltrane's playing, says Mike Brecker, had "a large, spiritual, mystical quality to it, and a gorgeous sound. From a technical viewpoint, it was outrageous." Coltrane's technique was hard-won—he was known to practice before gigs and recording sessions, during breaks and afterward. Their marriage, said his wife, was "ninety percent saxophone."

(© David Redfern / Redferns / Retna Ltd.)

When Branford Marsalis, shown here at a benefit for Benny Powell, switched from alto saxophone to tenor, it was like "finally finding the right woman." (John Pearson Wright/Time Life Pictures/Getty Images)

Michael Brecker during a 2001 Carnegie Hall performance celebrating the music of John Coltrane. Like many modern saxophonists, Brecker idolized Coltrane when Brecker first switched from clarinet to tenor saxophone. (Debra L. Rothenberg)

Even when practicing as a boy, Sonny Rollins, pictured here playing on the Williamsburg Bridge in Brooklyn in 1966, would go into a "reverie. I'd just lose myself. I was into heaven, another place. To a great extent, that still happens today." It's as though, he says, the saxophone is playing itself. (© New York Daily News, L.P. Reprinted with permission)

François Louis and his "diabolique" aulochrome, a double soprano saxophone.

The saxophone section of the Purdue University All-American Marching Band, shown here at the 2003 Indy 500 parade in downtown Indianapolis, occasionally invites middle-aged novices, such as the author, second from left, to march with them.

David grew up in Dallas, where he was smitten by the playing of Buster Smith, Charlie Parker's idol. "They called him 'Prof,'" David says. "He was a more aggressive player, he got all over the saxophone, his execution was faster than most other alto players. That's what Parker liked. I liked it, too."

David was also a scion of the noisy Texas tenor family fathered by Budd Johnson, Buddy Tate, Illinois Jacquet, and Arnett Cobb. In his early twenties, he would play bebop on weekends in the Woodmen Auditorium in Dallas, then rejoin Ray Charles on the road for weeknight gigs. Charles, who called his lead soloist Brains (he'd been given the moniker Fathead by a music teacher after flubbing a sight-reading test in high school), had recruited his octet in Dallas, where saxophone players were known to strive for a sound as big as the state.

Charles, who occasionally played alto saxophone, had a fondness for a tight horn section. "He borrowed a big-band concept and put it into a small group," says David. "We had a baritone, alto, tenor, and two trumpets. Other combos would do straight one-three-five voicings, but Ray would write parts for the horn that were the same as the ones he played himself on the piano. The harmonizing was more extended and sophisticated."

As it was for jazz, the 1960s was a great decade for the saxophone in popular music, even though by the time of the Woodstock festival the electric guitar had eclipsed it as the go-to instrument in rock and roll. Fats Domino, purveyor of New Orleans boogie-woogie, never had fewer than four saxophones in his band; his tenor player, Herb Hardesty, traded lead lines with Fats's vocals on 80 percent of the tunes. The avatar of funk, James Brown, had a five-piece horn section featuring searing sax chops by Maceo Parker and J. C. Davis. It's hard to find a Motown tune on which the tenor or baritone saxophone is not

---

tenor. The way he was soloing—he wasn't just playing blues scales—you could tell he had been listening to Coltrane. In fact, one of his first records was called 'I Remember John W. Coltrane.' It's amazing to think about. With the popularity of that band and their frat-house party music, who would have thought that the guy was playing Coltrane licks?"

the second, or, in the case of the vocal quartets, fifth voice in the music, responsible for every fill and solo. Junior Walker even persuaded Motown executives to record him and his All Stars with the saxophone as the lead voice.

Players like King Curtis and David Newman, though, always felt a little conflicted about the music. Among their peers, true respect was granted to the artful jazz saxophonists. But pop-music recording sessions and gigs paid the bills. "Eddie Harris used to talk about how all the saxophone players would sit around the bar and discuss who their favorite player was," says David. "Everyone had a different opinion. One guy would like Stan Getz, another Prez, another Hawk, someone else Sonny Stitt, Gene Ammons, or Coltrane—all of them great jazz-music players.

"Then they'd ask the bartender and he'd say, Junior Walker. Again, it was that soul thing. People loved it."*

The soul-jazz thing continues to thrive at the nexus of popular and jazz music, a fact Ron Blake discovered after graduating from Northwestern University and getting a gig with rhythm-and-blues organist Charles Earland, who died in 1999. With his formal education, Ron was schooled in many styles but was concerned that he might not choose the right one for Earland. "I was right out of college," Ron remembers, "and I said to myself, 'Just lay back, stay in the pocket, and keep it simple.' But then I looked down at the top of his keyboard and there's a picture of Coltrane. Earland was a soul-jazz Hammond B-3 guy who grew up playing saxophone. I was, like, Hmmm. This guy thinks like me."

It was an instructive lesson for Ron, a tall, wickedly handsome young saxophonist whose wide-ranging career illustrates how thoroughly the

---

*In 1961, Eddie Harris, a bop saxophonist in the smooth style of Stan Getz, recorded the theme from the movie *Exodus*, one of the earliest jazz-pop hits, which sold more than a million copies. After being criticized for "selling out," he refused to play the tune for years.

saxophone has penetrated all modern music* and continues to be an innovative force in new music. Following him from gig to gig over the course of a week can be dizzying. He might premiere an eccentric bit of "concert" saxophone music one night; play straight-ahead jazz with bassist Christian McBride the next; join the Yerba Buena ensemble for a high-spirited salsa-meets-hip-hop gig; perform tunes from his R&B–inflected album with his own band; then record a tribute album to Fela Anikulapo Kuti, the late Afrobeat star.

For Ron, who considers Lester Young his "root," the ease with which the saxophone traverses the idiomatic landscape guarantees its inclusion in new music. Growing up in the Virgin Islands, he listened to the sounds of the Caribbean—calypso, soca, steel pan, reggae, salsa, and merengue—as well as the Jackson Five, Kool & the Gang, and hard rock. The interbreeding of styles defined music's cutting edge—and no instrument was better suited to negotiating this alternative approach than the flexible saxophone.

Still, the widely eclectic Yerba Buena band, which first asked him to solo on two tunes it was contributing to a Fela tribute record, presented a challenge. Just where do you fit in with an ensemble that draws upon salsa, Cuban *son*, jazz, Latin rock, hip-hop, rhythm and blues, and club culture? And which references from Fela's Afrobeat should you insert into the middle of all that?

"When I checked out Fela," Ron says, "I heard a more contemporary sound that went back to my roots. In the Virgin Islands, there's a music called kwelbe, sometimes spelled quelbe. It had a washtub bass, banjo or ukulele, drums, and saxophone. The saxophone would play the melodies along with the vocalist or improvise over the form of the tune. It was a style you could hear a lot in Lester's music. It had never translated into calypso or soca, where the saxophone is used as part of a horn section. But when I heard Fela, I said, 'Oh yeah, it's like kwelbe but with a bigger groove. I get it.'"

---

*In commercial terms, at least, the pop saxophone reached its apotheosis in the late 1990s, when Kenny G became the best-selling instrumentalist of all time.

The Yerba Buena band, Ron says, wanted his jazz background to be evident on the Fela record. "So the connection there was to all the lyrical cats of the music—Coltrane, Shorter, Stanley Turrentine, and again, back to Lester Young. That's my root.

"What was remarkable to me was that, in examining these two saxophone styles from opposite ends of the idiomatic spectrum—kwelbe/Fela and jazz—you find they both have the same source. And that's also the amazing thing about the saxophone. However far you range, you still find yourself connected to everyone who's ever played it."

This love is for real, I've decided, and it's time to commit. I need my own horn.

Dave Hoskins, aka Junkdude, sells vintage saxophones from his home not far from the Columbus, Ohio, airport. He's one of hundreds of dealers around the world who swap, barter, and trade old horns—or at least those built before about 1965, the last days of Selmer's best Mark VIs. Dave had a couple of tenors made by SML, a Parisian saxophone manufacturer named after its founders—Strasser, Marigaux, and Lemaire—that he thought might be a good choice for me. In 1934 the trio raided the Selmer design staff and began producing horns they thought could steal a little bit of Selmer's business. SML made a few hundred saxophones a year until 1986, when it decided it could no longer compete with Selmer. The Junkdude, along with other vintage experts, believes the SMLs are vastly underappreciated and represent great value.

Dave has laid out the tenors he has—the two SMLs, an old Conn, a

Martin, and a Selmer Super Balanced Action—on a pool table off his living room. The SMLs, he says, date to the forties; he'll let me have either one for $1,600. Both have done some hard time. Neither one has a bit of its original lacquer—giving the horns a stressed look that's popular among serious musicians, many of whom also believe a relacquering can wreck a horn's distinctive sound. One is pocked and dinged; the other one, equally beat up, has been retrofitted with a microphone pickup. Dave, an affable fellow in his thirties, hands me a mouthpiece—a Morgan—and invites me to try them out.

After offering apologies in advance for my rank beginner status, I finger and blow one horn, then the other, but manage to elicit only a few squawks and moans from the instruments. The low notes don't speak for me at all—my breath passes silently through the horn without intruding upon the realm of fluid mechanics. I remember Ortley saying one night that sometimes the saxophone fights you, it just doesn't want to be played. But this is worse. Maybe these old codgers, after long and illustrious careers, just can't fathom closing out their days serving a novice. When Dave plays the horns, they project magnificently, with a husky, deep voice. I'd love to own one, but what's the point if they won't play? It's clear they don't like me.

I try the old Conn, a 10M, and the Martin, with pretty much the same result. Then I pick up the Super Balanced Action. Its serial number, 42668, dates its production to 1949, a year after the model, which featured a couple of ergonomic improvements over the popular Balanced Action, was introduced. It was fabricated at a time when Selmer was producing about 3,000 handmade saxophones a year—as opposed to the 17,000 the company's highly mechanized factory assembles today. Between 1948 and 1954, when the illustrious Mark VI debuted, Selmer made about 20,000 Super Balanced horns. The company's reference numbers don't distinguish among the various members of the sax family, but a good guess is that about 90 percent of them were altos and tenors. This one has been professionally relacquered and is engraved with a delicate but simple floral pattern. Dave got it from a local psychiatrist who figured he could buy a couple of new German Keilwerths for the price the SBA would fetch. The shrink used to lend it to a guy named Rusty Bryant, an R&B player whose group once included Nancy Wilson as vocalist, Dave says. He has no idea who owned it before. Because it's a high-quality Selmer, Dave says, he's asking $3,600 for the horn.

I strap on the instrument, and its pearled keys seem to rise up to meet my fingers. I depress them without blowing and they efficiently pass the commands along the elaborate network of tubes, rods, cross hinges, and rollers, causing the key pads to descend upon the tone holes with a satisfying clunk. The action is, well, balanced—beautifully, in fact; it's like the keys are powered with a hydraulic assist. I finger and blow a low C—for me the real test; I don't expect to be able to get the notes below it to speak immediately, but the C I should be able to hit—and the note pops out cleanly with a clear, liquid sound. I'm stunned. I press my luck and finger the lowest note, the B-flat, and the horn roars proudly.

Before I think too hard on it, I write Dave a check and flee with the instrument. I can't wait to meet all the personalities who inhabit this horn.

That night, after dinner, I pull the SBA from its case, rig up the mouthpiece, and, with great anticipation, blow. The horn responds with a hoarse squeak. I reach for the low notes. Nothing. A rising panic makes my head pound. Did the Junkdude do a bait and switch? Don't think so. It's more likely that the horn itself is doing an Adolphe, staking its claim as scion of the nineteenth century's most dedicated anarchiste de droite. Now what?

Here's what: the next morning, when I return the Armstrong tenor to the rental store and show a technician my new SBA, he tells me that the horn has been "laying a while." The kid leather pads that seal the tone holes are cracked and loose and several key bumpers are missing; it needs many adjustments and is probably acting a little deranged. Tell me about it: one minute it's singing joyously, the next it retreats into a sullen funk.

Talk about high maintenance. This love may be for real; I just hope I can find a horn to share it with.

8. THE NAKED LADY

For as long as he can remember, the voice of Sax has been in Ralph Morgan's head, occasionally disclosing tantalizing details of the esoteric science behind the instrument's invention. At the moment, Ralph, who makes hard-rubber mouthpieces in the basement of his ranch house in Springfield, Ohio, is smoothing the side rails of Illinois Jacquet's mouthpiece with a piece of silicon carbide paper laid across the surface of a perfectly flat piece of float glass. Jacquet had complained that he was unhappy with the tone in the middle range of his horn and had entrusted Ralph to perform whatever minor surgery was needed to improve it. Using feeler gauges that resemble mini–tongue depressors, Ralph has taken some key measurements—the angle and length of the facing curve, the size of the tip opening—and recorded them on a grid to compare them with those of a facing chart copyrighted by his father in 1940. He found the tip opening was half a thousandth of an inch off. "Now the D and E will be right back where they should be," Ralph says proudly as he cleans the mouthpiece.

For the past twenty years or so, Ralph, who has spent a lifetime around saxophones, has been searching for the instrument's Holy Grail: a design for the perfect mouthpiece. Every great player, alive or dead, has tried dozens of mouthpieces—long and short; plastic, wood, crystal, and rubber; square-chambered and round-chambered; and all the permutations thereof—hoping to tame the caprice of a horn that relies upon a sound-producing mechanism sensitive to barometric pressure, temperature, the quality of the material it's made of, and a dozen other factors, including whether the player has just had his teeth cleaned or is still getting over a cold. The collective agony endured by saxophonists searching for the "right" mouthpiece can't be underestimated. When John Coltrane, who practiced obsessively, once made a minor alteration to his favorite mouthpiece of the moment and ruined it, he couldn't bring himself to play for weeks.

Ralph makes mouthpieces with a round chamber—the way Adolphe Sax originally designed them. In the 1930s, when saxophones infiltrated big dance bands, designers discovered that a smaller square chamber enabled the horn to project more, enabling it to compete with the other instruments. In Ralph's view, the design change made no sense and sacrificed, among other qualities, the saxophone's ability to be played in tune.

A round, avuncular fellow with a hearty midwestern laugh, Ralph rises from a chair to give me a tour of his basement workshop. Pre-production paraphernalia occupy one corner. This is where Ralph mixes a chunk of rubber that's been machined into the rough shape of a mouthpiece, some red rubber dust, and powdered sulfur, mounts it atop a shrink pin, and bakes it in a convection oven until it slims down to the exact bore size of a saxophone crook. Nearby shelves are lined with hundreds of the coal-black accessories, all sitting astride their shrink pins like unidentifiable alien creatures in suspended animation. Another corner is host to Ralph's small finishing table, where he makes final adjustments after his two assistants work up the mouthpieces. On a remote bench is the prototype of a new saxophone he has designed and built, along with the tools he used recently to disassemble it following a road test by Craig Bailey, an alto player who tried it while on tour with Ray Charles. ("Ray was blown away," Ralph claims.) There are file cabinets bursting with catalogues, magazines, clippings, and odd bits of Saxiana. Shoe boxes bulge with dusty ligatures, horn crooks, and ancient mouthpieces, many of which would fetch a handsome price on eBay. Stumps of rock-hard grenadilla wood, from which he fabricates custom mouthpieces, are scattered around the floor. Many of the earliest saxophone mouthpieces were made of grenadilla, which is so dense it will not float in water. The pronounced grain of the wood added richness to the horn's midrange harmonics; the large chamber with comparatively thin walls accounted for the dark "fat" sound still sought by many modern players.

Born at the peak of the saxophone craze, Ralph is one of the last links to a grand era in American instrument manufacturing, a time when midwestern enterprise and heartland smarts gave birth to an industry that by the turn of the twentieth century began to overtake its European competitors and that, though it's since been swallowed up by conglomerates that mechanized production and is facing a new challenge from the Chinese, continues to dominate world markets today. The people who gravitated toward Elkhart, Indiana, which became the instrument-manufacturing capital of the world, were a zany, brainy, often self-educated group—eccentric designers, tool-and-die wizards, acoustical scientists, master engravers—almost all of whom were also highly skilled musicians. Ralph got his first job at the Selmer factory in Elkhart in 1950 drilling springholes and mounting posts on clarinets and flutes, moved through just about every facet of saxophone production, and closed out his career there as a regional sales manager, one of the top jobs in the company. Ralph's territory was a big chunk of the central United States, which he shared with a guy named Curt Guppert. Curt was a pilot who, when his eyesight went bad and he could no longer fly, retrofitted his Lincoln Continental to accommodate a 430-horsepower airplane engine and installed an instrument panel from a B-26 bomber on his dashboard. He trashed the thing when he hit a bull at 135 miles per hour on a one-lane highway in Texas. Like the other managers, Curt and Ralph could play all of the two dozen instruments they demonstrated and sold on the road.

Ralph and his buddy Curt were typical of the kind of guys who worked in Elkhart, which owes its existence to the C. G. Conn Instrument Company. Around 1888, Conn produced the country's first saxophone. The subsequent success of Conn saxophones and those of its chief American competitors, Buescher, Martin, King, and eventually Selmer, had powerful repercussions. It turned a quiet village along the St. Joseph River into the musical-instrument-manufacturing capital of the world; Elkhart remains home to nearly two dozen instrument makers. The companies' extravagant marketing campaigns helped make the saxophone the most popular instrument in the land, in turn encouraging an evolving idiom, jazz, to discover its most expressive voice. The saxophone itself was, in part, responsible for the school band movement and the introduction of music education programs to the nation's public schools—the first such curricula in any country. As with the saxophone's first manufacturer, however, none of this came without a price. The Conn company's success conferred upon its visionary founder, Charles Gerard Conn, enormous wealth and power—and led to his sad, penniless demise.

C. G. Conn was born in 1844, the year the saxophone debuted in Paris, to upstate New York farmers who moved to Elkhart when the boy was seven. In 1861 he enlisted in the Union Army, where he played cornet in a regimental band, then became a member of the First Michigan Sharpshooters, where he was promoted to captain before he was twenty. During a skirmish in Virginia he was taken prisoner and remained in custody, despite three attempted escapes, until the war was over. He then returned to Elkhart, where he opened a bakery and played cornet in the town band. To make extra money, he also made rubber stamps and replated silverware in a back room of his bakery.

Conn's introduction to instrument design came by way of a mouthpiece. After tearing up his lip in a fight, Conn searched for a way he could continue to play cornet with his troupe, the Haverly Minstrels, without wrecking his mouth. Having worked with Dexter Curtis, the inventor of the zinc collar pad for horses, in Michigan, he knew how to vulcanize rubber to metal and devised a cornet mouthpiece with a cushioned rim. When others expressed an interest in his lip-friendly design, he converted a sewing machine into a lathe and began making mouthpieces in his bakery workshop. He took out patents on the product in the United States and four other countries.

By 1876, he and Eugene Dupont, a French instrument maker who had moved to Elkhart, were making cornets—most notably the Four-in-One cornet, which could be played in four different pitches—in the back of the bakery. They were soon joined by Ferdinand August Buescher, who later founded the Buescher Band Instrument Company, manufacturer of the much-admired True-Tone saxophones, and John Henry Martin, whose son founded the Martin Band Instrument Company, producer of the Committee line of horns. In 1877 the partners bought an idle factory building, enticed other European artisans to join them, and shifted the Conn-Dupont Company into high gear.

Hardly deterred by a fire that destroyed his factory in 1883, Conn, sole proprietor of the company after his partner retired, soon established a subsidiary plant in Massachusetts and a retail store in New York City. He induced famous performers and conductors, including the trombonist Frederick Neil Innes and conductor Patrick Gilmore, to endorse his Wonder line of instruments. As Elkhart's first paterfamilias, he introduced a profit-sharing plan to his employees in 1891 and endorsed the establishment of a new union at his plant, Local 335 of the Metal Polishers, Buffers, Platers, Brass Molders, Brass and Silver Workers International Union of North America. (Their label proclaimed "Unity, Mutual Assistance, and Education.")

Conn took great pride in his saxophones which, by the early teens, accounted for nearly three quarters of his company's production and an even greater percentage of its profit. His early M series horns still fetch a handsome price on the vintage saxophone market, if only because of their desirability as art objects. Conn believed his instruments deserved elaborate ornamentation and devoted a huge wing of his plant to engraving. All of the work was done freehand, much of it by master engravers Charles and Julius Stenberg, who worked for a combined 136 years at the Conn company. Their engravings, which required about half a day per horn, followed the caprice of their particular mood and included images of the *Spirit of '76*, Leda and the swan, Saint George and the dragon, Uncle Sam, the god Mercury, the figure of Liberty, toddlers, kewpies, cherubs, satyrs, all manner of flowers and plants, geometric patterns, and scrolling. The M series horns featured the famous Naked Lady, which some embarrassed customers returned so that engravers could render the woman's torso in a more modest fashion. For a long time, serious players believed that the quality of intonation of the horn was directly related to the depicted size of the Naked Lady's breasts. Her expression varied, too—she was sometimes smugly satisfied, sometimes irritated—perhaps as a reflection of the engraver's current romantic life. Despite their great skill, the Stenbergs left the Naked Lady etchings to others. Low-affect Swedes who never spoke with fellow workers and rarely with each other, the Stenbergs were considered to be clueless when it came to describing the shape of a woman.

In the mold of Adolphe Sax, Conn had an outsize personality and a grand sense of his importance to the world around him. Big, blond, and rakishly handsome, with a prominent Irish nose, he was elected mayor of Elkhart in 1880, to the Indiana state legislature in 1889, and to the U.S. Congress in 1893. Like Sax, who also ran a publishing company, Conn followed his entrepreneurial instincts and political leanings into the publishing business. He founded *Trumpet Notes*, which later became *C. G. Conn's Musical Truth* and eventually *Musical Truth*, to help promote his instruments. He purchased the local Elkhart newspaper, the *Elkhart Review*, and renamed it the *Elkhart Truth*. While serving in the nation's capital, he took over *The Washington Times*.

Realizing that enormous profits awaited him if he could interest children in learning to play music, Conn established the Chicago School of Music in 1903; its graduates became teachers and instrument salesmen who fanned out throughout the Midwest, setting up private music schools and stores that could support the coming saxophone craze. It was no coincidence that major universities in Indiana, Michigan, Ohio, Iowa, and Illinois, all about equidistant from Elkhart, went on to form the center of advanced music education in America.

Like the designer of the monstrous Saxocannon and the steam-powered organ that could be heard anywhere in Paris, Conn was a wild-eyed big thinker who rarely shied away from a fight—and was often delighted to start one. When he heard that the Indiana and Michigan Electric Company was planning a hydroelectric dam on the St. Joseph River, he purchased several hundred acres four miles upstream from the project, where he planned to build his own dam and open a utility company. He lost the competition, at considerable expense. As publisher of *The Washington Times*, he used the newspaper as a soapbox to rail against vice in the nation's capital. His campaigns resulted in his being named a defendant in a costly libel suit. He lost another expensive lawsuit after he fell far behind in his payments to a former factory manager, William Gronert, to whom, as a production bonus, he had promised fifty cents per horn, never predicting, despite his grandiose visions, that the saxophone would become so wildly popular. In 1910 he was again forced to rebuild after fire destroyed his factories. Finally, after failing to meet payments on a $200,000 loan he had secured by pledging all of his worldly possessions, the hypomanic businessman was forced to sell his company in 1915.

Embittered by the loss, Conn fled his beloved Elkhart, home to a musical-instrument industry whose four-mile-long network of foundries, assembly plants, offices, repair shops, and subsidiary companies now formed the backbone of the town. Like Sax, who wrote a pamphlet on the health benefits of playing the saxophone, Conn had always had an interest in physical culture—before he started his company, he worked as a traveling salesman hawking "Konn's Kurative Kream." He found California to be hospitable to his oddball enthusiasms, which he detailed in several books. His last effort was titled *The Sixth Sense, Prayer, and Brain Cell Reformation*.

Conn died in 1931 at the age of eighty-six. According to his wishes, his body was returned to the town, now a city, that he helped develop. Some of the men he had personally hired still worked at the plant and took up a collection so that their impoverished former patron could receive an honorable burial.

Conn's successor, Carl Greenleaf, presided over the company's heyday, deploying his own spirit of invention. He retooled the Elkhart plant, fought to diminish the power of the union, and introduced stenciled engraving to reduce costs. Although the company continued to make a range of band instruments, Greenleaf expanded production of saxophones to 150 horns a day. The popularity of the saxophone had enabled other instrument makers—Buescher, Martin, Holton, and H. N. White, which made Charlie Parker's favorite, the King Super 20—to grab pieces of the ravenous market; at the height of the craze, they were producing a combined 6,000 saxophones a month. The quest for a competitive edge resulted in continuous subtle refinements of the saxophone's mechanics: in the twenties and thirties, forty-five patents relating to saxophones were granted by the U.S. Patent Office.

Unrestrained by truth-in-advertising laws or simple common sense, the competitors' marketing campaigns strove to outdo each other in their outlandish claims. "Learning to play the Saxophone is much the same as a youngster learning numbers and letters by moving blocks—and almost as simple," declared the Buescher company.

Conn linked its horns with the pursuit, and attainment, of the American dream: "Popularity, pleasure, a big income, all may be yours if you start now to cultivate your musical 'bump' with a Conn saxophone." To demonstrate the ease with which the instrument could be played, one of Conn's advertorials in *Musical Truth* showed a woman executing a somersault on the wing of an airplane while playing a solo. Conn's "Aqua Jazz" ad featured saxophonists toeing surfboards and playing one-handed on water skis. The Buescher company responded with clever schemes of its own. When Commander Donald MacMillan sailed for the North Pole in 1921, the company outfitted his crew with a Buescher saxophone.

Greenleaf's most profitable move was to involve his company in the emerging school band movement, an outgrowth of the rapid changes occurring in the country's public education system. Up to 1885, the American school curriculum was rigidly classical, modeled after a European system that emphasized foreign languages, physics, chemistry, algebra, geometry, and history. Despite the claim fifty years earlier by Lowell Mason, the conductor and music-education crusader, that any child could learn to sing, there was little teaching of vocal or instrumental music in the American school system. There were exceptions, however: Heeding Mason's advice, Boston public schools introduced vocal instruction. In 1857 the Boston Farm and Trades School established a school band, supported by school funds. And a high school in Middletown, Ohio, had a student "orchestra" in 1863.

The interest in teaching children music coincided with a growing interest in their welfare generally. Public high school enrollments rose from around 200,000 in 1890 to nearly a million in 1910. As cities grew and the pace of American life quickened, schools took on a greater role in providing leisure-time and enrichment activities. Several states formed associations starting in 1898 to organize school sports programs. Schools added cafeterias, nurses, and guidance counselors. Communities saw a need to provide suitable recreational activities for the growing youthful population. The National Recreation Association was founded in 1906, the Boy Scouts in 1910, and the Girl Scouts two years later. By then, 180 cities had public playgrounds, and playtime breaks, or "recess," were widely incorporated into elementary and secondary school curricula.

Within this climate, school bands began to thrive. By 1900 there were an estimated fifty school orchestras in the country, three times that many a decade later. In Connersville, Indiana, the supervisor of music, W. Otto Meissner, put together a school ensemble "to keep boys with changing voices interested in music." A pedagogy emerged that involved teaching children how to play in a band by actually having them play in the band from the very first lesson. Over the next decade, national educators' conferences repeatedly affirmed the value of music education, although instruction was still being provided by musicians from outside of the school system.

In 1920, Wisconsin and Michigan organized contests for school bands, followed by Montana a year later, and Wyoming in 1922. In 1923, Carl Greenleaf, then head of the Music Industries Chamber of Commerce, persuaded the Conn board of directors and his company's competitors to underwrite the first national band contest, which brought thirty ensembles from high schools, grammar schools, and military and preparatory schools to a four-day tournament at the Drake Hotel in Chicago. Reflecting the enormous popularity of the saxophone, the required piece for the competition was the Prelude from Bizet's *L'Arlesienne Suite* no. 1, which contains a saxophone solo.

The event encouraged the formation of thousands of school bands, many of whose directors were professional musicians who had lost their jobs in vaudeville. Instrumental music quickly captured a major share of funds budgeted for the teaching of music. Sponsors organized other national competitions—for soloists in 1929 and for vocal groups in 1936. The annual national band contest grew quickly and split into more manageable regional competitions. About 10,000 bands, orchestras, and choruses, 7,500 instrumental and vocal ensembles, and 15,000 instrumental soloists participated in the 1940 district and state competitions.

All this activity was an obvious boon to the instrument manufacturers. Greenleaf devoted saxophone profits to funding a new sales campaign. Fanning out across the Midwest, Conn salesmen would meet with local school boards and ask them to set up a meeting with students and parents. At the gathering the salesmen would describe the social benefits of playing in a group and would then call up a student from the audience who had no musical training and teach him or her how to play several bars of "America the Beautiful," usually on the saxophone, in less than fifteen minutes. They would then offer parents rental contracts for instruments on a six-week trial basis.

Greenleaf also committed the Conn Company as a major financier of the National Music Camp at Interlochen, Michigan (today an internationally renowned program); funded the initial publication of *Universal Teacher*, a method book for young band musicians; and established the Conn National School of Music in Chicago to develop the nation's first generation of public school band directors. Self-serving or not, the Conn Company's efforts, underwritten by its enormous saxophone profits, helped establish a musical curriculum in American public schools that became a model for the rest of the world. More than 100,000 student musicians march in college bands today, countless more in high school.

Ralph Morgan's education in instrument design began long before he joined Selmer, a French manufacturer that felt obliged to establish an early foothold in Elkhart. His father, Ralph senior, a designer for the Conn Company who had his own American-storybook personal history—his mother died when he was nine, whereupon he ran away to live on a Potawatomi Indian reservation in northern Michigan—taught him how to carve molds for saxophone keys. After school, Ralph would perfect wooden fabrications of the body and arm of a key or pad cup, and on Saturdays he and his father would drive out to the Routson Brass Foundry on South Main Street and fool around with the tool-and-die equipment. "Dad taught me how to take an empty gate of a sand caster, mix up my own molding sand, and tamp it in there," says Ralph. "He showed me how to push that key part in there, the one I'd carved, then throw on the parting, which is like talcum powder, put the top gate on, tamp that full of sand, pull it off, and there's the impression of half your key. Then I'd cut what's called a sprew hole, where you pour the metals through. Then he showed me how to take copper, zinc, and a few other things, put it in the crucible, melt it up, and make my pour through the sprew hole. When you were done, you had a brass key part."

When he was twelve, Ralph started working part-time at the Conn factory. "I apprenticed to the two old Babbitt brothers, Rollie and Jesse, who were some of the last ones who knew the proper design of a mouthpiece." By then, he also had a conditional (meaning underage) union card, which enabled him to play tenor saxophone in a traveling ensemble known as a territory band. A few years later, while still in high school, he was playing lead tenor in Artie Shaw's band; he then studied with Larry Teal at Wayne State University before being called up by the army air forces in 1943.

When Adolphe Sax stuck a bass-clarinet mouthpiece on an ophicleide (the same mouthpiece he had improved when he refashioned the bass clarinet), which gave him the crude prototype for a bass saxophone, he had only a vague idea of the importance of the mouthpiece proportions to the quality of the sound produced. As he developed the saxophone, Ralph maintains, Sax proceeded by trial and error to come up with the precise dimensions. Ralph says Henri Selmer, who would later buy Sax's workshop and whose sons would go on to build some of the finest saxophones ever made, was the first to "get scientific" about the design of the mouthpiece, in 1880.

Mouthpieces can have different dimensions, but all must obey certain rules, Ralph says. He shows me one that Henri Selmer carved out of grenadilla wood and describes its parts. There's the table, upon which the stock, or unscraped, portion of the reed lies. The window, the open portion of the mouthpiece, begins at the end of the table and is covered by the rest of the reed, from the shoulder, or beginning of the scrape, to its thin tip. The window is defined by its side rails and tip rail and curves ever so gently its entire length, creating enough space under the scraped portion of the reed for it to vibrate.

A couple of important variables come into play here (even before considering the size of the chamber, or interior portion, of the mouthpiece): the shape of the curve and its length. Both determine the size of the tip opening—the distance between the tip of the reed and the tip of the mouthpiece. Long and short facings require reeds of different strength and adjustments of embouchure. Narrow and wide tip openings also affect choice of reed and the dynamic range of the instrument.

"The facing curve allows the reed to vibrate at 100 percent efficiency," Ralph explains. "The scope of the reed's movement is like that of a fly rod. When you cast, the scope of the rod's movement near your hands isn't nearly as great as that at the thinner tip, which whips out farther. So on a mouthpiece, you have to construct a facing curve in such a way that at the millisecond each particular point on the reed reaches the end of its movement, it comes in contact with the side rail, which stops the vibration and causes it to spring back. If that particular point on the mouthpiece facing is a little too high or not far enough away from the tip, some guys say that note sticks in the horn or it's a wolf tone. It pops out a little brighter."

Of course, the notoriously unreliable reed can affect the execution of what Ralph calls a finite science. Most reeds are made of cane grown in the Var region of France. The *roseau*, or rushes, used for the reed are actually weeds that grow to about twenty feet. For years, producers have tried to cultivate the plant but have found that only the wild variety produces a quality reed. The region's reed carvers believe an ancient spirit resides amid the *roseau*; when the wind blows, its singing can be heard all through the Var.

The thin piece of cane, the only moving part on the saxophone responsible for generating sound, is remarkably athletic. To produce a pitch of A for one second (which would be fingered as a B on a

B-flat saxophone), the reed must vibrate 440 times, assuming the player is in tune. (Until the early twentieth century, "low pitch" A was considered to be 435 Hz, and "high pitch" A to be 457; many instruments were designated as such.) Press B (or concert A) again with the octave key, and it doubles its rate of vibration, to 880 cycles per second. When you finger a B-flat without the octave key (sounding A-flat on the tenor saxophone), it instantly decreases its rate of vibration to 462 cycles per second. As it arcs down to touch the side and tip rails with each flutter, the reed repeatedly seals and reopens the mouthpiece, acting as a valve that allows puffs of air into its chamber and setting up the wave patterns responsible for sound—a simple matter of fluid mechanics, says Ralph.

"It doesn't matter whether you're talking about fluid or air, both act the same when they pass over some path of resistance," Ralph says. "They show the same propensities for turbulence. When water in a creek hits a rock, it disturbs everything around and behind it. In a mouthpiece, the turbulence caused by air passing over a reed is noise."

The chamber, and the volume of air in it, constitutes the most important part of the bore of the instrument, says Ralph. "Its main job is to take a thin strip of air that's coming in between the tip of the reed and the tip of the mouthpiece and as nicely as possible form that into the round shape that it has to be to go into the end of the saxophone. That interior is shaped aerodynamically, not acoustically, so that the air will flow through it with the least possible turbulence. Musicians call it the core or center of the sound."

The biggest mistake any designer could make, Ralph says, is to make the interior square. It immediately changes the volume—a constant in the equation that governs mouthpiece design. A conical instrument like the saxophone, he says, works best when the volume of air in the mouthpiece is equal to that missing from the apex of the cone. "That's the first thing we change, and then we wonder why the instrument is out of tune."

Even the reason for the design change—to help the dance bands of the 1920s generate a big sound—was misguided, Ralph says.

"The goal was to make the sound brighter. Today we call that pro-jection, a misnomer. But if it's brighter, that's a sign it's producing more high harmonics, which are short wavelengths, and short wave-lengths don't travel anywhere." Another consequence of the smaller chamber is that the highest notes on the instrument will tend to be very sharp.

Like his father, Ralph has a photographic memory and easily calls up names, dates, and historical events. One cluster of his neurons is devoted to archiving weird science, some of which has found its way into his theories of mouthpiece design. He's particularly fascinated by some data developed by an acoustical scientist named Ignatius Gennusa, whom Ralph met in North Carolina in 1954. "Iggy found that if you take the blade, or scraped portion, of the reed and slice it in thirty-three equal horizontal sections—one for every note of the saxophone's compass—then measure the weight of each section and compute the basic vibrational frequency at which the mass or weight of that material will vibrate, you have in all respects the chromatic scale of the instrument that reed is going to play on. In other words, starting with the bottom of the scrape where it's thickest, that little section will vibrate at an exact ratio to the number of vibrations we assign to B-flat—or 462 cycles per second. The next section will vi-brate at the same ratio to B, the next to C, and so on.

"He spent thirty years working on the relationship between the facing curve and the configuration of the reed's blade," Ralph says. "Imagine that. Thirty years. I've only spent twenty designing my mouthpiece."

When he presented the saxophone to the world, sending into the universe a sound that had never before been heard in nature, Adolphe Sax challenged not only the livelihoods of other instrument makers but many of the then-accepted principles of the fledgling sci-ence of acoustics. In his many writings and rantings before courts of law, Sax stated that sound was a vibration, not an airstream, a fact confirmed and quantified in the late 1890s by Heinrich Hertz, who determined the number of those vibrations per second for each pitch. A fundamental principle of acoustics that Sax identified in constructing his saxophones was more difficult for his detractors to grasp: The timbre of the sound is determined by the proportions given to the air column by the proportions of the body of the instrument that contains it.

In lay terms, this meant that the nature of the sound of an instrument had little to do with the kind of material it was made of—whether wood, ivory, brass or other metals—and everything to do with its shape. The principle Sax had articulated, which to many seemed counterintuitive, explains why Charlie Parker sounded as good on a plastic Grafton saxophone as he did on one made of the finest French bell-metal brass. In defending this principle in one of his many legal battles, Sax, with typical disdain, described how his "adversaries" unwittingly employed it. "In negating the necessity of proportions," he said, "the hapless men are obliged to submit to them, for without them they would not be able to fabricate instruments. Only, routinely following a template, produced arbitrarily or by groping, they use proportion without knowing it, as Monsieur Jourdain writes prose." (Monsieur Jourdain is the boring, witless social striver in Molière's play *The Bourgeois Gentleman*.)

The acoustical underpinnings of the tuning of the saxophone were more mysterious. It was understood that an instrument made of a conical tube, like the oboe, bassoon, and now the saxophone, could produce all the even- and odd-numbered overtones of the harmonic series (and overblow in octaves, which meant the fingering for the first and second octaves was the same), whereas a cylindrical tube, like the clarinet, could not (it overblows by an octave and a fifth, requiring a different set of fingerings for the second octave). But in seeking patent protection, Sax argued that the position and height of the tone holes, the dimensions of the neck, and the size of the mouthpiece chamber were all precisely calculated and that the parabolic form of the upper third of the bore was responsible for proper tuning between octaves. He provided few details, however. In his first court case, a panel of experts determined that Sax's invention "forms a cone of which the walls have a specific curvature and which the Sax patent designates under the name of parabolic cone." But until Jaap Kool, a German acoustical technician, made a careful analysis in the 1920s of a Sax-built alto, no one really knew what that meant.

In *Das Saxophon*, Kool wrote that the forward side of the inner wall of the horn, where most of the tone holes are seated, forms a curve: if you look straight down the body of the instrument, or tube, the forward wall of the cone, which contains the tone holes, arches out of sight; you can't see all the tone holes without turning it upward. The back wall of the bore, conversely, is straight; you can see all the way down its length. A cross section of the instrument would reveal a slightly elliptical, rather than round, shape. The diameter of the bore does not increase uniformly but in a way determined by the geometric rules that govern a parabola. If the taper progressed uniformly down the tube, it would form a perfect cone—the shape of a bassoon, say, or an oboe.

The two different shapes of the bore's walls create an acoustical phenomenon not unlike that of convex and concave reflectors. Imagine slicing the saxophone bore in half from top to bottom and then taking a horizontal slice of each half. The slice from the straight side would be concave and would concentrate sound waves much the way a magnifying glass focuses light. The slice from the curved half would be convex, diffusing the concentrated waves that are being directed at it from the opposite wall. So in addition to traveling straight down the tube and reflecting back, sound waves, both focused and diffuse, are also bouncing horizontally off its sides, adding and subtracting from each other. Kool concluded that this frenetic activity accounts for the saxophone's mellow, rich tone.

Another way to understand what's happening in a saxophone is to think in aerodynamic terms. In a clever primer titled "The Acoustics of the Saxophone from a Phenomenological Perspective," John-Edward

Kelly, a concert saxophonist and pilot who now lives in Germany, uses Bernoulli's law of differential pressure, a basic principle of aerodynamics, to explain the saxophone's remarkable resonance. Bernoulli's law states that when a fluid, such as air, flows over a surface quickly, it exerts less pressure on that surface than air flowing more slowly over the same surface.

When applied to an airplane wing, the law explains the phenomenon of lift. When an airfoil passes through an air mass, the air, parted by the wing, attempts to remain stable or preserve homeostasis, a fundamental law of the universe. If the wing were perfectly flat, it would slice through the air in a straight line, or perhaps wobble a bit as it encountered differing levels of air density. The air itself would travel at the same speed across the flat top and flat bottom of the wing. But the bottom surface of an airplane wing is flat, and the top surface is arched at the leading edge. That means that air traveling around the curved top surface travels a greater distance than the air moving in a straight path below. That, in turn, means that the air on top is traveling faster than the air below. According to Bernoulli's law, the faster air on top exerts less pressure on the wing than the slower air on the bottom; the difference in pressure between the two surfaces generates lift.

Kelly correlates the airplane wing and the saxophone bore. The longer upper wing surface corresponds to the arching parabolic wall of the saxophone, the straight underside to the straight wall of the horn. Because the curved wall is longer than the straight wall, the airstream, or "soundstream," travels down along the two surfaces at different speeds, exerting less pressure on the curved side, more upon the straight. The asymmetrical pressure creates an unstable environment that greatly intensifies the resonant excitation of its walls. Regardless of how many tone holes are open or closed, the instrument's entire length is encouraged to vibrate enthusiastically.

In addition to explaining the saxophone's unique acoustical properties, Kelly's pamphlet mourns the modifications introduced by modern saxophone makers that largely eliminated the parabolic shape of the original saxophone—"an aesthetic atrocity directly comparable to the horrors of genetic mutation," he writes. "For the sake of accuracy, the so-called saxophone really ought to be given a different name."*

As a design purist, Ralph Morgan wouldn't disagree with that suggestion, although he finds it challenging to modify new equipment so that it sounds like the old. As we've been talking, Ralph has been filing down a chip on an old white plastic mouthpiece made by Arnold Brilhart, a saxophonist with the California Ramblers, a popular orchestra in the twenties. Brilhart later became a maker of much-sought-after mouthpieces. This one is called a Tonalin, made for a tenor. The design is a compromise between old and new—its chamber has two flat sides and a rounded top and bottom. This one also has a thin stress fracture on the inside of its neck (the "throat"), although Ralph doesn't think that will affect its playability. After taking final measurements and wiping it clean, he attaches a reed with a ligature and hands it to me. "Let's play it and see how it sounds," he says.

Unfortunately, Ralph has only an alto saxophone, so he suggests I play the chromatic scale on the newly conditioned mouthpiece alone so he can check out my embouchure. Try as I might, I can barely get a squeak out of it. "Think about blowing up a balloon," he says. "It's push, not blow." After I struggle some more, he tells me I'm biting down too hard. "Make believe you're going to push a pea through a peashooter. You wouldn't bite down on that." Pretty soon I'm able to coax a lower sound from the device. "You're getting there," Ralph says. "Just remember, it's a breathing instrument, not a blowing instrument. It's not the speed of the air that makes the reed vibrate, it's the pressure of the air."

As I continue to try to find notes that correspond to a simple Western scale on the mouthpiece, Ralph opens a Selmerpak and

*For more from Kelly, see Chapter 12.

pulls out his Mark VI alto, a 145,000 series, which dates its manufacture to 1966. He rigs up a Morgan alto mouthpiece, fixes it to the crook, and plays notes up and down the chromatic scale. The horn has a beautiful rich tone, although because it hasn't been played in a while a couple of the keys are sticking. Then he hands it to me. Although the first note I played on a saxophone was on an alto just like this one, I've gotten used to the more friendly tenor, and instead of eliciting a resonant long tone, as I did the first time I played the alto, I find myself lost in the land of accidentals. "You're playing some kind of Chinese scale," Ralph says, laughing. "Maybe it's a Doric mode, where the third and fifth don't sound." In my confused attempts to get a decent sound from the instrument, I bite harder and the instrument, egregiously offended, howls in protest. "Now you're doing what we used to call a nanny goat," Ralph says.

I give up. I'm not sure how my long day with Ralph has devolved into a lesson; saxophone players just can't help themselves, I guess. Thankfully, I've got a plane to catch and bring the lesson to a close. As Ralph walks me to the door, he says, "You have a tenor, right?"

I nod.

He hands me the Tonalin. "Here," he says. "This is yours. You'll need it."

9. DIABOLIQUE

Shrinking into a corner of the lobby of the Maison de Radio France in Paris, a postmodern concert hall along the Seine in the shadow of the Eiffel Tower, François Louis clutches an instrument case to his chest, nervously shifting his weight from foot to foot. He has just witnessed the formal debut of his new instrument, the aulochrome, which, his friend Joe Lovano assured him after he played it during a visit to François's workshop in Belgium, contains "the sound of the third millennium." François is discreetly trying to eavesdrop on audience members' conversations as they leave the hall, hoping to verify Joe's pronouncement that "this is the horn everybody will be playing a hundred years from now."

An hour earlier, Fabrizio Cassol, a young Belgian saxophonist with long and tight Kenny G curls, had walked to the front of the concert-hall stage carrying the delicate instrument, an elaborate conjunction of two soprano saxophones. Backed by the Baden-Baden and Freiburg Symphony Orchestra from Germany—an ensemble whose instrumentation includes a giant, hand-cranked roller assembly that re-creates the sound of waves crashing onshore, a brass gong the size of a double-garage door, and other unidentifiable noise and percussion devices—Cassol began his solo with a piercing trill that seemed to emanate with a kind of surround-sound ubiquity from every nook of the hall. The sound was so attention-grabbing and extraordinary that many in the audience spontaneously sprang to their feet and cheered for thirty seconds before settling down to listen to the rest of the piece, *Fanfare III, pour aulochrome et orchestre*, which the orchestra had commissioned from the Belgian composer Philippe Boesmans for the instrument's debut.

François, a round, rumpled, bespectacled fellow with half a century's deliberations on the nature of things creasing his brow, had worked nonstop on the aulochrome for two years, starting with two crude Borgani soprano bodies that he welded together. In his workshop in Ciplet, Belgium, he constructed his own tubes, rods, cross hinges, keys, pads, rollers, guards, and vents, as well as the horn's double mouthpiece and ligature. Widely known for his exquisite handmade silver and wooden mouthpieces—Lovano, David Liebman, Michael Brecker, Wayne Shorter, and David Sanborn are just a few of his clients—François also invented a new fingerboard mechanism for the aulochrome that he believes could improve all conventional saxophones. One table of keys, each key split in half, runs down the center of the double instrument. The top half of a key plays the horn on the right, the bottom half the horn on the left.

Now, as the concert hall empties, it's clear that the twinned horn's first performance, which was broadcast on national radio, has been a succès d'estime. Everyone, it seems, professes to be awed by the ethereal voice of the new instrument, although the Boesmans composition had only vaguely explored its unique sonic properties. French, German, and Belgian television crews are scrambling to arrange interviews with François. As his friends, who had come from New York, Brussels, and Berlin, surround François, Lee Konitz, the alto player who accompanied Miles Davis on *The Birth of the Cool* in 1949, declares that "the aulochrome makes me want to play for another seventy-five years," although he privately concedes to a friend that at times the polyphonic horn resembled the blare of "a fleet of taxicabs at rush hour in Times Square."

But François, holding the cased instrument in a death grip under his arm, has grown increasingly dispirited. There is only one aulochrome in all the world, and he is feeling uneasy about his chances of hanging on to it. What his supportive friends don't know is that it is already the object of a custody battle among competing interests, all of whom think the unusual horn was their idea or that a few Euros contributed during the design stage entitles them to ownership. Lawsuits have been mentioned and, unbelievably, even threats of physical harm to its gentle inventor. François is flat broke, in debt to family and friends, and doesn't see how he can defend himself. He has created a monster, he says in a cab as he flees the reception. "It's *diabolique.*"

Of course, if you were the spirit of Adolphe Sax lying smugly in your grave, all of this would seem very familiar—history repeating itself—not to mention justified. The saxophone has a molten soul, it was forged in a crucible fired by wild-eyed genius and tempered to resist all proprietary assaults. Those who try a little too hard to probe its mysteries, or exploit them, are often doomed to repeat the fate of its inventor.

François is the most recent of a long and eccentric line of acoustical gearheads who have been captivated by the brilliance of Adolphe Sax's invention and compelled to try to improve upon it. Sax himself set the tone for this spirit of zany innovation. In addition to his "quadruple bastard"—the saxophone joins parts of the ophicleide (its conical tube), the clarinet (its mouthpiece), and the flute (its keywork), all of which are held together by the construction material of the brass family—Sax assembled many other instrumental Frankensteins. A kind of clavier-timpani (picture kettle drums linked by a keyboard) might have been his wildest recombination.

In 1866, when Sax's patents expired, other manufacturers were able to tool up quickly, perhaps because they'd been counterfeiting saxophones all along, as Sax alleged in his raft of lawsuits. The lack of specifications was not much of a deterrent: his competitors fabricated a mandrel around which they could hammer out the approximate shape of the horn, then proceeded by trial and error—or "groping," as Sax might say—until they found the proper placement for the tone holes. The French firm Millereau-Schoenaers immediately began producing saxophones in 1866, followed later by Couesnon, Gautrot, et Cie (some of Sax's biggest tormentors); Buffet-Crampon, Goumas, Evette, and Schaeffer; Lecomte; and Fontaine-Besson. Around 1900 the Selmer Company purchased Adolphe Sax's Paris factory, which was then being run by his sons, and in 1920 it established a satellite assembly plant in America.

The application of fresh minds to Sax's masterful creation resulted in two important improvements: the adoption of the simplified fingering for the left hand developed in 1832 for the flute by Theobald Boehm (the Boehm system), and the introduction of a single automatically selected octave key. (Early saxophones had two octave keys.) In the early 1900s, Couesnon made a saxophone with a chromatic scale of three octaves from G for a virtuoso in the Garde Republicaine, and in the 1920s, Selmer designed a horn with a four-octave range from A. In the 1950s a designer for Leblanc, Charles Houvenaghel, designed "le Rationnel," on which all the tone holes are open (Sax's design required three notes, G-sharp, D-sharp, and C-sharp, to be closed at rest). A new coupling mechanism enabled the player to lower the pitch in the left-hand key bank one semitone by depressing the first, second, or third finger of the right hand. Although ingenious, the Leblanc system was up against more than a century's worth of pedagogy and methodology and never achieved commercial success.

Odd, often ingenious crossbreeds also became saxophone legatees, joining Adolphe's large family of instrumental freaks. As saxophone sales began to slow in the late twenties, the instrument manufacturers began experimenting with hybrids and other peculiar variations. Buescher built a curved soprano that could be played with one hand and a straight alto, later nicknamed the stritch by Rahsaan Roland Kirk, who played one. King introduced the Saxello, a B-flat soprano saxophone with a partially bent bell and a slightly bent neck. Conn, which maintained a full-time research laboratory, designed two completely new instruments. The Conn-O-Sax was a straight F alto with a small bulb of a bell at the end, a cross between a saxophone and a heckelphone (itself a rare sort of wide-bored baritone oboe). The F Mezzo Soprano fell between the size of a soprano and an alto. Both instruments, which required expensive new tooling by the plant, had the misfortune of being introduced shortly before the Great Depression and sold poorly despite their elegant design. In the thirties, the finely constructed and mellifluous Mezzo Sopranos were consigned to Conn's repair school, where they served as crash-test dummies for students learning how to fix dents and dings. In 1974 the saxophone was introduced to the microchip, leading to a marriage that produced the Lyricon, an electronic instrument that converted a player's wind pressure and fingering into synthesizer control information.

Amateur designers were also tinkering with the horn. In the thirties, Billy True, a musician from Steubenville, Ohio, patented a design that linked three saxophones, enabling the player to deliver three-part harmony. One saxophone was played by the right hand, another by the left, and the keyboard of the horn in the middle was manipulated by an elaborate system of wires and pulleys operated by the feet. Another hobbyist designed a fingerboard that snapped on and off for easy maintenance. Basement tinkerers carried on Sax's mad science, producing, among many other bizarre musical creatures, the Clar-O-Sax and the saxobone, a saxophone with a trombone mouthpiece. Producing a crude forerunner of François Louis's aulochrome, saxophonist George Braith welded two horns, a soprano and a straight alto, in 1979 into his Braithophone.

The European contributions to this freak family included the Saxi, which was described as the missing link in the saxophone's evolution, although no description was given of its predecessor. A product of Couesnon et Cie of Paris, the Saxi was shaped like a meerschaum pipe and had six finger holes and two keys, along with an F-sharp key and an octave key. The "little brother" of the saxophone came with its own method book, which made clear how seriously the instrument was to be taken: "A very close, detailed, laborious study of the Table (finger chart) is not expected, nor even advised. A general idea is the thing to get."

Between 1924 and 1930 a German designer, Richard Oskar Heber, built one hundred instruments he called normaphones, offering them in four different sizes. The novelty instrument, a valved trombone to which a saxophone bow and bell were attached, exemplified the era's reigning marketing strategy, which was applied to nonmusical products as well: an association with the saxophone, particularly its sexy shape, could boost the sales of just about anything.

The cleverest addition to the extended family was the slide saxophone, which seemed to arrive in response to shifting tastes in music. The movable tones of the Middle East and Asia were infiltrating American music, most notably on Broadway, and were also making their way into early jazz. The saxophone was capable of bending notes, but a slide mechanism, like that of a trombone (or normaphone), would enable a player to glide even more gracefully from one pitch to another. Thus, in the 1920s, came the saxoprano, the Royal Slide saxophone ("a combination of Saxaphone [*sic*], trombone, and Frisco whistle which gives its musical voice a cello effect"), the English Swanee Sax, and the Mello-Sax.

Swanee, an English company, produced an entire set of slide saxophones. The basic design consisted of a straight conical tube bisected its entire length like a sexy ballgown slit from thigh to hem. A thin metal bar with a handle slid up and down the tube, closing the opening like a zipper. It was described in promotional literature as "a perfect reed instrument—easy to play—yet it can be studied." Like all of the other zany hybrids, however, it wasn't.

Perhaps the greatest assault on the integrity of Adolphe's invention was launched by Rahsaan Roland Kirk, who often played three saxophones at once—a tenor, the defunct Saxello (which he called a manzello), and the "stritch." Kirk, who was blind, had a technician add extra keywork, rods, springs, and levers to the instruments. After suffering a stroke that paralyzed one side of his body when he was thirty-nine, Kirk had his tenor modified so that it could be played with one hand. The horn generously accommodated the changes, lost none of its range or intonation, and served its master well until he died a year and a half later.

But the resilient saxophone, which had no predecessors,* has resisted all attempts at substantial modification. Although Adolphe Sax lost a few of the many proprietary battles he had with his enemies, his design has prevailed over all challengers. Aside from Kirk's brief embrace of the "stritch," the straight alto, none of the new instruments ever attracted a famous proponent; each occupies its own barren twig on the saxophone family tree. Aside from a few minor alterations to its shape and some ergonomic improvements, the saxophone has remained pretty much the same since Sax won his patent for it in 1846.

At least until now.

François Louis is not unaware of the similarities between himself and the creator of the horn he is trying to reinvent. He, too, survived a calamitous childhood, health problems as an adult, and the destruction of his workshop and business. And a Belgian doctor tried

---

*The principle of joining a reed to a conical bore had been around for a couple of centuries. The Hungarian tarogato, which has a conical bore and a double reed, dates to the thirteenth century. An Argentine instrument called a signal horn consisted of a bull's horn with its narrow end shaved down to accommodate a thin reed made of bone that was attached with thread. Other instruments, including the shawm, dulcian, oboe, and bassoon deployed the idea. But the brass saxophone, with its covered tone holes, can be thought of as a unique application of this idea.

to interest him in converting a mouthpiece into an inhaler that would teach asthmatics how to breathe properly. Adolphe invented an inhaler too—the Goudronnier Sax. As for his tormentors . . . it's best to leave that subject alone, François says with a wave of his hand.

Like Sax, the young François had the same impishly perverse interest, however unconscious, in destroying himself. "It made me crazy not to understand the way something worked," he says, sipping coffee at a table in his small workshop, which doubles as a living space, in the tiny village of Ciplet, Belgium. "I once stuck a wire into an electrical outlet because I wanted to feel what was in there. I was almost electrocuted. Another time I turned on the gas stove to see what happened, how much spark you needed to ignite it. I almost blew up the house."

François, one of seven children, grew up in Brussels, as did Sax after his family moved from Dinant. Like his father, an architect, François was interested in all things mechanical; he built a crystal radio before he was ten. An indifferent student, he was pulled out of high school by his parents after a month and sent to a technical school, where, on the first day, he was given a set of drawings and a billet of metal and told to get to work. "You had to make a cylinder with a cone and some other parts," says François, whose perpetually sly smile, nest of frizzy, untamable hair, unruly beard, and wireless spectacles fit his reputation as the village genius. "There were ten stages and none of the other students, who had already been there a month, had moved beyond the fourth. At the end of the day I gave the instructor the completed project. He said, 'Who gave you that?' So I split. I couldn't go with those stupid guys. I wasn't going to spend two years to learn nothing."

François went back to regular high school, began working part-time in a motorcycle repair shop, and conceived a new double cylinder for a two-stroke engine—a concept that, independent of his efforts, was incorporated into motorcycle-engine design two years later. He developed a peculiar affinity for and insight into the engines. "By examining the parts, I could tell exactly how someone was riding that bike, whether he was tense, nervous, or respectful of the bike's limits."

As a child, he had listened in his bed at night to John Coltrane and Sonny Rollins—"Sonny is still the master; in each note he tells a story"—on Belgian jazz radio. Approaching adulthood, he felt a "responsibility" to involve himself in an artistic discipline. "It had always been easy for me to shape materials," he says. "But to go deep within yourself, you need resistance. I had never played a musical instrument and I chose the saxophone."

François took lessons, practiced diligently, but couldn't achieve the "enormous and fabulous" tone obtained by his idol, Rollins. "I became obsessed with the mouthpiece question," he says. "I knew that's where it all started. I analyzed the mouthpiece and described in words the sound I wanted. My idea of a color was amber, with a little transparency. Not yellow or red or orange, but dark and light together.

"I realized it was the same problem an engine has with the airstream. When it's interrupted by a valve or piston, it creates a shock wave that directs energy backward. When the valve opens, it goes forward again. The best thing is to have the valve open while this energy comes together so the shock wave doesn't go against the airstream. In the mouthpiece, I knew I had to synchronize the phases of this shock wave with the waves of the reed. The meeting point of the two waves is in the chamber, so if you make a chamber that resonates at all frequencies, then it can be in phase with any frequency."

He had the idea that a spherical chamber would accomplish his goal, unaware that the original Adolphe Sax mouthpieces also had a round chamber. He hollowed out his working mouthpiece and discovered it had "twice the sound in dynamics and volume." His teacher was impressed with the result, so François made a mouthpiece for him, too. He carved another mouthpiece from a chunk of ebony and took it with him to a jazz summer camp. "I had a huge sound," he says. "Everybody wanted to play my mouthpiece."

François began making and selling the pieces to local musicians. "Each one got better. My goal was to find a design that was universal and flexible enough so every player could find his own way and the sound that comes out is the result of what you put in and not the result of the mouthpiece itself. I wanted to make the mouthpiece as invisible as possible, so you could change the tone colors but keep the color you want at every dynamic and every place on the register."

By 1979, then in his mid-twenties, François was working constantly but making little money. "The pieces were expensive, about $100, but each one took two weeks to make." He had taken apart his own horn a number of times to make adjustments and began doing a little repair work on the side. "Compared to race engines, a horn was easy," he says.

In 1981 he got an unexpected break. He was visiting his sister in her guitar shop in Brussels when a heartbroken Billy Mitchell, who had played first tenor in Dizzy Gillespie's band in the fifties and was then touring with the Count Basie alumni band, stepped into the shop. It was a Monday, the instrument repair shops in town were closed, and Mitchell was desperately seeking someone to fix his horn. It had fallen out of an open case and none of the keys closed.

"I hadn't had much experience, but I said I'd try," François remembers. "I looked at it and really concentrated for half an hour. I moved each key to see how far away from the tone hole it was. Then I motioned with the horn and said to him, 'It fell like this, right?' And he said, 'Exactly like that.' So I held it close to my body, tried to feel it from everywhere, took the bell and the body and scrunched it. I just wanted to apply the opposite force. I knew the material— you have to go over a little too far to get it back to where it was supposed to be, but I was nervous. I mean, I could ruin the horn forever. But when he played it, it was like new. So he invited me to the concert—I'd never met anybody like this, a true legend—and after he finished one solo his eyes opened and he was looking right into mine. He screamed, 'François, you saved my life!' We hung out till five in the morning. I asked him to try my mouthpiece, and he loved it and ordered one. And that was the first step."

François officially started his business and was soon making mouthpieces for David Sanborn, Bob Berg, Michael Brecker, Joe Lovano, Tim Ries, Chris Potter, and David Sanchez. He charged $600 for a silver mouthpiece, $800 for a wooden one. He would take on a commission only if he could meet the player and talk to him at length about what kind of sound he wanted. "It would take three hours to answer all my questions," he says. "I analyzed all the information, his tensions, how he talked, what he liked about the sound of the recordings he was happy with.

"But I pulled back. I got to the point where I could listen to a player's ten records without meeting him and tell how he was likely to treat a waiter in a restaurant. It was too much. Sound is always the vehicle of emotion, your inside is there in your sound. But I wanted no more emotional perceptions. I decided to respect the artist's privacy and mine. I was making too many judgments and judgments are always weak, only true for a second."

He moved to a bigger workshop in Brussels in 1989 and for the next five years worked ceaselessly on his mouthpieces. Five years later his back was shot and required an expensive operation, which kept him off his feet for six months and forced him to sell all his tools and close shop. After he recovered, he moved to Ciplet, built another workshop, and slowly reestablished his mouthpiece business. He also designed a metal ligature and licensed it to a distributor. Then, as the aulochrome was beginning to take shape in his mind, the ghost of Adolphe Sax appeared. Returning home late one night in 1998, François was flagged down by his neighbor, who delivered the news that his workshop, in which he had also been living, had been destroyed in a fire. "I lost everything—my tools, nine saxophones, all my books, clothes, everything. I'd exchanged money for a trip to New York and that was destroyed, too. All I had were the clothes I was wearing and my plane ticket."

He arrived in New York with a plastic bag containing a pair of underwear and socks he borrowed from his neighbor and spent the next couple of weeks at the home of Tim Ries, the versatile young saxophone player. When he returned to Belgium, he found that friends had organized a benefit concert for him—the club held only 400, but 200 others demanded to be allowed to stay outside on the street so they could contribute their admission fee.

So again, like Adolphe Sax doggedly pushing beyond each shop-closing bankruptcy, murder attempt, fire, or life-threatening illness, François rebuilt his workshop, which he currently lives in. A cinderblock square finished in stucco and roofed with slate that is set before a verdant pasture, the building is devoted entirely to utility. There's a minimal galley kitchen, outfitted with a portable gas burner, a microwave stove, a coffee maker, and a sink, where François has been known to produce some legendary dinners. A large table, on which the aulochrome now rests in an open case, consumes an adjacent eating area. The rest of the room is filled with workbenches, two lathes, a drill press, hundreds of tools, cylindrical chunks of brass, and small boxes filled with metal posts, springs, mounts, and other finely machined parts that make up the architecture of a saxophone's tablature. Brass shavings litter the floor. In the center of the space, a circular staircase leads to a sleeping loft.

The rural life calms François. Ciplet is the quintessential European village, surrounded by fallow fluorescent-green fields and bifurcated by narrow, potholed roads that curve blindly around a few old imposing brick houses. François can get to Brussels in less than an hour to hear a friend's gig; if he's seeking inspiration, Adolphe Sax's birthplace, Dinant, where 10,000 saxophonists have been known to gather in the town square to summon Sax's spirit on the anniversary of his death, is only sixty miles away.

François was motivated to create the new instrument by the "deep ancestral need for polyphonic playing." He had named it after the ancient Greek aulos, a reed-blown double pipe. Like the saxophone's, the bore of each pipe of the aulos was conical, making it, according to Jean-Marie Londeix's mythical schema, a prototypical Dionysian instrument; not surprisingly, it had been used in fertility rituals and to induce trance states. *Chrome* refers to the aulochrome's ability to produce virtually any color in the musical spectrum.

Although it took him two years to build, the aulochrome had been taking shape in François's head for almost two decades. He has always been intrigued by limits—"Specifically, I don't like them," he says. Like most good players, he has learned to play higher harmonics on the horn—"My highest note on the soprano is the same as my highest note on the baritone." But ever since he got good enough to contemplate the possibility, he has been obsessed with going beyond the horn's limit in the lower register. Some players will raise their knee to a tenor to muffle the bell and drop the horn's very bottom tone a half step from B-flat to A (sounding G), but that's the lowest note the instrument will play.

François had studied the nature of differential tones, which are produced by two different notes sounding at once. The difference in frequency of the waves of the notes produces "beats," the undulating pulsating sound (wah-wah-wah) that can also be heard when two instruments playing the same note are slightly out of tune. The two waves add to and subtract from each other—they alternately add to the total amplitude, or volume, and subtract from the total frequency of the sound. For instance, if one horn sounded A at 440 Hz and another sounded the note a bit more sharply, at 460 Hz, the lowest note heard in that pulsating wah-wah cycle would be at the differential—20 Hz, right at the bottom of the threshold of human hearing. The lowest sounds created by this acoustic phenomenon, says François, are virtual bass notes, which can be heard (assuming they're within the range of human auditory perception) only if the two waves are in phase in both time and space. (Rahsaan Roland Kirk tried to accomplish this by playing two horns at once.) The aulochrome, with its two mouthpieces and two pipes, can send any combination of notes into space simultaneously. The resulting differential notes can drop down to the point at which they can't be heard, only felt.

Slight differences in tuning of the aulochrome's horns—one is a little brighter than the other—creates a variety of other eerie effects. The two mouthpieces are perfectly tuned, François says, but have the potential for unusual harmonization. The most extraordinary effect involves the sound's location: listeners can't place its origin. "And that has a very powerful emotional impact," says François as he lifts the aulochrome from its case. "A big part of the emotional characteristic comes from the fact that you cannot describe for yourself the sound you are hearing, nor where it's coming from. It's like it's unknown, from another dimension, something that your heart hasn't recorded yet. To some people it's spiritual, to others it's scary."

He raises the instrument to his lips, then lowers it again. His cherubic face suddenly droops into a mask of defeat. He says he doesn't feel like playing. Next to the instrument case is a stack of letters from various parties—the unwitting successors to Sax's tormentors, the Association of United Instrument Makers—who are clamoring for a stake in any future revenues. In addition to inventing a new member of the woodwind family, François has designed key mechanisms that offer almost no resistance—a modification that could be worth a lot in royalties. He has begun recording the design specifications of the new instrument on a CAD-CAM program because, as was true of Adolphe Sax and his early instruments, the specifications exist only in his head.

He turns the instrument in his hands, looking at it with a mix of pride and fear. "I'm thinking of taking it apart," he says. "It's *diabolique*."

I've picked up the Super Balanced Action from the shop—the overhaul came to $695. The repairman also affixed a metal ring around the throat of the Brilhart Tonalin mouthpiece that Ralph Morgan gave me to secure the hairline crack—another fifty bucks. I bought a ligature for $50 and still need a strap, a reed case, a mouthpiece cap, a silk swab to clean the inside of the horn, and a bottle of preservative to treat the leather tone-hole pads. While I'm at it, the technician suggests that I buy a better case, because the SBA is too fine and delicate an instrument to be rolling around inside the fifty-five-year-old Selmerpak it came in. I'm now into the horn for well over five grand. This thing has got its clutches in me big-time.

I go straight from the repair shop to my Tuesday night lesson and ask Michel to try it out. He puts his Otto Link mouthpiece on the crook and runs through the horn's entire compass. The bottom has a rich, deep, gorgeous tone, the high notes are clear and in tune. "Wow," he says. "This sounds better than mine."

When he plays it, anyway. I've got the floppy $2\frac{1}{2}$ reeds I was using on the Selmer C-star mouthpiece that came with my Armstrong rental. The reeds are too soft and close down the Tonalin mouthpiece in the horn's upper range. Michel adjusts the reed so the tip extends just beyond the end of the table. The high notes are still hard to coax out of the horn, but the bottom register now sounds great.

Near the end of the lesson, my band mates, Ortley, Craig, and Dan, drift into the rehearsal room and ogle my pricey new acquisition. I hand it to Ortley and he drools over it, blows five notes, then howls with glee. "Talk about friendly," he says. "That low C just sits there, at your service."

To help inaugurate the horn, Michel decides to stick around and play with us for a while. Tonight he has his tenor, so he and I play "Watermelon Man" in unison, trading a couple of choruses with Ortley on alto, while Dan plays piano, and Craig the bass guitar. The sound of the three horns together is transporting and I'm overwhelmed with gratitude. How many beginners get to play with real musicians? Toward the end of the tune I find a very clever phrase—the SBA trying to impress me with its latent creative ability, it seems. As I repeat it again and again and then close the song with a variation on the neat little figure, Craig smiles. "At first I thought that was just a lucky string of notes you played," he says when we finish. "But then you backed it up." He nods toward Michel. "You're a credit to your teacher."

Maybe so. But on the next tune, "In a Sentimental Mood," which, at a recent family meeting, I was told I could no longer play within a hundred yards of my wife or children, I blank out in the middle. I've practiced this song every day for the past two months, but am now completely lost. So much for the slow embossing. At times like these I get some perspective on my supposed prize-student status. I think of Mozart and how, after hearing Allegri's Miserere, composed in nine parts for two choirs, performed in the Sistine Chapel, he went home and transcribed the work note for note. Or how Mendelssohn, after leaving the score of A Midsummer Night's Dream in a London cab, simply rewrote it from memory.

Now those two guys must have done some really slow practicing.

10. PERSONAL SOUND

In a remote subterranean rehearsal room in the performing arts building at East Stroudsburg State University in Pennsylvania, Dave Liebman has his hands around the throat of a young
man blowing on a tenor saxophone. Dave's a pretty fiery character,
and an innocent observer of this scene might be inclined to jump
into the fray and try to save "Lieb" from ruining his career as an educator. In fact, though, he's not strangling the guy; he's attempting
to demonstrate to his student how the muscles of his throat expand
and contract—or should—with each note he plays, just the way
they do when he sings. As the player, a high school student from
Nashville, attempts a two-octave interval that peaks somewhere in
the altissimo range of the horn, Dave relaxes his hands—and one of
his cardinal rules. "This is one of the few places where I'd say you do
have to bite down a little to get that note to speak," he says. Almost
immediately, a circuit breaker in a closet trips and all light is instantly vacuumed from the windowless room. As if on cue, Dave

screams, "I take it back. My God, it must be the ghost of Joe Allard. I'm sorry, Joe. I'll never say that again."

Allard is the legendary saxophone teacher, universally regarded as a sweetheart of a man, who taught at the New England Conservatory, conducted summer camps and gave private lessons in New York. Although he's not so presumptuous as to make the claim, Dave, one of his former students, is the legitimate heir to the late guru's pedagogy. Lieb's book, *Developing a Personal Sound*, which is popular among serious students, acknowledges its debt to Allard, who believed that blowing the saxophone and creating a unique sound should be as easy as breathing. One of Allard's rules was that a player's embouchure should never change no matter how high he's reaching. When necessary, it appears, he disconnects himself from the eternal music of the spheres long enough to pull the plug on his occasionally wayward protégés when they ignore his manifesto.

Since 1987, Lieb has held a one-week boot camp for serious saxophonists in this quiet Pocono college town not far from his home in the Delaware Water Gap. This year's group of eighteen are all alumni and range from prodigiously talented high school kids who slouch sleepily in their chairs to middle-aged men who obsessively tape-record all eight hours of each day's proceedings, which include serial speed-rapped commentaries from Lieb. The students are asked to prepare two pieces of music they'll play before the group, many of them note-for-note transcriptions of famous solos from Gerry Mulligan, Stan Getz, or Wayne Shorter, say, or thirty-two-bar accompaniments to a Miles Davis tune. The week concludes with each player soloing with Dave's band at the nearby Deerhead Inn, where Lieb and his neighbor, Phil Woods, frequently engage in some friendly cutting sessions.

Dave is a motormouthed former Brooklyn boy who played with Elvin Jones and Miles Davis in the early seventies, has written numerous compositions, including some chamber music, and has played in a number of all-star bands. Occasionally, Joe Lovano, Mike Brecker, and he tour as "the Three Tenors." The son of New York City schoolteachers, he takes the business of instruction very seriously. "One by one, eighteen guys," he says of this year's group. "You try to spread the word, tell the truth, get them to appreciate and understand the music, and build a better world." But his week of master classes is also part performance art, starring Lieb. Slight and bald, with limpid blue eyes and an intelligent face, Lieb will perch on a high stool before his captives and alternate lengthy disquisitions on the end of artistic freedom, the brilliant scatology of William Burroughs, or the pathetic state of leftist politics with gossip from his own career, usually drawing on his experiences with the socially dysfunctional Miles Davis. His raps can be like stream-of-consciousness poetry—colorful, biting, reactionary, irreverent, and often deeply personal.

After the lights come back on, Dave summons to the front of the class a college student named Danny, who's in his final year at the New England Conservatory. "Man, it seems like you've been there forever," Dave says. "The minute you graduate you've got to get the fuck out of Boston. It's a motherfucking WASP tight-ass holier-than-thou town. Talk about a glass ceiling." Danny, in shorts, flip-flops and a T-shirt, rolls his eyes. He has studied with Lieb for years and this diatribe is not new to him, although the others find it entertaining. He launches into an atonal sonata, a piece from a study book titled *25 Caprices*. When he finishes, Lieb compliments him effusively, then offers more critical observations. "You played it note for note the way it was written. That's good, but not great. There were no dynamics, the piece had no inflection. In my mind, if you're going to play classical music on the saxophone—and I'm not saying anybody should—there are only two ways to do it. You play it as an exercise, to develop your technique and fingerings. Or you play it like a ballad. To me there's nothing in between. Fuck what the music says, play it the way you want to hear it. If it's predictable, cats don't listen."

He reaches for Danny's tenor. "I see you got a new mouthpiece," he says, admiring the shiny new metal Otto Link. "How many do you have now?"

"Six," Danny says.

Lieb pushes back on his stool. "Just a start. Man, I don't care who you are, the search for the perfect mouthpiece never ends," he says. "You're looking for that combination of feeling and hearing—so that it feels perfect and sounds perfect every day and night. You never get a hundred percent of both. There's this illusion that, Okay, if I get this kind of reed and that kind of ligature and put it on this mouthpiece, then I'll really be able to do some serious shit. It's very humbling. So you're always going for whatever you can get. It's a serious Zen exercise. You have an idea of what you want and what it feels like because you've had a moment when, for a minute, that was it. It's humbling until the day you die.

"You don't ever need to apologize for your desire to find a better horn," he tells the group, "even if you're deluding yourself. It happens to everybody, even the best. I knew this guy in Chicago, a horn dealer. Sonny Rollins is in town one day and calls him up, says he'd like to come by and try some of his pieces. The guy gets excited and calls his friends, tells them to make up an excuse to come in because Sonny's going to be there playing every one of his horns all afternoon. So Sonny's there and all the guy's friends are there and Sonny proceeds to play one note, the low B-flat, on each horn before trying the next. It was the only note he played all day."

The morning's second performance is from a self-taught thirty-year-old psychologist from England who also has an advanced degree in music theory. When he's finished, he recommends to the class that they learn something about Alexander technique, a type of therapy that seeks to promote physical health by increasing body awareness. Although great musicians make it look easy, playing the saxophone is an incredibly complex activity, he says, a fact made more obvious when you look at an anatomic representation of the motor strip, a linear map of the body's muscles from head to toes, that's laid out on top of the brain. The muscles of the face and pharynx take up about 40 percent of the motor strip, and those of the hands another 30 percent. That means almost three quarters of the part of the brain that masterminds motor function is involved either passively or actively in playing a simple arpeggio. "We all tend to tense up when we play," he says. "This might help you become a better player."

The suggestion launches Dave into a discussion of performance anxiety. He talks about drugs, their prevalence among musicians, particularly in the forties and fifties, and how the personal strength required to overcome addiction is artistically often very liberating. "It's right after a cat cleans up that you want to pay close attention," Lieb says. "Look at Wayne Shorter's influence in the sixties. It's immense. He's cleaning up and he starts to burn, he's like light. When a cat is full of heat and fire and excess, when he's put all that bad shit behind him, he's often totally uninhibited. That's his best period. Look at Trane. There's 'Surrey with the Fringe,' then he cleans up and you get *Round Midnight* and *Blue Train* in '57. When you're listening to a cat who has his fly open, his zipper's down, his dick is on the table, he's totally abandoned, that's when you really want to check him out."

He goes on to tell the group of his own attempts to find pathways to his creative center, ranging from drugs to Scientology. He brings up Miles, describing how before a gig he would sit by himself in a corner, staring at the floor, widening the already considerable distance between him and the members of his band, who imagined that the prince of darkness was lost in a reverie of cosmic thoughts. "But you know what?" Lieb says. "I think he was just nervous and he was thinking about the first few notes he was going to play in the set, just to get him through. Although you never knew what Miles was thinking. If you dared to ask him a question, you often got a mysterious answer. During the time we were playing the tunes from *On the Corner*, I often felt superfluous and I said, 'Do you really need me?' He thought about it, then looked at me with those eyes that seemed focused from a thousand miles away. He said, 'The people like to see you move your fingers.'"

The group laughs and Dave pauses to catch his breath. "But here's the deal," he says. "Before a gig you can get high, you can pray, twist yourself into a pretzel like some fucking yogi, get rolfed, have sex, or talk to your mommy on the phone, but none of that shit matters. What matters is the music. If you focus on the music, it will get you through and your voice will be there, loud and clear."

Assuming you have one, Dave confesses later as we lunch at a nearby Friendly's. The process of finding your sound can be torturous, it can take decades of serious playing, but it always involves imitating someone else's first, and then, as Mingus said, being able to conjure up the rest of the history of the instrument. On the saxophone, that means being able to mimic the tones of a dozen or so distinctive voices—Hawk, Hodges, Webster, Prez, Parker, Getz, Cannonball, Trane, Rollins, Coleman, Konitz, and Brecker are a good start—and then abandon them all to find your own.

"There was a stage when I didn't know who I was," Dave says. "I was well into my professional career, and every day it was apparent that I was speaking through somebody else. It was disturbing and I was worried: How do I get out of this thing? I stopped listening to Coltrane. I stopped listening to jazz. I tried Indian music. I wanted it to be easy, like taking a pill. There was a lot of pressure in the sixties to do something new. No one should sound like anyone else. But I was playing like a schizophrenic."

Eventually, he fell back on the teachings of Joe Allard. "Joe always said let the voice box do its job," Lieb says. "The voice box will react to what you tell it to do through your ear. When you talk you don't think about the tone or pitch or modulation of your voice. The same is true of playing the saxophone. Relax the voice, don't do anything that tenses you up, don't play with your head down, don't have your lip over your teeth because it creates tension in your throat. All those books that say it should feel like a yawn or say an *O* or feel like you're smiling, they all generate more nervous energy. The point is to do what you do when you talk. The point is to do nothing."

The head of a player, says Lieb, is essentially a sound box. "On a saxophone, the reed is the vibrating substance," he says, "but if it's vibrating out in the air, there's no sound. Similarly, the string is the vibrating substance on a violin, but if you stretch it out in the air and draw a bow across it, it makes no noise. It comes down to the body of the violin, or, in the case of the saxophone, not just the bore of the instrument but how the player's oral cavity is shaped. Everyone has a different cubic volume of air in there."

By doing nothing, Lieb says, your own voice, your personal sound, will emerge. "And that's determined by your anatomy, your bones, the shape of your throat, the size of your vocal cords and larynx, where your tongue is, the density of tissues in your head. The nuance comes from how you typically express yourself, your background, where you emphasize, inflect, or bend a word when you're talking, how you feel about the content. The saxophone is the only instrument capable of reflecting those personal characteristics.

"But first you have to get to neutral. You have to remove all encumbrances, any tension that inhibits you from being who you are. Everyone has a personal sound. It's just a matter of being able to let it out."

Once it's "let out," the sound of the saxophone, personalized by every player, has a unique effect on the listener. As an ever-rhapsodizing recent convert, I've been told by many people that they also "love" the sound of the horn. It seems like a mundane comment until you realize that, with the exception of the four members of the string family and perhaps the oboe and the Indian chenai, most instruments fail to elicit such reverence for their sonority. No one ever says he loves the sound of the piano, or the trumpet, or the flute. He may be moved by the arrangement of notes, intervals, and melodies played on those instruments, but their actual sounds, uniform in tone throughout their entire compass, are less than transporting.

My own unscientific, completely anecdotal research reveals that the sound of the saxophone touches many women in a very special way. When I mentioned this to saxophonist and educator John

Handy, he nodded and told me a story. Between his gigs with Charles Mingus many years ago, he often went to Southern California to sit in with local jazz bands at dance halls and cantinas along the Mexican border. "I remember one time I made my way to the bar between sets," he says. "These three men got up from a table in front of the stage where they'd been sitting with their girlfriends or wives. They came up to me and said, 'Quit messin' with our women.' Only they put it even more bluntly. All I'd been doing was playing. I'd like to think it was because I presented an image of a big, beautiful sexy icon onstage. But I think most of the time I was sitting down."

Players often attribute the horn's seductiveness to its similarities to the human voice, an intuitive observation that turns out to be scientifically accurate. On a spectrograph, which measures the frequencies of sound, the most pleasing human voices tend to have a rich complexity, just like the saxophone.

"The thing that's different about the sax is that it's not really smooth," says Rob Haupt, a research scientist at the Massachusetts Institute of Technology's Lincoln Laboratory who also plays and collects saxophones. "On an oboe, for instance, you get a pure sound, a lot of energy in the main frequency. If you look at its sound on a spectrograph, you see the main peak right in the center of the graph. To the left and the right, at the higher and lower frequencies, there's not much energy.

"On a saxophone you hear things other than that main pitch. Any given note is extremely complex. And what you see on the graph— Wow! On the graph you see all this vibrational energy scattered throughout the full range of frequencies, from high to low. You just can't get a complex sound like that on a clarinet."*

---

*The timbral differences in various makes and models of saxophones have long been one of saxophonists' favorite topics. As an acoustical engineer, Haupt has the advantage of adding scientific analysis to subjective opinion. He once analyzed the difference between an early Mark VI alto, which has a short bow, and a later-series model, in the 90,000 range, which has a slightly longer bow. Keeping the conditions as uniform as possible—using the same

That "outrageous" wave form, says Michael Brecker, makes the sound very moldable on the part of the player. "It's peculiar how one is able to project one's own persona and musical sensibility through the saxophone to such a degree that one's presence can be identified so quickly," he says. "It's uncanny, really. I see it as being vocal in that way, not so much that it sounds like a human voice but that it accomplishes the same purpose, except nonverbally."

In addition to mimicking the breadth of the human voice, that complexity enables the saxophone, like a shaman who refuses to have his photograph taken for fear of losing his soul, to resist attempts to quantify or capture its unique acoustical properties. Unlike virtually every other instrument, it has been found by recording technicians and musicians to be nearly impossible to sample in any realistic way.* The same, of course, can be said of the human voice. Digitized versions of it—on phone-mail systems or automatic public-address announcements—are instantly recognizable as false. The wide variation in voices has also thwarted efforts to build a reliable speech-recognition machine.

The vocal quality of the saxophone—or rather, its musical vocal quality; vaudevillians routinely squawked and yammered through the instrument—was first fully expressed by early black American saxophonists, Archie Shepp maintains. "As an instrument of the human voice, the saxophone came to life through black men," he says as he packs his bags in Manhattan's Gramercy Park Hotel for the trip back to Paris, where he now lives, after a rare two-night gig at Bird-

---

mouthpiece and reed, applying the same air pressure—he recorded the sound of each and found that the long-bow saxophone was not as complex. What it did have was more power, the result of a design tweaking that began in the 1930s, as saxophones strove to be heard in swing-band ballrooms, and continued through the sixties, as they competed with the sound of electric bands. "There weren't as many overtones on the long-bow but you could play louder," Haupt says. "There was a lot of energy in the main pitch, which gave it a purer sound."

*Frederick L. Hemke, an esteemed saxophonist and teacher at Northwestern University, remarks that his electronic saxophone is capable of sounding like just about any other wind instrument—except a real saxophone.

land. "There were many excellent white European-American performers who played complex things with great skill. But they all sounded alike. They had no identity on the instrument.

"African music is vocal music and tends to be tonal," says Archie, who, as a poet, playwright, educator, and composer is one of jazz royalty's most voluble and elegant representatives. "Words take their meanings from their endings—a high, low, and medium ending mean three different things. This is carried over to music, the bending of notes on either side of the center of the pitch, which is totally outside the European concept of timbre. But in the hands of Hawkins, Lester Young, and Parker, with that ancient African tradition supporting them, the instrument took on a distinctive identity. Later, there were several great white players, as there are today. But when it first matured, it was a black instrument. The saxophone was outside the system and the Negro was on the fringes of society. Together they found their voice."

Evoking the human voice, the saxophone works its magic on a receptive listener by exciting ancient reward and arousal systems in his or her brain, pathways that have evolved to light up, say, at the sound of a mother humming while nursing or soothing a child. Psychologists have long been intrigued by the link between music and nonverbal aspects of speech—and how emotion can be mediated by both. The British philosopher Herbert Spencer first proposed this relationship in 1857 in an article titled "The Origin and Function of Music." He explained the characteristics of both vocal music and vocal expression in physiological terms, declaring that both were premised on "the general law that feeling is a stimulus to muscular action." In lay terms, this meant that emotions influence physiological processes—when you feel fear you run, when you feel sadness you wring your hands—and these in turn influence the acoustic characteristics of speech and singing: fear is accompanied by a scream, the wringing of hands by a moan or a sob.

The link between emotion and action—the nonverbal utterance, whether a yelp or a whimper—is an adaptive mechanism that evolved to aid human survival and can be readily observed in non-human primates. It also gave rise to music, many theorists believe. The nineteenth-century polymath Hermann von Helmholtz, a pioneer of music psychology, concluded that "an endeavor to imitate the involuntary modulations of the voice, and make its recitation richer and more expressive, may therefore possibly have led our ancestors to the discovery of the first means of musical expression." The composer Richard Wagner seconded this idea: "The oldest, truest, most beautiful organ of music, the origin to which alone our music owes its being, is the human voice."

Consequently, instruments evolved that could imitate or evoke those vocal qualities. Marcel Proust observed that "there are in the music of the violin . . . accents so closely akin to those of certain contralto voices that one has the illusion that a singer has taken her place amid the orchestra." Another French writer, Stendhal, a great fan of music, said that "no musical instrument is satisfactory except in so far as it approximates to the sound of the human voice."

When he released *A Love Supreme*, John Coltrane said that "as long as there is some feeling of communication, it isn't necessary that it be understood." But that hasn't deterred modern music psychologists from trying to tease out which performance and acoustical cues most effectively aid that communication. In the past decade, researchers have conducted more than a hundred studies that explore music's ability to evoke in the listener the five "basic" emotions—happiness, sadness, anger, fear, and love/tenderness, which appear in musical scores as, respectively, *festoso*, *dolente*, *furioso*, *timoroso*, and *teneramente*—or the hundreds of subsets of those emotions. Patrik N. Juslin and Petri Laukka, psychologists at Uppsala University in Sweden, have done meta-analyses of studies examining expressive musical cues, including tempo, sound level, timing, intonation, articulation, timbre, vibrato, tone attacks, tone decays, and pauses. Sadness, they have found, is associated with slow tempo, low sound level, legato articulation, small articulation variability, slow tone attacks, and dull timbre. Happiness is associated with fast tempo, high sound level, staccato articulation, large articulation variability, fast tone attacks, and bright timbre. The combination of cues that is most expressive, according to listeners—and very similar to the combination that evokes sadness and tenderness—includes legato articulation, soft spectrum, slow tempo, high sound level, and slow tone attacks. Sounds that mimicked so-called separation calls—sobs, cries, and moans—were the most poignant of all. Some instruments, obviously, are more capable than others of delivering these cues. Arguably, the saxophone, with the sounds of dozens of instruments tucked into its complex wave form, can deliver almost all of them.

For at least one saxophonist, little distinction exists between the expressive cues he issues on the instrument and the weight and meaning of his words. In fact, the poet Robert Pinsky says, when he plays the saxophone—he has played the horn, semiprofessionally and recreationally, all his life—he's trying to do the same thing he does when he "fits the words together" in a poem.

"The horn is connected to what I do as a writer because it's on a completely physical scale and an infinite scale," says Pinksy, who was poet laureate of the United States between 1997 and 2000. "Theoretically, the cone of a saxophone goes on forever, giving the sounds that come from it an infinite quality. But it's given its expression by a human. I try to do something with the vowels and consonants of words that makes them musical—infinite—but the medium is my voice, or anybody's voice who is reading the poem, which means that the medium is inherently on a human scale—on a physical scale, like the saxophone.

"I would trade everything I've written if I could play the saxophone the way I want to. If I could sell my soul and just be tremendous, a monster, I'd be a tenor player. But I can't. I'm not musical enough. The closest I can come to what the saxophone can do is with words."

"Your sound is everything," says Phil Woods, as he sips a muddy espresso in the living room of his home near the Delaware River in eastern Pennsylvania. "You know it when you've got it, and you know it when you don't."

Crusty and sardonic, now in his early seventies, Phil is iconic among both jazz fans and players, the legend from Springfield, Massachusetts, who sounded so much like Charlie Parker that he felt obliged to marry Bird's widow and raise his kids. A Juilliard graduate, he's recorded hundreds of albums with everyone from Dizzy Gillespie and Benny Carter to Paul Simon and Billy Joel, composed saxophone sonatas, and scored and played on such movies as *Blowup*, *Reds*, and *The Hustler*.

The night before, Phil had made a guest appearance at Birdland with Bill Charlap, a hot young pianist who was in Phil's quintet a few years ago. Phil has recovered from a bout with prostate cancer but needs oxygen supplementation because of emphysema and has curtailed his performances. It was moving to watch him blow his heart out during a solo at the end of the set, then wait patiently while the band brought the tune to a close, no doubt desperate to get at his tank backstage.

Before us, on a coffee table, is my Super Balanced Action, which I've brought along to encourage Phil's thoughts about the importance of good equipment to developing a personal sound. It serves instead to elicit first a couple of stories about virgin saxophone experiences. Phil lost his innocence at age twelve when he discovered his uncle's alto in a case under the wicker sofa in his grandmother's bedroom, bundled up and hidden away like a pair of sexy underwear or an embarrassing "adult" toy. "I liked it because it was all shiny and gold with the pearl keys," he says. "At the time I was also into toy soldiers, which I made by melting down the lead in old batteries. I think in the back of my mind I was saying, If I melt this sucker down I could make a golden horde of warriors that would take out the whole fucking block! Some people mistook this avaricious intent for an interest in music, so after my uncle died I was given the saxophone. I put it in the closet, never melted it down. A couple months went by and my mother said, 'Well, Philip . . .' When she called me Philip I knew something was up. 'Your uncle went to a great deal of trouble to leave you the saxophone.' Even at twelve I realized death could be construed as a great deal of trouble. 'You should take a lesson.' So I looked in the Yellow Pages and got a teacher named Mr. Harvey La Rose. That's when my life changed."

After a few lessons, Phil discovered that "I could play the goddamned thing without trying. I was put on earth to be a saxophone player." He graduated high school at fifteen, studied awhile at the Manhattan School of Music, then four years at Juilliard, supplemented by private lessons with the pianist Lennie Tristano. He also received a practical education. He recalls one of his first tours in the early 1950s with an all-star band: "I sat right behind Lester Young and Bud Powell. We had Al Cohn on tenor, myself, Conte Condoli, Roy Haynes, and Sarah Vaughan. We left in the middle of January in a storm, sleeting rain, snow blowing sideways on the bus. I said to Al, 'I got to take a piss, I wonder if the guy's going to stop.' 'Sure, go ask him,' he says. So I go to the front of the bus. I'm just a kid and I say, 'Excuse me, sir, but I have to go to the bathroom.' He says, 'Do you now, young man?' So he opens the door, going about eighty down the turnpike, and I'm hanging out there trying to piss. It's a different world now. You don't learn that up at Berklee anymore. But it fit with the life of the saxophone player really good."

Not much later, he found himself playing at a strip club in Greenwich Village, where he got an unexpected lesson on saxophone sound, and how an obsessive focus on the importance of equipment can be completely misleading, from Charlie Parker.

"I was playing 'Harlem Nocturne' ten times a night at the Nut Club," he says. "I wasn't happy with my setup—I didn't like the reed, the ligature, the horn. I gotta get some new equipment, that's what's holding me back, I kept thinking. Somebody said Parker was across the street jamming at Arthur's Tavern. So there's Bird up on the bandstand, scuffling on a baritone sax that the painter Larry Rivers gave him. There's a guy on the piano who had to be a hundred and fourteen years old. On the drums is this guy's father, playing a snare drum that was like a pie plate. I used to see Bird at Arthur's Tavern and he'd say, 'Did you eat today?' He was a very kind man, he always knew who the young guys were in town. He might not know my name, but he always kept his eye on the brood. I learned a lot from that.

"I said, Mr. Parker, maybe you'd like to play my alto. He says, 'Yeah, this baritone's kicking my butt.' I flew back across Seventh Avenue, got my horn and brought it over, and he played 'Long Ago and Far Away' by Jerome Kern. I'm listening and it occurs to me that there's nothing wrong with my saxophone, nothing wrong with my setup, it sounds just fine. He says, Now you play. I did my imitation of the master and he says, 'Sounds real good, son.' I levitated back over Seventh Avenue and played the shit out of 'Harlem Nocturne.' I never looked for the magic ligature, the magic mouthpiece, the magic reed. Instead I started practicing."

That's not to say he's resistant to all bouts of covetousness. Spotting the Brilhart Tonalin Ralph Morgan gave me, he says, "I want your mouthpiece." Echoing Bird, Phil assembles my horn, then says, "Now you play." Fearing a reprise of my disastrous lesson with Ralph, I hook the instrument to a strap around my neck and tentatively finger the keys. "Well, you look like a saxophone player," Phil says with a little laugh.

I try a couple of scales I know, or knew yesterday, anyway. The horn is a little hesitant, skittish, but doesn't fight me. "What you gotta do is get more lip out," Phil says. "You're playing it like a clarinet. If you tighten up and strain, you'll maybe get the F, but you'll never get higher than that without killing yourself."

I play a couple bars from Sonny Rollins's great calypso tune, "St. Thomas." After hitting a few clams, I begin to get it right. "Not bad," Phil says. "You've got a good tone." He points to the pinky finger of my right hand. "But keep your fingers in, you're waving this fucker way out here." I play it a final time, error-free, then stop to catch my breath.

As though channeling Bird again, Phil says, "Sounds real good, son."

A saxophone, too, has its personal sound. A less agreeable way of putting this is to say that the saxophone is notoriously unreliable. For all its bluster, it's a delicate instrument. Its mix of materials—the wood of the reed, the leather of the key pads, the fragile brass—are vulnerable to all sorts of environmental pressures. The intricacy of the mechanisms that control and open the keys is sensitive to the merest bump or knock. Along with the unique physiognomic properties each player brings to the horn, these factors account for the saxophone's malleability—and for its ability to rebel, surprise, or just resist being harnessed altogether. A player who demands a precise response from his instrument will never be happy playing the saxophone. As the tenor saxophonist James Houlik says, most players tend to be the "cowboy daredevil type. An equipment breakdown on stage is just another welcome challenge."

Lee Konitz generously refers to that unpredictability as flexibility. "It's a daily challenge to confront the instrument," he says. "It often dictates to you and you can never predict what it wants to say. After playing it for all these years I have to continue to flex on it or lose contact altogether.

"The hardest thing about the saxophone is that you can't count on it. That's something a trumpet player doesn't have to deal with. His mouthpiece and horn is a big piece of metal that stays the same forever. When he has a gig at Carnegie Hall, a certain degree of confidence in his equipment is his birthright. But when a saxophone player does the gig, he's scared as hell that the reed that sounded great in his living room now won't work at all, and that no matter how great he is he might start getting a leak right at middle C."

Konitz has respected the saxophone's fickle nature ever since he opened a tenor sax case when he was twelve and was immediately "dumbfounded" by the smell of the new purple velvet protective lining and dazzled by the horn's beautiful architecture. "I was immediately fascinated with the key structure and trying to make a new sound," he recalls as he fends off the sweltering summer heat in the living room of his Manhattan apartment. (His primary residence is in Germany.) "I'm still trying to do that. There's never been a time in my life when I've felt that that's solved and I can move on to something else."

Konitz, born in 1927, came of age when the saxophone was just beginning to find its voice in jazz and there were just a few important role models. "I liked Johnny Hodges, and there was Chu Berry, Lester Young, Benny Carter, and of course Hawk. But the guys in the big bands, too—Corky Corcoran and Tony Pastor were lead players in Artie Shaw's and Benny Goodman's bands. We all loved those people and thank them for doing the initial exploration on the instrument."

Like everyone else, he was awed by Charlie Parker. "Bird influenced everybody," he says. "But by his early thirties, he felt pressured to come up with something really new, and that's a big job after you've done what he'd done. So he checked out, I think."

Unlike many of his contemporaries, though, it never occurred to Lee to try to imitate Bird's sound or technique, which earned him a reputation as the anti-Parker. "The saxophone is basically like a megaphone that you sing through," he says. "So why would you want to sing like someone else? I tried to discover their secret and move on." Similarly, when he heard Paul Desmond, he decided to change his sound because it was too close to Desmond's, even though he felt that Desmond was imitating him. "My idea, more modestly, was just to continue looking around and making different sounds. I opened my throat, tried a double lip, tried to become aware of the airstream as an integral part of blowing the horn." Throughout his entire career, he says, his goal has been to become as loose as the instrument he plays—"to become as intense as possible without getting tense"—and to be as unpredictable as the saxophone.

"My approach has been never to take the saxophone for granted," says Lee, a slightly shy, quiet man whose furry white whiskers travel down his neck and disappear unfashionably into his shirt. "Every day I feel like I'm starting anew. I pick up the horn and work on the simple production of sound, reformulate all the things I remember from the day before, and try to proceed to the next level. What I don't do is try to achieve the same sound I got the day before, assuming it was a sound I liked anyway. I'm not the same as I was the day before, nor is the horn.

"If you're going to play the saxophone, you have to be prepared for constant change. It's built into the instrument. It's why it works so well in jazz, a free music. I saw Zoot Sims near the end of his life and he was still trying to play like a hipster. I thought, That's not right, he should be playing like a man close to the end of his life. I think if we're coordinated in the production of our music we can be fulfilled by playing on the very first level of our reality. Instead of trying to swing and play hot and fast like a young competitor, what could be more meaningful than playing a nice melody even with the lowest amount of energy?"

Being open to the saxophone's shifting physical state is key to successful improvisation, he says. "It's a question of looking for what I don't know," he says. "That's also what I understand jazz to be: improvised music. A lot of great solos we know and love, like Hawkins's on *Body and Soul*—don't tell me that was improvised on the spot. He was laying for that one. Parker also played what he knew much of the time.

"When I go onstage I don't know the first note I'm going to play," he says. "There's that feeling of anxiety—that's what I've been trying to perfect all these years. And when it's going great there's a feeling that the music is playing itself and I'm standing there and enjoying it. It feels like nothing I've ever heard before. It's a subconscious state; I always get to some part of it. It doesn't have to be spectacular. I can be satisfied playing at a lower level, knowing that's all I can do at the time. It's essential that we like ourselves enough to be able to enjoy the process at all levels."

In keeping with his desire to be surprised, Konitz has returned to playing a sixty-five-year-old Selmer Balanced Action, a 21,000 series, that he bought in the 1940s for $200 and then lost about thirty years later. In the 1970s he visited the Selmer factory in Paris, where he was given a Mark VI to try out on the road. When he returned, he was told he could keep the VI—a famous player's actual possession of a horn is the best advertising of all—and that his Balanced Action had been misplaced. "I said, Okay, I'll play the VI," Konitz remembers, "but I always wondered what happened to the other horn. One time they told me they sold it, another time something else. I never got a satisfactory answer. Finally, after about twenty years, I again asked Patrick Selmer and he said, 'Oh, that's in our museum.' And I said, 'Give me that horn, man!' And I got it back. Now I go through my closet and try the horns, seeing if one indicates more than another. And I keep returning to the Balanced Action."

That decision, he says, is based on more than just nostalgia. In the same way he's eager to play every day to chronicle the latest changes in his three-quarter-century-old body, he's curious to hear what morphological changes have occurred in the saxophone he's been playing nearly all his life, too. "Coordinating the two of us is a very organic process," he says, "because the horn is changing as much as I am."

For the past twenty years, Bill Singer has been observing saxophones grow and change in the small repair workshop he operates on West Forty-third Street in New York City. Bill is one of a handful of top-tier technicians, including Roberto Romeo, Perry Ridder, and Joe Sachs, to whom professionals will entrust the care of their precious horns, whether they're in need of a simple "tweaking" or a complete overhaul. "A lot of the research on saxophones happens right here or at the other guys' shops," he says. "The repair guys—and the musicians—are the scientists."

The top customer-scientist in Singer's laboratory is David Sanborn, who usually books Bill three or four days a month to massage his horns. Bill will bring a small packet of his handmade tools to Sanborn's apartment on the Upper West Side of Manhattan, and the two will conduct experiments. They'll replace a silver screw with a gold screw and assess the change in sound. They'll change the height of tone holes—"Some instrument makers say the height of the E-flat tone hole can make or break a saxophone," Bill says. They'll try different materials as resonators (the slightly domed center of a key pad, usually made of metal or plastic, that reflects sound back into the horn when the tone hole is closed). They'll replace or minimize the tiny pieces of felt and cork affixed to the horn to buffer the moving metal parts. "Dave probably knows more than most repairmen," Bill says. "He taught me that the weight of materials you put on the horn does things to the sound," Bill says. "For instance, some repairmen will use any kind of glue to attach a key pad. I use stick shellac because it hardens and won't muffle the sound. But even then, using more or less can affect the tuning."

One regular renovation involves replacing those key pads, which perform the vital function of providing an airtight seal of the tone holes. "No two pads are the same," says Singer, a tall, lanky man with a boyish face and a well-tamed thatch of short, wavy brown hair. "One may be thicker than another. Some soak up moisture— okay, spit—and some don't. Only two companies in the world make pads, and a few years ago one of them suddenly started using a real thin designer leather. I called them up and said, 'You're changing the sound of half the saxophones in the world.' They'd never even thought of that."

A repairman's greatest challenge, Bill says, is to respect the "looseness and wildness" of the saxophone. "You don't want to squelch its rebel spirit," he says as he places a leak light into the body of a Mark VI alto he's tweaking. "In fact, you want to bring that out. Some repairmen tighten up the horn too much, closing down the sound of the instrument. With a flute or clarinet, one tiny leak prevents it from playing. With a saxophone you want to be flexible. In fact, David Sanborn sometimes introduces small leaks to his instrument to gain an edge to his sound."

Over time, Bill says, a saxophone evolves, partly a result of the many repairs it has undergone, but also due to organic change—the erosion of gold plating or the peeling away of lacquer. A lot of change occurs in the neck. "When the neck is bent into its curved shape, it becomes a unique entity," he says. "No two necks are the same—you simply can't duplicate what happens on a molecular

level. There are lively and dead spots on the neck, parts that will vibrate and other parts that will not. So when you play, moisture vibrates off the lively parts and collects in the dead parts, over time
creating little microcosms of oxidization that become bumpy. As the
airstream passes over them, they help excite the wave, creating swirls
that enrich the tone. That process continues to occur over the entire
life of a horn. The last thing you want to do is take a wire brush and
clean that out."

As a horn doctor, Bill establishes an intimacy with his patients that,
in some ways, even their owners cannot achieve. "Each horn has its
own vibe," he says. "Some horns come in here and you can see they've
been at the heart of the music. Their vintage, the wear on them, the
evidence of past repairs, you can feel that they've been at the center of
the history of the music. They wear their scars, and badges of honor,
like people.

"When I do an overhaul, I strip [the saxophone] down to the
point where it looks like a tin can. Where each key was, there's a needle spring, which is made out of a sewing needle, or blueing metal,
that's tempered so it can bend and hold pressure on the key. I play
those needle springs like a kalimba, or thumb piano, and every horn
will play its own tune. Some sound like they're in Eastern scales.
These horns may have been through fifty years of playing, have
made maybe some of the greatest recordings ever, but they've never
played the tune I play on them. Each horn plays a song that only I
get to hear."

As do many players, Singer believes the newer instruments can't
compare to the older ones. "The keyboards are more comfortable
and the tuning is better on the new horns, but they have no soul,"
he says. "The old horns just sound better. They reflect the level of
craftsmanship that went into them and the quality of materials. After World War II, Selmer bought bombshell casings made of high-
grade brass that bordered on bronze. A few years later they were
making the Mark VIs, the best saxophones ever made. Then, at
some point in the sixties, a lot of people felt the VIs being produced

suddenly weren't as good as the earlier ones. They probably ran out of high-grade brass.

"Today, saxophones are built by robotic machines. The tuning is very precise. But how do they age, how do they sound a few years later? The companies do no research. But the repairman does. We analyze them, strip them down to nothing, analyze them in their naked state, build them back up into something better. Above all, we listen. We honor their sound."

11. *PROVOCATEUR*

In the Land of Symphony, where all the subjects are shaped like cellos, the Queen is hosting a ball. As couples twirl about to a Bach minuet, the Princess gazes longingly across the Sea of Discord to the Isle of Jazz, where a different musical event is taking place. Hot music is blistering the walls of the royal palace, where everyone is shaped like a saxophone. The saxophone King, slouching on his throne with his crown tilted at a rakish angle, taps his foot to a jungle beat pounded out by a multiarmed saxophone cavorting atop a drum kit. Lady saxos shimmy and shake and boogaloo. The joint is jumpin'.

After stretching a curved saxophone into a telescopic eyepiece, the young saxophone Prince espies the Princess across the water and begins to woo her with his sultry tones. She answers his choruses by writing prim musical notes and giving them to a bird to deliver to the Prince, whose father is now being entertained by a writhing belly dancer. The saxophone Prince, an aggressive young fellow on the make, hies across the water to join his sweetheart and is promptly thrown in a jail, shaped like a metronome, by the symphonic King's authorities. Upon learning of his son's confinement, the jazz King declares war. Brass instruments with cannonlike bells rise up out of the palace and bombard the Land of Symphony with jazz notes. The Land of Symphony responds with huge orchestral blasts. After a barrage of sixteenth notes destroys the jail and springs the Prince, he and the Princess head out into the Sea of Discord, using an eighth note as a paddle, and begin to founder. Seeing their children in distress, the two empires declare a cease-fire and dispatch a saxophone skiff to rescue the young royals. United in their love for the heir and heiress, the two kingdoms make peace, and wedding bells chime for the saxophone King and his newly beloved, the Queen of the Land of Symphony. After the ceremony, the new couple inaugurates the Bridge of Harmony that now joins the two lands.

This cartoon, titled "Music Land," one of Disney's many Silly Symphonies, was released in 1935 and cleverly illustrates polite society's long-standing disdain for the racy saxophone.* Latter-day Savonarolas have stalked the horn since its invention, hoping to still the perverse voice of Sax and preserve moral order. Throughout its history the saxophone has encountered various incarnations of the crusading fifteenth-century Dominican monk who tried to destroy all musical instruments capable of making a "licentious" sound.

But the cartoon also underscores the instrument's uncanny ability throughout much of its short history to have an impact beyond the

---

*Some of the most inventive and entertaining saxophone playing can be heard on cartoons. The Hollywood studio orchestras, says Loras Schissel, music historian at the Library of Congress, were some of the best ensembles in the world. "Warners and MGM had amazing orchestras," he says. "They could sound like the best Viennese orchestra. But the cartoon work was reserved for the varsity players, the people who could manipulate their instruments to make it sound like Bugs Bunny really was flying off a cliff or slamming into a tree. They might spend all day recording an Eric Korngold score for an Errol Flynn swashbuckler, then haul out these mind-boggling charts written by Carl Stallings or Scott Bradley, who made the music as hard as they possibly could. They'd sight-read the charts while the cartoon was screened before them and have a wonderful time."

music world—whether acting as a highly visible symbol of equal opportunity for women in the 1920s, voicing the tenor honkers' social protest, giving expression to the spiritual yearnings of the 1960s, broadcasting defiance to the regimes of Communist countries, or funding music education in American public schools. In advertising, the simple inclusion of a saxophone in a magazine layout of, say, shoes, confers upon the product youthfulness, sexiness, and a slightly subversive sense of cool. Its appearance in movies usually signals a scene of emotional, most often erotic, power—"The time you usually hear it," says Phil Woods, who has played on several movie sound tracks, "is when they're fuckin' or dyin'." Worldwide, its very shape is iconic.

As with so many of its other traits, the saxophone comes by its sense of self-importance naturally. In promoting his invention to military officials and members of the royal court while fending off attacks from his jealous opponents, Adolphe Sax turned the instrument into a political animal, and it has remained one ever since. Its prominence on the political landscape was apparent in 1849, three years after Sax persuaded the French government to include saxophones in military bands, when King Louis Philippe was deposed. One of the first acts of the republic's new administration was to banish saxophones from the military bands and restore the more conventional instruments they had replaced. Three years later, when Napoleon III became head of state, his very first decree, two days after assuming power, was to reintroduce saxophones to the ensembles. That determining the fate of the saxophone should be the emperor's first order of business seems almost as preposterous as that an American presidential candidate, almost 150 years later, would woo a late-night television audience, and the electorate, with his saxophone licks—his choice of instrument revealing, to many of his detractors, everything they needed to know about him. In fact, they would probably argue, it was emblematic of the seedy behavior that eventually destroyed his presidency.

But that's the saxophone: seductive, itching for a fight, eager to lead its followers astray, always poking its bell into other people's business.

When he was growing up in Leningrad, now called St. Petersburg once again, Igor Butman wasn't concerned that his choice of instrument, the saxophone, might land him in jail. But the stories his father had told him about Russian saxophonists who were alternately sentenced to Siberian lockdown and released to swing freely again occasionally gave him pause. Born in 1961, Igor first attended "pioneer houses," where kids could study art or music, then entered the Rimsky-Korsakov Music College when he was fifteen. Although artistic pursuits were then sanctioned by Communist authorities, officials had a history of reversing policy without warning. "Stalin had called artists, musicians, and actors engineers over people's souls," Igor says as he sips coffee in the backyard of a friend's Manhattan townhouse. "No one has ever forgotten that. And where jazz music was concerned, there was a saying, *Segodnia on igraet dzhaz, a zavtra rodinu prodast*: Today you play jazz, tomorrow you betray the motherland."

Igor, a stocky tenorman with a broad, friendly smile and reddish blond hair, is in town with his big band to appear onstage with Wynton Marsalis and the Lincoln Center Jazz Orchestra in a sort of large-scale cutting contest. Host of a weekly television show, *Jazzophrenia*, and part owner of Le Club, Moscow's most popular jazz joint, he is often referred to as Russia's most famous jazz musician. He has earned his credentials. Like some other European players who try to distinguish themselves from the Americans, he has virtuosic talent—an ability to get around the horn with mind-warping speed. But he is also known for his canny harmonic improvisations and distinctive tone, which he says he eventually acquired after trying to imitate Cannonball Adderley, John Coltrane, Sonny Rollins, Michael Brecker, and Branford Marsalis. "When you're born," he says, "you listen to the voices of the people around you and then you start speaking. You don't think about it, and eventually you have your own voice. It's the same with the saxophone."

Between his father and his teacher, Gennady Goldstein, nicknamed Charlie for his Bird-like skill, Igor had heard of many cold war–era Russian saxophonists whose voices had been silenced by the Siberian chill. "It often depended upon relations with the United States," he says. "When things got better and we wanted something from the U.S., the saxophonists were allowed to be free and play jazz. When they got worse, they'd go back to jail."

As elsewhere, the saxophone appeared in Russia not long after its invention. By the 1860s, military and court wind bands included the instrument. It was added to the Navy Band in 1873 and, on the recommendation of Nikolai Andreyevich Rimsky-Korsakov, removed a year later because "climatic conditions unfavorable to the saxophone—that is, the cold and dampness while playing the saxophone outdoors—affect its harmoniousness and good tone."

After the Russian Revolution in 1917, says Igor, officials expressed ambivalence toward the horn. "It was the instrument of black slaves, so at first the commissars of the People's Party said it was okay," Igor says. "Bands from France and America—the Russians called them Chocolate Boy bands—were allowed to travel through the country. Sidney Bechet came to Russia. Classical music accepted the instrument, too—Shostakovich and Prokofiev included the saxophone in some of their orchestral works. But in the early thirties, Maxim Gorky published an article in which he said that he'd been to a jazz club where the saxophone was making a terrible noise, and he declared jazz the music of rich, fat people—the capitalists. A few years later, during Stalin's Great Terror of 1937, many saxophonists were shot or exiled. The saxophone was considered a dangerous capitalist instrument and a symbol of the tsarist past."

If they survived the purges, saxophone players went underground, to resurface after World War II. "We had been allies, so jazz was again okay," says Igor. "But during the cold war of the fifties, saxophonists were sent back to Siberia." There, many found opportunities to play for jazz-loving prison officials who, removed from the seemingly omniscient purview of state censorship, sometimes escorted them under guard to perform for officials at other labor camps.

Because party officers assigned to rooting out jazz actually enjoyed the music, some saxophonists thrived in an underground club scene. Leonid Utesov's big band, the country's most famous popular ensemble, found that it was able to offer sizzling jazz performances as long as it appeared to be satirizing the Americans. "Officially, the party line was, 'From the saxophone to the switchblade is only one step,'" says Igor. "In other words, playing the saxophone is one step from being a murderer. You'd see the phrase in the newspapers. But meanwhile, you could hear it played in clubs every night."*

One consequence of the periodic purging was the elimination of any formal saxophone instruction for much of the twentieth century. Igor's generation was the first to benefit from the more relaxed attitude toward the instrument by the Communist authorities of the seventies and eighties. Now the saxophone, once the symbol of a personal autonomy that threatened state authority, is again iconic, for another reason. "Because it was prohibited for so long, it's very hip," says Igor with a twinkling smile. "Ladies come up to me and tell me it's their favorite instrument."

During the same year Stalin was unleashing his Great Purges, prompting Russian saxophonists to take up the flute or cello, the Nazis were also training their sights on the "decadent" music of the West and the sinuous purveyor and symbol of "Judeo-Negroid" music: the saxophone. For many years, Germany had been one of the few countries able to resist the hegemony of the horn. After the German instrument maker Wilhelm Wieprecht challenged Adolphe Sax in 1845 about the provenance of the instrument and was humiliated when his claims were proved specious, Germany expressed little interest in the saxo-

---

*The Voice of America also effectively sent the sounds of jazz across the Russian airwaves. During one of those moments when the authorities eased their enmity toward the West, in 1962, Phil Woods toured Russia with Benny Goodman. He says, "You'd hear people whispering to you from the bushes, 'Dizzy Gillespie! Thelonious Monk!' The Voice of America educated the whole world about jazz, but we never had a Voice of America for America. So our country is woefully ignorant about this music."

phone for the rest of the century. (After all, it was irredeemably French.) In 1902, during a trip to Paris, the German composer and pianist Gustav Bumcke bought eight saxophones from Adolphe Sax's son, established a saxophone class in Berlin, and by the 1920s had done much to promote the instrument in German classical music and the conservatory. As the jazz age heated up, cabarets and nightclubs were also filled with the sounds of keening saxophones. But to nativist Nazis, the instrument was a dangerous interloper.

In 1937, as the Great Terror tore through Russia, the Nazis mounted a five-month touring exhibit titled *Entartete Kunst* ("degenerate art"), which featured paintings, books, sculpture, and other artwork created by the mentally ill, Communists, Gypsies, homosexuals, Jews, and others they considered to be subspecies of the human race. A year later, they staged an exhibition called *Entartete Musik*, listing famous works by Mendelssohn, Mahler, and Schoenberg as examples of unacceptable compositions. Among the many other composers who were declared to be degenerate was Anton Webern, a follower of Hitler but a friend of Schoenberg, a Jew, and thus tainted by association. The most prominent items in the exhibit, though, were representations of what Joseph Goebbels referred to as "Americano nigger kike jungle music."

To advertise the exhibition, the Nazis retooled a poster from the 1927 jazz opera by Ernst Krenek, *Jonny Spielt Auf* (Johnny Plays On), morphing the poster's handsome black jazz musician into a wild-eyed, thick-lipped simian creature in a cockeyed top hat and tuxedo, sporting the Star of David on his lapel and a ring in his ear, fingering a saxophone with a huge bell. The poster and its saxophone-wielding subhuman came to symbolize all that was inferior and evil in the West; it announced the exhibition to be *eine Abrechnung von Staatsrat*, or a statement of national standards. Those standards thereafter required light orchestras to restrict the use of saxophones of all pitches and to substitute for them an appropriate stringed instrument—a violoncello or viola—or a German folk instrument.

Also in 1937, Japan, Germany's factotum, began the National Spiritual Mobilization campaign, designed to rid the country of "enemy" music. The "lascivious" sound of the saxophone was a primary target of the campaign. All bands were ordered by the Japan Music Culture Association to reduce their number of saxophones "to rid light music of the stink of jazz." Officials decided that even if they couldn't eradicate the saxophone altogether, they could at least sanitize its name and, they hoped, the musical company it kept. From then on, they declared, the saxophone would be called "bent metallic flute."

Yuri Yunakov was born in Thrace, Bulgaria, but grew up speaking Turkish because the town was fifteen miles from the border with Turkey. As a Rom, or Gypsy, he also grew up around the Romany language, which has its origins in Sanskrit and has much in common with modern Hindi, the language of northern India, whence the Rom began their fitful migration at the turn of the first millennium. A generation or two ago, his family abandoned its real surname, Ali, and adopted a Slavic one. To be a Rom in Communist Bulgaria was hard enough without also attracting the special persecution reserved for Muslims.

Yuri and his mentor, clarinetist Ivo Papasov, a Turkish Gypsy, are responsible for creating a style of music that Bulgarian Communist authorities considered dissident and subversive—a hyperactive, trance-inducing idiomatic hybrid called wedding music. Starting in 1983, Yuri played with Papasov for ten years and then, when his star eclipsed his mentor's, formed his own band, becoming the most famous musician in the country both for his playing and his defiance of the authorities. While Communist officials in Russia were relaxing their attitudes toward the interloping saxophone, Bulgarian apparatchiks were stepping up their campaign against the voice of protest, which emerged defiantly, despite their efforts to suppress it, from the bell of Yuri Yunakov's saxophone.

His technique, characterized by long phrases of precisely articulated notes delivered at an impossible speed and interrupted by short legato phrases, is stunning to behold. "Before me, no one plays the saxophone like this," Yuri says. He may be right. Imagine a triple-tonguing Wiedoeft played at twice the speed, add to it the improvisational skill of Bird and the harmonic flights of fancy of Coltrane or Coleman, overlay it all with a tone of iron, and you get some idea. The style of music is equally complex—an extraordinary mix of sounds and odd, shifting meters from Indian, Turkish, Arabic, Rom, and Balkan traditions seasoned by modern jazz and electric rock.

Because the music had no relation to what authorities considered a national style, it was outlawed. "The state wanted to present an image of Bulgaria as a homogenous population of Slavic Eastern Orthodox Bulgarians," says Yuri, a huge bearded man, as he sits with an interpreter in the living room of his American record producer. "Bulgaria had a famous national orchestra with handmade instruments that they thought represented the peasant folk culture. Our repertoire was clearly non-Bulgarian and our instruments, like the saxophone, had come from somewhere else. So we were thrown in jail."

At first, weddings, out of sight and hearing of official censors, seemed like a safe place to play the frenetic music. The band would play for hours and the guests, like their dervish ancestors, would dance until they dropped or entered an altered state. The demands on Yuri, a former professional boxer, were considerable. "People would save up their entire lives to have a big wedding for their child, and music was at the center of it," he says. "The point was to dance. But sometimes a single dance would go on for five hours in 2/4 rhythm. Do you know how many improvisational solos you have to play in five hours, what good lips you have to have?"

As the band's subversive repertoire became more popular and compact discs of the music were distributed underground, the weddings turned into spontaneous music festivals. "Eventually, thousands of uninvited guests would turn out," says Yuri. "Everyone from an entire region would gather. Roads for many miles would be blocked with cars. We were like rock stars."

As Bulgaria's most popular musician, Yuri was well rewarded for his efforts. "You have to tip the musicians," he says, "so we would walk away with satchels of cash." But the authorities decided to make an example of him to other musicians who might aspire to the same status. After each show, he would be thrown in jail for fifteen days and his head would be shaved. Eventually, he applied for and was granted asylum in the United States.

After the Communist bloc disintegrated and other musical styles were allowed, the craze for wedding music faded. "The height of wedding music was at the country's most oppressive time," says Yuri. "The more resistance to creativity there is, the better the result. It's why the saxophone was the perfect instrument for this kind of subversive activity. The more resistance there is when you blow, the better the sound."

In 1951, when the Catholic Legion of Decency screened *A Streetcar Named Desire*, Elia Kazan's film adaptation of the scorching Tennessee Williams play, its members found themselves uncomfortably aroused by one particular scene. After being abused by her husband, Stanley (Marlon Brando), during a drunken card game, Stella (Kim Hunter) flees to an upstairs room in their New Orleans apartment building. Stanley is thrown in a shower to cool off by his poker buddies and emerges repentant. Dripping wet in a clinging white T-shirt as he kneels at the bottom of a wrought-iron staircase that separates the two apartments, he begs for forgiveness, howling like an abandoned child. Her fear melting in the swelter of passion, Stella slowly descends the staircase, bosom heaving, magnetically drawn to her beautiful, powerful, savage husband. After placing his head against her newly pregnant belly, Stanley picks her up and carries her off to their bedroom. The heat left in the wake of the tormented couple fairly incinerates everything around them.

After reviewing the movie, the Legion of Decency demanded that a number of scenes be censored in the scorching film, including this one. The vivid depiction of such base eroticism, it declared, was a violation of common "decency." Its decision had nothing to do with what actually took place on the screen, however. Rather, the censors were offended by the voluptuous saxophone solo that accompanied Stella's lustful surrender.

The score's composer, Alex North, fearing the legion's denouncement as much as modern filmmakers dread the damning effect of an X rating, immediately changed the instrumentation from what the censors called the carnal saxophone to French horn and strings. The scene remained; only the score was changed. The substitution satisfied the censorious legionnaires. In 1993, when the movie was released on DVD, the original saxophone cue was restored to the sound track.

Streetcar, says Fred Karlin,* a composer and movie score historian, was a landmark use of the saxophone, even though it took forty years for it to be heard by the general public. In the twenties and thirties the instrument had contributed to the scores of film shorts and movies about jazz —"Saint Saxophone Opens Up Them Jazzy Gates," announced an advertisement for *Jazz Heaven*, a movie featuring Duke Ellington's Jungle Band that opened at New York's Globe Theatre in 1929. "And it was used for lightness and comedy," says Karlin. "After *Streetcar*, it could still provide a comical touch, as in *The Pink Panther*. But from then on it most commonly evoked the dark world of the hard-bitten detective or gave voice to lust, as it did in *Last Tango in Paris*. It's also been a good choice for exploring the psychotic, as in *Taxi Driver*, or depravity, brilliantly articulated by Ornette Coleman's free-jazz styling for *Naked Lunch*."

In the opinion of Loras Schissel, two other orchestrators of the same era made brilliant use of the saxophone—perhaps because both played the instrument. "David Raksin's theme from *The Bad and the Beautiful* perfectly captures the siren-song quality of a rotten Hollywood director who's a genius and screws everybody," says Schissel, who also loves Raksin's main-title saxophone solo for the

*Fred Karlin passed away in March 2004.

1961 movie *Al Capone* and his score for *Too Late Blues*, featuring Benny Carter on such tunes as "Sax Raises Its Ugly Head."

Schissel's other favorite score accompanies *A Place in the Sun*, the adaptation of Theodore Dreiser's novel *An American Tragedy*, for which Franz Waxman used a saxophone solo to tie the young couple together with a sense of youth and sensuality. "It was a searing melody that you associate with a slightly disreputable woman," says Schissel of the score, which won Waxman an Oscar.

Karlin, who has compiled a list of what he considers to be the one hundred best film scores, considers composer John Barry's use of solo saxophone to trip the audience's "known emotional triggers" in *Body Heat* another groundbreaking moment for the instrument. "There was no romance involved," he says, "only sex and eroticism. The saxophone completely captures that. For all its lustiness, the saxophone can sound terribly alone at times."

Ronny Lang, who played the *Body Heat* solo, remembers that Barry liked Paul Desmond's "ethereal" sound and asked him to replicate it in the movie. Lang, who has played on the scores of more than 900 movies over a forty-year career, was known for being able to play in almost any style—a talent that allowed him to perform solos as various as Henry Mancini's noirish theme song for the police-detective television show *Peter Gunn* (nicely caricatured on the "Guy Noir, Private Detective" segment of Garrison Keillor's *Prairie Home Companion*) and composer Bernard Herrmann's in-your-face psychotic choruses in *Taxi Driver*.

"But it was always the sound of sex," says Lang, who played in the Los Angeles–based Les Brown band before working for motion-picture studios. "It got to be almost a cliché. André Previn, who used to work a lot in movies, once told me, 'If I hear another slurping alto saxophone solo in a bedroom scene I'm going to throw up.'"

Ironically, given the saxophone's ability to draw attention to itself, its movie-score players, until recently, were never acknowledged in film credits for their work. One of his few credits, says Lang, was on Clint Eastwood's *Bird*. "I play in this one scene where there's a guy who's a really bad saxophone player," he says. "Clint kept telling me to make it worse, make it worse. He wanted me to squawk and honk like Big Jay McNeely. I ended up getting a splitting headache.

"But I got credit—for being a horrible saxophone player."

Every morning, on my way to work, I walk through Pennsylvania Station, where, interrupted only by train-departure announcements, an endless loop of cheerful light jazz fronted by a soprano saxophone spills from hundreds of speakers throughout the hub, spurring millions of travelers in a brisk and orderly fashion toward their destinations. In the crowded elevator to my office, similarly bland and pleasant saxo-Muzak distracts passengers from the discomfort of being a little too close to their colleagues. Once settled at my desk, I may tune the television to an all-news channel just in time to hear the show's saxophone-heavy theme song announce a commercial break. The advertisement itself, for a new sports car, has a hip solo saxophone sound track. If I malinger and try to catch a few minutes of a rerun of *Sex and the City*, I may arrive just in time to hear a lusty saxophone solo provide the coda to the romantic misadventures of the love-starved quartet. A few clicks away, a local sports wrap-up show may be announcing its start with a frenetic run of saxophone licks, the musical analogue of a football running back cutting and weaving through a line of defenders. Sensitized to the sound of the instrument, I find it inescapable.

At least I don't live in Europe. Whereas the sound of the saxophone seems to have penetrated every American medium, abroad it's the image of the horn (which unconsciously evokes its hip sound) that's ubiquitous, particularly in print advertising, where it's used to sell everything from aftershave to microwave ovens. For the past several years, its presence across the commercial European landscape has been documented by Bernhard Habla, a music researcher at the University of Music and Dramatic Arts in Graz, Austria, and the head of the International Society for the Investigation and Promotion of Wind Music. The findings of his latest survey have been compiled in a paper titled "The Iconography of the Saxophone."

Throughout musical history, Habla notes, a few instruments have become associated with nonmusical events or activities. Putti trumpeters provide their blessings in paintings depicting sacred scenes. Thanks to the paintings of Peter Brueghel the Elder, the bagpipe has come to symbolize the peasant dance at farmers' festivals. The flute has long been associated with romantic shepherd scenes. The Celtic harp is the state insignia for Ireland. The French horn is used as a signaling instrument in the hunt and to announce the arrival of mail; the postal horn emblem can still be found on many European mailboxes. The saxophone is the newest member of this iconic instrumental pantheon. Wherever it appears in a nonmusical context, says Habla, it symbolizes "fun and action, youth, style, the atmosphere of the Big World and, based on its associations with jazz and rock, an America with unbounded possibilities." In the mid-1980s, the Citroën car company apparently attempted to capitalize on all these associations when it introduced the newest addition to its automobile lineup, the Saxo.

To support his thesis, Habla's forty-page manuscript is illustrated with 130 examples of advertisements that contain the saxophone as an accessory, as well as other iconographic uses. Paging through this document, it's amusing to contemplate the kind of brainstorming session that resulted in the decision to illustrate the cover of a cookbook with a vegetable saxophone. What's the subliminal message conveyed by the saxophone propped in a corner of an otherwise empty room that's just been renovated with beautiful parquet flooring in the magazine advertisement for a wood company? "*Wer kocht* (Who's cooking?)," the ad copy asks in a pitch for a self-cleaning electric oven as a handsome and carefree young couple entertain each other—they're cookin', apparently, both literally and musically—in a saxophone duet. The Sigl brewery encourages its customers to "Keep on swinging" by topping off a saxophone with a sudsy head of beer. In a multipaneled newspaper advertisement for the Arosa ski resort in Switzerland titled "Two winters in the life of the bachelor tenor," a debonair saxophone is depicted schussing down ski slopes, then meeting a lady alto with whom he spends the rest of his vacation. The next summer, the couple return to the beautiful green mountains at Arosa to hike and swim. But by winter the tenor is again skiing alone because his lady alto wanted to get married. He loved her but, well, he's a swinging tenor saxophone. Marriage doesn't fit his profile.

The horn is casually, sometimes absurdly, positioned in dozens of advertisements for women's and men's clothing, travel agencies, appliances, cigarettes, carpeting, banks, insurance companies, cars, whiskey, home entertainment centers, circuses, flea markets, motor sports, and the Green political party. A real estate company trying to sell new apartments uses the saxophone as a decoration piece kept in a glass case, or as the leg of a chair or a lamp stand—clear evidence of the apartment complex's sense of cool. Unsurprisingly, many of the pictures are provocative: a series of ads for a radio station features a scantily clad woman in a military hat with impossibly long legs straddling a huge saxophone. Another image, of a beautiful woman in a summer dress playing the horn while walking the bar in a nightclub, is actually an advertisement for the shoes she's wearing. A close-up of her face reveals that her embouchure and blowing technique might best be suited to a different, more intimate, activity.

Habla has included other offbeat imagery as well: Barbie and her saxophone as accessory; a scene from *Some Like It Hot*, in which Marilyn Monroe's character reveals her special feeling for a "tenor-man"; a program from the Saint John Coltrane African Orthodox Church; a Keith Haring saxophone graffito; pages from a German comic book in which Donald Duck scuffles with his saxo-playing neighbor. Habla includes pictures of famous people who play the saxophone as a hobby—Thailand's King Bhumibol Adulyadej, who in 1996 celebrated the fiftieth anniversary of his coronation by playing the saxophone, and, of course, Bill Clinton.

Although the abundance of saxophone iconography is overwhelming, Habla says his presentation can't possibly convey how often the instrument is used as a sales tool. "It is almost impossible to survey how often a saxophone has been shown standing in a corner, or lying on a chair or on shelves in advertisements," he says. "You get the impression that saxophones normally lie around in every room of the house like old newspapers."

The Super Balanced Action has changed everything. It's beyond preten-tious for me to own a horn this good, so I've been working hard to earn its trust. I practice every day and on Tuesday nights get my band mates to back me up on my expanding repertoire. My current goal is to play like Billie Holiday sings, since Miss Lady Day once said she tried to sing like Lester Young played and that would leave me only a degree or two of separation from Prez, whose music I'm currently stuck on. I've been listening hard to Lester and other early jazz-saxophone titans—Hawk, Johnny Hodges, Ben Webster, Benny Carter. I'm not sure I'll be able get beyond Lester, though, because his sound is just so sweet.

    Ownership has somehow convinced me that I'm no longer a student but a player, a member of a special brotherhood. When I'm discouraged by my progress, or lack of it, I consult the elders in my new fraternity. The other night, completely flustered by my pathetic attempts to play arpeggios at a marking above the larghetto setting on my metronome, I gave up and be-gan paging through a biography of Jean-Marie Londeix, the now-retired French master saxophonist. I turned to a passage in his diary where he

*complains of subtle imperfections in his sound when he fingers F-sharp.
He again would have to change the shape of his mouth and the placement
of his tongue and lips, he lamented, "and then patiently do the same thing
on each following note. Will I never move beyond this level of working?"
Londeix had been studying the saxophone for ten years at that point. I've
been at it for eight months. Chastened, I set the metronome at 50, in the
mid-largo range, quietly thanked M. Londeix, and got back to work.*

    *But my lesson this evening with Michel is a struggle. I've been out of
town for five days, unable to practice, and my embouchure, such as it is, has
gone slack. We began with our usual long-tone warm-up, concentrating on
attack and release, coming to the note cleanly and backing off at the end.
We're trying to "tighten up the air column," Michel says. We've also been doing tonguing exercises, which have proved daunting. To articulate a note,
you first establish sufficient back pressure while preventing the reed from vibrating with the tip of your tongue—sort of like flooring the accelerator in
a car while holding down the brake. When you release your tongue, the note
should pop out crisply. If you're tonguing the notes of a scale, it's essential to
have your fingers and darting tongue working in concert. It sounds simple
but it's incredibly complex. What other activity requires you to rehearse the
synchronous movement of your tongue and fingers?*

    *Nevertheless, at the end of the tonguing torture Michel compliments
me on my sound. "I like it better than mine," he says. "It's boomy, edgy,
it's got a lot of roundness to it."*

    *Me? I have a sound now, too? It's like acquiring a new persona—
becoming a father for the first time or discovering that you have a middle
name. How odd to think of a simple respiration being launched in my diaphragm, making its way through my lungs, throat, and mouth, squeezing
down a conical brass tube, funneling itself into waves of energy that set into
motion ambient molecules of air as it spills from the bell of the horn—and
conferring upon me an* identity *as it becomes sound. My sound. Have I
really achieved that milestone? If Mingus is right—you have to be able to
conjure all the voices of the past before you find your own—there's no way
I could have my own sound. I mean, I'm still stuck back with Lester.*

    *But I'll take the compliment. With the saxophone, you never know:
my sound could easily disappear tomorrow.*

12. LEGIT

When Don Sinta began studying with Larry Teal as a young saxophone prodigy in the fifties, he was given very specific instructions about whom he should *not* sound like. At the time, only two styles of playing, both of them European, were considered acceptable when performing, say, Jacques Ibert's *Concertino da Camera* (1935), Bizet's *L'Arlesienne* suites, or Heitor Villa-Lobos's *Fantasia* (1948)—three of the better known compositions in the "legit" saxophone's emerging repertoire. One was the "dark," German sound exemplified by Sigurd Rascher, a master saxophonist who had fled the Nazis in 1939 and settled in upstate New York, where he gave master classes when not performing recitals and concerts around the world. At the other end of the tonal spectrum was the "bright," French sound associated with the equally legendary Marcel Mule, head of the saxophone class at the Paris Conservatory of Music, who, like Rascher, had done much to promote the saxophone as a classical instrument. Teal, a homegrown American who had been appointed professor of saxophone at the University of Michigan in

1953, the first such appointment at a major American university, was partial to neither, but he was particularly disdainful of the French sound, so prominent on Mule's recordings of the thirties and forties. "Whenever he found out I had a Mule record he would confiscate it," Don says. "He could hear it in my playing. He'd say, 'I told you not to listen to those records.'"

For the rest of the century, the debate regarding the German and French styles of playing dominated American saxophone pedagogy, fueled in part by the apparent determination of each camp's virtuoso to outlast the other's. Finally, in 2001, both expired—Rascher at the age of ninety-four, Mule at one hundred. Since he succeeded Larry Teal as head of the saxophone department at Michigan in 1974, Don Sinta, widely recognized as one of the concert saxophone's most talented performers and distinguished educators, has seen hundreds of colleges and universities establish strong and well-subscribed saxophone departments—yet the French vs. German thing refuses to go away. Most teachers, and their students, continue to line up behind the legacies of Mule or Rascher, or side with the third, "American," school founded by Larry Teal (and carried on by Don Sinta), who advocated a sound somewhere between those of the two Europeans.

"How you put forward the idea of different schools of pedagogy is still a sensitive issue," Don says. "When you say the Mule sound is brighter than the Rascher sound, some people resent that. So how do you find words to describe these ideas without alienating people who embrace them? I'm a Teal student, and my tone is different from both of them. But the English say my sound is too goddamned tubby. I guess, like everyone else, I should resent that. But I don't know what it means."

Is it any surprise that even in the seemingly genteel world of the classical, or concert, saxophone, Adolphe Sax's obstreperous hybrid should stir anger and discord? Or that hundreds of years of hostilities between two European neighbors should be distilled into an argument about the saxophone's "true" sound?

For Rascher acolytes, the issue has been reduced largely to a matter of equipment. Followers are urged to play instruments made before

1920, or early models by Buescher, which maintained Adolphe Sax's original bore size, and the instrument's prominent parabolic shape, until around the Depression. (Early Conns did, too, but their manufacturer's name didn't possess such Teutonic cachet.) Mouthpieces, too, should resemble those made by the Belgian inventor, with a hollowed-out chamber, deep baffle, and a large round throat. In his many writings, Rascher declared that the alterations made to the instrument so that it could compete with noisier instruments in dance bands had ruined the tone "which so had delighted the great musicians in earlier times." Rascher maintained that the older horns sounded the way Sax intended them to. "Anything else," says Don, "was considered a bastardization, a remove from the true tradition. But the original Ford also started with a hand crank in front of the car."

Disciples of the French sound, on the other hand, play mostly Selmer and Buffet instruments (both of French origin, of course), which are known for their cheerful, bell-like clarity. Their pedagogical lineage in America traces back to Frederick Hemke, who studied with Marcel Mule in 1956 at the Paris Conservatory and won the top prize in his class, and Eugene Rousseau, who sat at the master's feet in 1960. They went on to develop the highly esteemed saxophone programs at Northwestern and Indiana University, respectively, from which hundreds of Gallic-toned players graduated and themselves became founding professors of saxophone programs around the country.

The politics of tone have been argued in all the places academics are known to squabble—in journals, at lectures, and at symposia. An occasionally disputed issue concerns the premiere of Jacques Ibert's *Concertino da Camera*, which was written for Rascher. Disciples of Rascher and Mule both declare their man to have given the first complete performance of the work around 1935. They have also disputed the "invention"* of the altissimo register, the notes above

---

*In fact, on his earliest saxophones, Adolphe Sax included a third octave vent for the altissimo range, enabling musicians to play naturally in the upper octave without resorting to false fingerings and distortions of the embouchure.

the natural range of the horn. Rascher published *Top-Tones*, an altissimo exercise study, in 1941, but in 1963, after Muleites claimed their patron saint had been fingering the high notes years before, he declared that, having thought a little harder on the matter, he'd actually been working on the technique since the late twenties. In fact, H. Benne Henton, a soloist in Patrick Conway's and John Philip Sousa's bands, was well known for his altissimo playing as early as 1911, and E. A. Lefebre before then. And it's doubtful that Mule, who loathed modern saxophone music and the extended techniques often required to play it, was ever interested in playing outside the horn's natural range.

Feelings have been sufficiently bruised for the Rascherites to threaten to withdraw from the North American Saxophone Alliance, an organization of concert players and scholars that also publishes the *Saxophone Symposium*, and form their own group. At the World Saxophone Congress, a biannual gathering of teachers, composers, and performers that Don Sinta helped organize in 1970, some members of the two schools still refuse to speak to each other. A couple of Rascher followers, finding all the feuding beneath their dignity, have packed up their vintage saxophones and moved permanently to Germany.

To Sinta, the bickering reflects a long-standing inferiority complex on the part of concert saxophonists, who, particularly in America, have been refused permanent chairs in symphonic orchestras. "Since we don't have a place in history, we're all trying to make this critical decision of which way we go," says Don. "A clarinet or flute player can at least get in a ballet orchestra, an opera orchestra, or a symphony orchestra. But we have none of those places open to us. So if we're going to make it, we're either going to get recognized in the academic world or in the very limited world of professional performance."

The modern version of the long-standing tonal debate, says Don, is being argued in small performance spaces—or wherever people gather to hear new saxophone art music. Does the French players' vogue for the avant-garde, with its emphasis on speed, multiphonics, circular breathing, slap-tongue, and extended techniques, represent a viable artistic and commercial future for the concert saxophone? Or does the refined, controlled, and mannered style of the Rascherites and their descendants, who are retroactively trying to link themselves to a classical tradition the instrument was never a part of, have more appeal?

"Having lived through the late sixties and seventies and played a lot of avant-garde music, I happen to be coming from a more pragmatic standpoint," Don says. "My sense is that in our culture we've moved away from the avant-garde. Don't get me wrong. All the saxophone players around the world are playing better than ever. The benchmark continues to go up. The quality of playing in some of our college programs is scary. Many of these kids are commissioning composers; everybody's getting new music. When we have a World Saxophone Congress, there are 200 world premieres. This is unprecedented in the history of wind instrument playing.

"The question is how we get an audience to embrace what we do. It goes way beyond whether the 'sound' should be French or German."

Adolphe Sax was well aware that one of the challenges facing the saxophone was its lack of repertoire; not long after receiving his patent, he established a small press in Paris and eventually published three dozen original compositions for his horn. Intrigued by its possibilities, some composers experimented with saxophone parts in new works. Jacques Fromental Halévy used the extraworldly thrum of a quartet of bass saxophones to describe the ascent of the spirit into heaven (articulating the "anguish and despair of humanity on the Last Great Day," in the words of the famed Boston music critic Philip Hale) in his opera *Le Juif Errant*, which premiered in 1852. The Philadelphia composer William Henry Fry scored for the soprano in his *Santa Claus Symphony* (1852), for soprano and bass in *Hagar in the Wilderness*, and for tenor in the symphonic poem *The Dying Soldier*, both of which premiered in 1854. The Belgian violinist and composer Jean Baptiste Singelée composed at least thirty solo and ensemble works for saxophone, and the British composer Caryl Florio added two pieces for saxophone quartets and a quintet for piano and four saxophones. Other prominent European composers who endorsed the new horn's use included Ambroise Thomas (in *Hamlet*, 1868), Jules Massenet (*Herodiade*, 1881), Joseph Arban, Jules Demersseman, Hyacinthe Klose, and Louis-Adolphe Mayeur. Despite the prominent exposure, though, the instrument remained something of an outsider, an arriviste, to classical purists. Most symphonic orchestras refused to formally admit the saxophone, and only one nineteenth-century piece, Georges Bizet's *L'Arlesienne* suites, has been considered good enough to make it into the concert-saxophone canon.

"In the classical world, the saxophone has had a pretty rough time making a case for itself," says Gunther Schuller. "I think that happens to any latecomer or outsider. Its aspiration to become a part of the symphony orchestra may have been misguided in the first place. Did it really think it could improve eighteenth-century classical music?"

As a musician and composer equally at home in jazz, classical and modern art music, Gunther has a well-informed perspective on the saxophone's struggles in the concert world. A French-horn player, he joined the Cincinnati Symphony as principal horn at seventeen and the Metropolitan Opera at nineteen and recorded with Dizzy Gillespie and Miles Davis (on *Birth of the Cool*). Schuller wrote what is still considered the most illuminating exegesis of the new American music, the two-volume *History of Jazz*. He has created more than 160 compositions and pioneered the Third Stream movement, a fusion of classical and jazz music to which he recruited collaborators such as Ornette Coleman, Eric Dolphy, and Charles Mingus. In 1970 he wrote *Jazz Abstractions* for Coleman, a piece featuring saxophone and string quartet in which Coleman plays freely, backed by strictly notated strings. More recently, in 1999, he composed a sonata for Kenneth Radnofsky, a professor of saxophone at the New England Conservatory, of which Schuller was president for ten years.

When he took that job, in 1967, a "legitimate" saxophone program did not exist, even though NEC had been the first American conservatory to offer saxophone instruction, in 1882. Gunther quickly hired Joe Allard, a Manhattan studio player and instructor whose students included Lee Konitz and Eric Dolphy. "It was shocking that a major conservatory like New England didn't allow students to apply on saxophone," says Gunther as he hunches over a table at a Manhattan jazz club, where he's been listening to his son Ed's new band. "That was a real blemish. But it was still struggling to be heard. Up to the forties, a person playing so-called classical saxophone was considered some strange outside figure, like someone playing the theremin."

The problem, despite Rascher's and Mule's efforts to commission new works, was the quality of the literature. "At the turn of the century, people were filling out the limited repertoire by playing transcriptions of Bach and Fauré, because there just wasn't much else," says Gunther, a large man with an inviting smile and a thick, Mozartian sweep of white hair. "And, of course, those works sound better played by the instruments they were written for."* Still, he says, the saxophone had demonstrated early on its potential to add color and character—even in compositions that seemed to include it almost as an afterthought.† Gunther has conducted Richard Strauss's *Symphonia Domestica*, which premiered in 1904, with and without the trio of saxophones Strauss offered as an option, and says their inclusion richly adds to the piece.

---

*While the quality of the literature was a problem, quantity was not. Jean-Marie Londeix has catalogued more than 3,000 pieces for saxophone written between 1844 and 1969. The combination of the saxophone craze of the 1910s and 1920s and the school-band movement produced a flood of literature—overtures, choruses from operas, marches, serenades, as well as original light music composed by the virtuosos of the era, including E. A. Lefebre, G. E. Holmes, and Rudy Wiedoeft.

†The Australian-born composer and pianist Percy Grainger made many transcriptions of early music for the saxophone and discovered that the instrument's tone quality, especially in an ensemble setting, very closely duplicated the sound of medieval instruments.

"They do nothing but double other instruments," he says. "There are a couple of fugues in the piece where the bass saxophone doubles the cellos. But I love it because it adds an openness, even a roughness, and a kind of bucolic energy to the music that's lacking without it."

Around the same time Strauss was finishing up his *Symphonia*, the concert saxophone was being tucked under the matronly wing of its first important American patron, a society lady from Boston who began commissioning works for it from early-twentieth-century composers. Although most of the pieces she commissioned—twenty-two in all, including Claude Debussy's *Rapsodie*—are all but forgotten, Elise Boyer Hall significantly advanced the saxophone's reputation as a serious instrument suitable for an orchestral or chamber setting.

Hall, whose Beacon Hill ancestors dated to the early colonists and included the famed architect Charles Bulfinch, was the widow of Richard John Hall, a Princeton-educated surgeon who had become renowned for performing the first appendectomy with only regional anesthesia. Hall used cocaine in his experimental nerve blocks and became hopelessly addicted to the drug. After spending eighteen months in a mental hospital fighting his dependency, he suffered a complete nervous and physical collapse. While in California helping her husband recover, Elise contracted typhoid fever, which impaired her hearing. Her husband suggested she learn to play the saxophone, hoping the ear training would prevent further loss. Elise, who had studied piano in Paris, found a farm laborer who had a saxophone and began taking lessons from him.

After her husband died—of systemic infection following a burst appendix—she moved back east and headed the Orchestral Club of Boston, an amateur musical society. She appointed Georges Longy, a French oboist who occupied the principal chair at the Boston Symphony Orchestra, as instructor and conductor of the club. Her first commission was Charles Loeffler's *Divertissement Espagnol*, which she and her club premiered in Boston's Copley Hall in 1901, the same year she induced Claude Debussy to write a work for the saxophone. Although Debussy quickly cashed the check from the woman he referred to as "*la femme saxophone*," *Rapsodie* did not premiere until 1919, a year after his death, having been completed by his French contemporary Jean Roger-Ducasse. Over the intervening years, Hall also commissioned *Choral Varié* by Vincent d'Indy, *Legend* by Georges Sprok, and Henri Woollett's *Siberia–Poeme Symphonique*, among other works. As a saxophonist, she appeared in twenty-eight concerts, rarely failing to provoke a reaction from the audience, which was unaccustomed to seeing a woman play the horn. She died in 1924.

Hall's greatest accomplishment may have been to expose the instrument to previously disdainful critics, who associated the saxophone with vaudeville and amateur home music. After hearing Panis Angelicus, a tenor solo from César Franck's Mass that had been arranged for the instrument, the critic Philip Hale wrote: "It is a pity that the literature of this peculiarly impressive instrument is not larger . . . for this instrument is something more than the plaything of a clarinetist and it should be nobly, not flippantly, played."

Most of the music Hall commissioned, though, was of less than memorable quality. Although Debussy's name added cachet to the saxophone repertoire, *Rapsodie* is considered one of his more lugubrious compositions—not surprising, perhaps, since he disparagingly referred to the saxophone as an "aquatic" instrument. And Loeffler, some years after the debut of the composition, did everything he could to bury *Divertissement Espagnol.* In a response to the San Francisco critic Alfred V. Frankenstein, who inquired about the work, an assistant wrote, "Mr. Loeffler, who is ill at present, wishes to say to Mr. Frankenstein that the work for saxophone and orchestra is not published and that the score has been destroyed as well as the parts. The work was less than unimportant and hence its destruction is of no loss to the world."

In the 1920s, Gunther Schuller points out, the saxophone was used effectively in "high-quality music," such as Modest Mussorgsky's

Pictures at an Exhibition and Darius Milhaud's *Creation of the World*, which substituted a saxophone for viola. "Marcel Mule and his friend Jean Françaix wrote quite a few pieces for quartet in the thirties," Gunther says. "The concerto by Paul Creston, a major work, premiered in 1941. But if you add all that up, that's an insignificant number of uses of the instrument prior to World War II.

"It's not surprising that people should have argued so long over how the saxophone should sound, because it was an unconventional instrument trying to fit into conventional music. That's what academics do when there's not much to fight over. Rather than address the problem—finding people who could write in new ways for the saxophone—they fell back on a convenient scapegoat: that old French-versus-German thing."

The jingoistic pride that has in part fueled the debate over the proper saxophone sound is, in fact, somewhat misplaced. Although he was born in western Germany, Sigurd Rascher, pioneer of the "German" sound, was actually of Danish descent. But where there's a good fight to be had, the saxophone doesn't get hung up on details.

Rascher's anointed successor, John-Edward Kelly, isn't German either, but he very capably continues to wave his mentor's flag from the purported home of the "dark" sound. An American who now divides his time between Oslo, where he teaches at the Norwegian State Academy of Music, and Düsseldorf, where he is a professor at the Robert Schumann Academy of Music, John-Edward is widely revered as one of the classical saxophone's most distinguished performers. Like his teacher, Sigurd Rascher, he has done much to advance the repertoire: in the past twenty-five years, nearly 200 pieces have been written for him. He has memorized them all. "It's about becoming a part of the music," he says.

John-Edward was invited to live with Rascher and his family for two years in upstate New York while studying with the master, taking four classes a week for as long as six hours at a time. "The thing

I appreciated most about him was his attitude toward music," he says during a rare visit to the United States. "He believed that music is one of the great accomplishments of human history, central to the identity of the human being, who he is, and that we have to take care of that identity, it doesn't happen by itself. He had a complete revulsion toward commercialism in music, and this spoke to me strongly.

"As for his playing, he accomplished unbelievable things for the saxophone, not only in terms of the repertoire he brought into the world but also by winning serious, broad-based respect for the instrument. In his lifetime he played with all the world-class conductors—George Szell, Eugene Ormandy, John Barbirolli, Leonard Bernstein—conductors who had never before played with a saxophone soloist."

Affirmation of Rascher's tone and technique was also granted by an equally important source, he says: Adolphe Sax's daughter. "In a famous letter directed to Mr. Rascher after a Strasbourg concert in 1934, she said in very explicit and enthusiastic terms that Rascher had played the saxophone as her father had always dreamt it would one day be played."

A tireless proselytizer for the instrument, Rascher helped the saxophone achieve "aesthetic respectability," *The New York Times* declared in 1939, when he was the first solo saxophonist to play with the New York Philharmonic in 3,543 concerts. The designation on the program of Rascher as a soloist was itself something of a watershed for the instrument. Previously, on the odd occasion when a symphony conductor deigned to include the horn in a performance, he would refer to its player as a saxophone "operator" or "technician."

But Rascher also had a reputation as a tyrant. He often insulted students and was rarely complimentary of others' playing. He encouraged isolationism among his followers; strict constructionists of Rascherism still prevail at the State University of New York at Fredonia, Syracuse University, the University of Louisville, and Florida State, where students are strongly encouraged to play the proper equipment. His love-hate relationship with the horn was apparent in his many writings. He referred to popular saxophone tone as "vulgar" and "obtrusive," and prudishly lamented the "temptation" of jazz and R&B players to "give expression to and stimulate certain emotions which should better be kept in the background." "The saxophone," he warned, "can exalt in sheer beauty or wallow in profanity. It is an instrument that calls for decisions of musical conscience and moral judgment."

In 1981, four years after he played his last recital, Rascher asked John-Edward Kelly to take his place in the famed Rascher Quartet, which is today led by Rascher's daughter, Carina. John-Edward moved to Germany, where the other members lived, and performed with the ensemble for ten years before striking out on his own as a soloist. "A lot of people have called me a clone of Rascher," he says. "They've obviously never heard my playing; I don't play like my teacher. The one thing we do share is the attitude that the changes that have been made to the saxophone acoustically have been extremely detrimental and that the instrument that has been put on the market since the 1940s is in the strictest sense no saxophone at all."

The changes in the shape of the bore and the proportions of the mouthpiece have amounted to a bastardization of the instrument, he says. (Some might say a bastardization of a bastardization.) "On the original-style saxophone, the fundamental relationships of the overtones remain the same," says John-Edward, who plays a Buescher Aristocrat built in 1928 that closely resembles Adolphe's original design. "The fundamental color does not change between pianissimo and fortissimo. But the harder you blow into a modern mouthpiece, the more you stress the higher partials in the overtone series, for the simple reason that the mouthpiece, the inside of which is smaller than the beginning of the bore, offers no inherent resistance."

Acoustical resistance is a fundamental component of every traditional instrument—whether the tension of a violin string or the tautness of a drum skin, which resists prolonged vibration. In conical wind instruments such as the saxophone, resistance must be produced before the cone begins because the cone can offer none itself.

(Think of a garden hose attached to the small end of a funnel. You could never fill the large end with water, because its conical shape produces no resistance, allowing the water to flow through unimpeded.) Resistance in a saxophone is produced in the mouthpiece, whose inner dimensions are significantly larger in diameter than the beginning of the instrument's bore, John-Edward explains. The compression of the airstream helps balance the overtones of the saxophone. The alterations made to the mouthpiece in the thirties and forties—its chamber was made roughly equal to the shape of the bore—corrupted the tone of the instrument, he says, making it incompatible with other instruments and discouraging conductors from including it in their orchestras. The change, undertaken to make the instrument louder, was the result of "a conspiracy of ignorance and poor taste." It seriously denigrated Adolphe Sax's original tonal conceptions and is "tantamount to a tragic catastrophe in the history of the saxophone."

John-Edward also shares with his mentor disdain for avant-garde (read: French) saxophone music. "I don't like squeaks, noises, and farts," he says, "so I try to avoid composers who write squeaks, noises, and farts. I'm not sure experimentation in composition has brought contemporary music anywhere. In fact, it's accomplished the opposite; it's made it a more isolated domain within music. My personal conviction is that if it doesn't sing and in some way dance, it isn't music."

A self-proclaimed "outcast in the saxophone community," John-Edward, like his mentor, is not shy about discussing the corruption not only of the instrument but of its players. "The saxophone has justifiably been vilified in the symphonic setting," he says. "I have many friends who are conductors, and they often complain that they dread any kind of piece with a saxophone in the orchestra, because most players have no culture in their tonal development, a limited ability to play in tune, and don't blend with other groups in the orchestra. Saxophonists for the most part have done an extremely bad job in becoming musicians."

Part of that has to do with what Rascher might call players' lack of "moral judgment." "When you have that kind of flexibility and huge dynamic range in an instrument, it's just like freedom in society. Freedom without discipline does not work. If you have no self-control in your playing, it's worthless."

With his refined views, John-Edward has found teaching to be frustrating. "One boy came to a master class of mine and he did not know how to phrase, how to make the form of the composition become part of the musical experience for himself or how to convey such an experience to a listener. I asked what works he knew of. Brahms? 'No.' Schubert? 'Who?' This is a saxophone player with an advanced degree. Saxophone players tend to look to other saxophone players for inspiration or some kind of standard, which is a horrendous mistake. When one plays, you want to hear the history of the Western canon, not the history of saxophone players."

Since Adolphe Sax's was a fiery personality, John-Edward is not surprised that the contentious voice of Sax should continue to rile the classical world. "But one quality of his has generally not been reflected in the saxophone-playing community," he adds. "Sax was a man of very great character. Unfortunately, we've seen too many saxophonists who have been too ready to compromise in that area; I'm not sure he'd be happy about it. And I'm convinced he would absolutely hate the modern saxophone and much of the modern music played on it. He was a very cultured man."

If John-Edward Kelly is the latter-day embodiment of Sigurd Rascher's ideology, Claude Delangle might fairly be described as an updated personification of Marcel Mule's. He has clearly adopted the gentle manner of the man known to his students as *le Maître*. When I was in Paris, he invited me to sit in on a performance-critique session he would be conducting with six of the twelve fortunate students selected from regional conservatories to study with him at the Paris Conservatory of Music. In a large studio on the second floor of the conservatory, Claude, a thin wisp of a man with bright blue eyes, a fashionably decadent week's worth of whiskers, and a thatch of sandy hair, listened intently as each student, all established players in orchestras or other professional ensembles, performed before him. Reading from notes he had scribbled on the score, Claude would offer a detailed analysis, balancing measured praise with critical insight, his students hanging on his every word. He would flip back through the score and have the student replay certain passages, sometimes singing along with him or her. Occasionally, but not often, he would reach for his own new Selmer alto and play just enough to demonstrate his point.

There was reason for his restraint. As good as his students were, a single note from Claude's horn instantly pointed up the difference between a star and a mere professional. Like John-Edward Kelly, he is one of a small cadre of internationally known saxophone soloists, and is particularly revered among American academics. As a student at the Paris Conservatory in the late seventies he won several first prizes for both solo and chamber music performances. He became a full professor at a regional conservatory in 1982, and by 1986 was being recruited by Pierre Boulez, among other well-known conductors, as a soloist. As one might expect of a pedagogical descendant of the master, Marcel Mule, he has recorded all of the pieces from the standard saxophone canon, if only so that he will never have to play them again. More significantly, he has worked with modern composers such as Luciano Berio, Philippe Hurel, Gerard Grisey, and Michael Levinas to create sophisticated new works. His latest venture, he tells me, has involved working with Chinese and Japanese composers to bring the saxophone into traditional Asian music.

Claude, who now has the job once held by Marcel Mule, met *le Maître* in 1967. Claude was ten at the time, and Mule was about to retire from his position as professor of saxophone. Tall and kindly, Mule was jurying the recital at which Claude was performing. "My dear boy," Mule said to Claude, who had been playing the saxophone for a year. "You have a beautiful tone quality!" Years later, in 1978, Claude took a few lessons from him. "He would focus on pitch and some elements of technique, but mostly he was a motivator," says Claude. "I think the greatest effect he had on his students was psychological. He offered encouragement and support. He was a very nice man."

Claude is only the fourth professor of saxophone at the Paris Conservatory, the mecca of the academic saxophone. In 1988 he succeeded his mentor, the late Daniel Deffayet, who held the job for twenty years after Mule retired. (Mule was appointed to the position in 1942, ending a seventy-two-year hiatus that began when the chair, held by Adolphe Sax, was eliminated because of financial constraints.) Like Mule, who began playing at age seven and was soon performing in a small-town band in Normandy, Claude discovered an almost instant affinity for the saxophone.

"It was very strange," he says as we lunch at a bistro not far from the conservatory. "I didn't choose the saxophone. I knew I wanted to play a wind instrument, and I didn't think it mattered which one. When I was a young boy, my father brought me to the *conservatoire* to try different instruments. In five minutes I chose the saxophone because of the shape and the sound. Or it chose me. Something entered me like a virus and I knew I wanted to do it for life."

As a child learning to play the instrument, Claude listened to all of Marcel Mule's recordings and studied the method books he wrote—no small task, as Mule designed many complex études for his students. Early in his career, while a member of the Republican Guard's wind ensemble, Mule formed a quartet; to make up for the lack of music, he had more than a hundred classical pieces transcribed. Over the course of his long career, hundreds of compositions for saxophone were dedicated to him, many of which he never got around to playing. Among the more notable was Heitor Villa-Lobos's estimable *Fantasia*, which was written (in 1948) for soprano saxophone, strings, and three horns. Upon his retirement from performing in 1958, Mule was made a Knight of the Legion of Honor, the highest distinction that can be awarded to a French citizen, for his efforts in advancing the classical saxophone.

But like his rival, Sigurd Rascher (whose recordings and method books were available just about everywhere but France), Mule was stubborn—a mule. Whereas Rascher disdained modern equipment, Mule refused to acknowledge the worth and viability of modern composition and advanced playing techniques. He loathed alternative modes or styles of playing that produced variations in timbre and tone. In the seventies, when French avant-garde composers associated with the conservatory in Bordeaux began focusing their far-out ideas on the saxophone, Mule was not shy about expressing his disdain. "Modern" music, he said, could be appreciated only by those who were "sick in mind." One of the compelling ironies of his and Rascher's lives is that, as hard as each worked to advance the classical saxophone, together they presented a formidable obstacle to its finding its natural place in new music.

As perhaps the most influential saxophone educator and performer in France, Claude Delangle feels obligated to "kill any bad talk about others in class." But Rascher's problem, he doesn't mind telling me, had little to do with music. "It was psychological," he says. "He considered himself too much like the absolute leader. It was difficult for him to allow that other people could do things differently and that they might be interesting. But perhaps Mule was like that, too."

Interestingly, a rivalry not unlike that between the two dead masters has been playing out within the cloistered world of saxophone pedagogy in France for the past thirty years. In 1970, Jean-Marie Londeix, the esteemed recitalist and then head of the saxophone class at the Bordeaux Conservatory, announced that he would henceforth play only music that was newly commissioned for the saxophone. His repudiation of the old saxophone canon helped establish the Bordeaux program as the home of experimental music, pitting it against the more conservative, Mule-influenced Paris school. Until they died, both Mule and his successor, Daniel Deffayet, sparred repeatedly with the feisty Londeix over the future of the French repertoire.

Today, Claude says of the ideological arguments, "that little world still exists, but people are meeting and working together and exchanging ideas." Still, in deference to his mentors, he is aware that he has an almost historical obligation to disapprove of the upstart Bordelais school of modern composition. Ironically, this puts him in league with his "German" counterpart, John-Edward Kelly, who also disapproves of "music without melody." In fact, when Kelly and the Rascher Quartet once performed in Paris, Claude went backstage after the concert to introduce himself in hopes of discussing the future of the neoclassical saxophone. But it seemed as if the spirits of their stubborn old mentors, perhaps goaded by the ghost of Adolphe Sax, would not allow the rapprochement.

"He refused to shake my hand," Claude says. "He said we have nothing to talk about."

13. INSTRUMENT OF THE FUTURE

In 1944, Vincent "Jimmy" Abato was twenty-five and had recently been named principal clarinetist with the New York Philharmonic. He was also a closet saxophonist accustomed to playing in jazz joints after his concert hall gigs to pick up a little extra money. It was an arrangement he was very happy with, wearing his tuxedo in one venue and a porkpie hat in the other. "But I was a classical guy in my heart," Jimmy, who lives in Florida, tells me during a trip to New York to visit his daughter. "How many times can I play 'I'm Getting Sentimental Over You'?"

Jimmy, one of the first American saxophonists to develop a viable career playing classical music, had been wrapping his lips around one mouthpiece or another since he was seven years old, when his older brother, just home from a stint in the National Guard, gave him a clarinet. Two years later he was enrolled at the Peabody Conservatory, not far from his home in Baltimore. At thirteen, he was playing saxophone in a speakeasy up the street. "My brother bought a Martin saxophone from a pawnshop and gave it to me," he says in a rapid, staccato delivery reminiscent of a tough-talking James Cagney. "It was right after Roosevelt repealed Prohibition, and every nook and corner had a saloon. I didn't go too far in school because I was playing every night. I'd fall asleep in class. So I dropped out of high school."

Despite his lack of a degree, he was given a scholarship to the Juilliard School of Music because of his prodigious talent on the clarinet. In no time at all, he was earning two dollars a night playing saxophone at the Fordham Swing Club. "But at Juilliard, the saxophone was taboo," says Jimmy. "When my professor learned I was playing saxophone he said, 'Don't you ever mention that instrument in this class or I'll take that scholarship away from you.'"

After graduating from Juilliard, Jimmy played with the Glenn Miller band for six months before joining Paul Whiteman's orchestra, playing clarinet for both ensembles. When his wife became pregnant, they moved back to Baltimore, where he auditioned for and won a chair in the local symphony. By supplementing his monthly legit concerts with nightclub work, he made a decent living. Then, when the clarinetist for the CBS symphony orchestra in New York was killed in a car crash, the conductor, Howard Barlow, sent for Jimmy. "I had a New York union card," says Jimmy, a fireplug of a man not much over five feet tall whose eyesight has been sadly diminished by macular degeneration. "Suddenly I was making $300 a week."

And not long after that, he joined the New York Philharmonic. "And this is where the saxophone comes in big-time," says Jimmy. "There was an American composer named Paul Creston, and he loved the saxophone. The Philharmonic agreed to premiere his saxophone concerto, and they engaged a French saxophonist named Marcel Mule. He was fair, although he had a vibrato you could drive a truck through. Well, this bogus report comes over the radio that Mule was killed in the war. Creston's concerto was already on the schedule. They panicked. They called me in, I was a young kid, I'd never played a concert saxophone solo in my life, and they said,

'Abato, look, we got this thing scheduled.' I said, 'What are you people? Nuts?'

"Talk about getting nervous. On the afternoon of the performance, the conductor gets sick, so a new guy comes in. This was my first performance as a saxophone soloist in a major orchestra in a major work and I swear to God, I wished Hitler would drop a bomb on that place so I wouldn't have to go onstage.

"But that launched my career. I guess I did all right. After that, the clarinet was second."

One reason Jimmy Abato went on to have a successful career as a concert saxophonist was that he was principally a clarinetist—and a clarinetist, unlike a saxophonist, was able to find a permanent position in an orchestra. Historically, if a part came along for a saxophone, a clarinet or flute player was asked to handle it, whether he knew how to play the saxophone or not. Jimmy's versatility encouraged orchestra managers to include pieces for the saxophone because he was an exceptional performer. But along with Mule, Rascher, and a few others, he was a rarity—although, like them, he tried to become part of the solution. For many years, he gave private lessons to elite students in a music studio on Forty-eighth Street in New York.*

The lean talent, says Tim McAllister, a professor of saxophone at the Crane School of Music, State University of New York at Pots-

---

*Charlie Parker often rented a studio next to Jimmy's. "The studios weren't soundproof, and I could hear him practicing and then stop when I'd talk to a student," Jimmy says. "I used to talk about intonation, the blend of colors in your sound, control. The sound of a saxophone is all about control. One day I hear a knock on the door. He says, 'Mr. Abato, do you mind if I sit in on your lesson?' I said, 'Come on in.' After it was over, we went to a place called Jim and Andy's, a hangout for musicians where they could get food and a highball. We were sitting at the end of the bar, talking, and all of a sudden he started to cry, tears running out of his eyes. He says, 'You know, I must have hurt a lot of young saxophone players.' I say, 'What are you talking about, you're the god of this thing.' He says, 'No, I never liked the way I sounded, and I'm sure kids all over who listen to my recordings think this is the way the saxophone should sound.' He liked what he was doing, but didn't like his sound, and he felt like he'd badly influenced a whole generation of saxophone players."

dam, partially accounted for the lean repertoire. Even the finest compositions could not take full advantage of the saxophone's unique characteristics. "Composers were reluctant to include saxophone parts because they couldn't be guaranteed that they would be played well," says Tim. "And when they did include a part, they had to make sure it could be played by another instrument in case they couldn't find a capable saxophonist." Some composers took more drastic measures. Ingolf Dahl's Saxophone Concerto, which premiered in 1949 and was considered a major addition to the saxophone repertoire, drew extensively upon the altissimo range, but because few performers were capable of reaching that far, he eventually struck those passages from the score or included alternate passages in a lower register.

Yet even today, with an extraordinary number of talented saxophonists available, players of other woodwind instruments are still often asked to handle any parts for saxophone, however rarely they're included, in the orchestral setting. "It's really bizarre that we have this level of playing that's exceedingly high but the orchestra is still revolving around poor playing," says Tim, who happens to be one of those exceptionally gifted saxophonists he's referring to. "It's a modern-day reflection of what was going on a hundred years ago."

Tim, in New York to perform with the PRISM Quartet, for which he plays soprano saxophone, is one of America's bright young stars both in teaching and in performing. Since graduating from the University of Michigan as the first saxophonist to win the School of Music's highest performance award, he has stretched out in a number of recordings, ranging from early conventional repertoire to challenging art music from avant-garde composers such as France's Christian Lauba and the Americans Elliott Carter and Milton Babbitt. He is also a learned historian of the instrument.

Old prejudices against the saxophone die hard, says Tim as he catches a quick meal at a Thai restaurant before his PRISM concert. After the turn of the twentieth century, through the efforts of Elise Boyer Hall and others, the instrument was close to establishing a permanent spot for itself in the orchestra. A number of Russian, English, and German composers were premiering pieces featuring the saxophone. "Into the 1920s," says Tim, "you see the saxophone appear a lot in true concert-orchestral music. It was beginning to add so much; when it comes in, it completely changes the timbre and sound. European orchestras had no difficulty accommodating these changes. But by the late twenties, the American Symphony Orchestra League decided it had had enough: it basically banned the use of saxophone in standard instrumentation. There was a coup to stop its infiltration."

The banishment was designed to "protect high culture," says Tim. "The amateur movement, with all of its self-taught musicians, had produced widespread poor playing. Plus, the saxophone had all those bad associations and low-life connotations. Even in *L'Arlesienne* suites, the most distinctive early work that includes the saxophone, it represents the commoner, the music from the streets."

The lack of formal saxophone instruction available to serious students reinforced its image as a lowbrow instrument. A handful of music schools taught the saxophone before 1900; as its popularity exploded in the following decades, and as the band movement spread throughout schools across the country, many conservatories and academies added programs—the Chicago Musical College in 1919, the Philadelphia Musical Academy in 1924, the Wisconsin Conservatory in 1926. The University of Southern California started teaching the instrument in 1934, the University of Iowa in 1935. By 1940, fifty-three music schools included saxophone instruction. But nearly all of the instructors, from primary schools to conservatories, were performers, most of them self-taught. (In 1920, there were more than 120 different method books for saxophone.) They often knew more about "dirt choruses" and "blue notes" than they did about proper embouchure. Even Larry Teal, founder of the country's first doctoral program in saxophone, received a total of only five weeks of instruction on the horn.

The instrument's association with dirty dancing and jazz, the devil's music, didn't help, either. In 1924, *The Etude*, a popular music teachers' magazine, published a series of essays by American composers on the new music. In one, Henry F. Gilbert described how the saxophone had been "exploited" by jazz. "This has been done in a way to make the angels weep (with laughter)," he wrote. "Originally an instrument having a richly pathetic and lyrical tone quality, it has been made to perform all sorts of ridiculous stunts, amounting to an indecent exposure of all of its worst qualities. It is as if a grave and dignified person were forced to play the part of a clown at the circus."

Sadly, some of its own performers also felt compelled to disparage the instrument. Clay Smith, the high falutin Chautauqua circuit player and columnist, had famously referred to saxophonists who played anything other than "dignified" music as "human hangnails." In *The Art of Saxophone Playing*, America's first saxophone professor, Larry Teal, noted the "great deal of disdain held for the instrument, much of which is justified." The standard of playing, he maintained in his 1963 introduction, was not yet high enough to guarantee a conductor a competent performance. The composer Walter Piston, who played saxophone in the United States Navy Band after World War I, complained in his book on music theory, *Orchestration*, that the saxophone had become "tremulous, oversweet, sentimental and is almost invariably played out of tune" and "cannot be used successfully in instrumental combinations." Sigurd Rascher, as many of his students know, regularly echoed Teal's lament, and his protégé, John-Edward Kelly, has kept the negative undercurrent flowing.

As college-level saxophone instruction in America expanded in the 1950s and 1960s, the number of competent "legit" players multiplied every year. Yet the exclusionary policy of orchestra managers and conductors, whether encoded or passively de facto, remained in effect. Teachers began encouraging saxophone students not only to learn to play all the saxophones competently but to double on other woodwinds, such as clarinet or oboe, as well. "It was the only path to a job," Tim says.

Today, says Tim, legit saxophonists no longer aspire to joining the symphonic orchestra. The concert saxophone simply has too much of its own original music to play, and its composers and players are the ones doing the hiring and booking the halls and theaters. The oft-cited strategic departure came when Jean-Marie Londeix boldly announced in 1970, after premiering Edison Denisov's demanding *Sonate*, that he would play only new music written specifically for saxophone. But Tim maintains that the real road to modernism for the concert saxophone began in America—although Londeix was still the first important player to step onto the path. At a time when Pharoah Sanders, Albert Ayler, John Coltrane, and Ornette Coleman were searching for new sounds in jazz music, "legit" players had also been dabbling in experimentation, primarily in the horn's upper register.

"American educators contributed a lot to this turning point. In 1966, Londeix made a trip to Interlochen," says Tim, referring to the famed music school and camp in Michigan, originally founded by the C. G. Conn Company, to which many of the country's top students and educators flock each summer. "He and Don Sinta met for the first time and would stay up all night listening to recordings. Sinta's role models were Freddy Gardner, H. Benne Henton, and Al Gallodoro; all of these guys were playing up in the altissimo range very naturally. The French were aware of that register, but put a cap on it. They told composers that they went to F-sharp and that was it. If the composers wanted anything above, that they'd have to write *fortissimo* and give them a chance to blow and push so the note will speak.

"Sinta told Londeix that to play altissimo, it was important to play soft, beautiful, vibrato, to make a sound like a voice or stringed instrument. Londeix said that was impossible. They stayed up all night and Sinta taught him, up to double C-sharp. A few years later, Londeix premieres the Denisov sonata, which goes up to double C-sharp and has multiphonics, and plays it again at the 1970 World Saxophone Congress. He completely steals that thunder. Afterwards he announces that he will play nothing that's old and his announcement redefines everything in the concert saxophone world. At that point, the entire body of literature began to change. Whereas the older stuff could be played on any instrument, the new saxophone music could not be replicated by others.

"But it was really a reflection of what had been going on in America in the late fifties and sixties. There were some interesting things being written for the concert saxophone, but not that many people knew of them. And that literature has just exploded ever since."

Later that night, Tim and the other members of the PRISM Quartet play a small sampling of that new literature in a program that features all British composers, most of whom are in their early thirties. The compositions are quirky, challenging, and often fun. One piece in particular, "Selected Movements of Great Masters" by Michael Finnissy, illustrates the freedom the horn now enjoys. Melding exercises in harmony composed by the late Paul Steinitz, an English conductor and expert in the music of J. S. Bach, with the simulated enactment of nursery rhymes and the bawdy humor of Shakespeare, the piece is as much theater as it is musical performance. With each quartet member representing a different "great master," the performers engage in a number of harmonic conversations with each other, frequently interrupting their playing to scratch their heads or blow their noses or mime other ordinary gestures. The composition, cheerfully defiant of the convention and formality of concert and chamber music, allows the saxophone to enjoy the freedom it has in every other idiom it has penetrated and conquered and to reveal, even in the "classical" format, its true rebel nature.

Frederick L. Hemke, now the dean of saxophone education in America, has been waiting almost fifty years for the symphony orchestra and its audiences to embrace the saxophone, and he believes that the moment has almost arrived. But it won't be because orchestra managers and conductors suddenly find a role for the instrument in their presentations of classical music. It will be because those programs finally catch up to the saxophone's lively and progressive repertoire.

"We're going to see a tremendous transition in the next few years," Fred explains as he swivels in a chair in his office at Northwestern University, his oval white beard glistening in the sunlight pouring through a window that looks out on Lake Michigan. "Most of the symphony orchestras are in trouble because they've been getting their financial support from old-timers who want to hear old music played on dead instruments. Now the old-timers are dying off, and the affluent baby boomers who are replacing them want something different. They've been exposed to new music in college and elsewhere, and that's what they're going to want to hear. If the orchestra managers want their money, they're going to have to give them new music. And more music is being written for the saxophone than for any other instrument."

Not that he's entirely dismissive of the old music. He has played, at one time or another, almost every major piece in the conventional saxophone canon. His recordings with the Chicago Symphony Orchestra include *The Age of Gold* by Shostakovich, Ravel's *Bolero*, and works by Rachmaninoff. "But those chestnuts are over and done," he says. "If we stick with the Ibert *Concertino*, which is beautiful, for the rest of our lives, we too will die just like the dead instruments of the symphony orchestra."

Since he began teaching at Northwestern in 1961 (he received a permanent appointment in 1964), Fred has guided about a thousand saxophonists through the university's elite music program. Hundreds of them have gone on to teach at universities and colleges—"Even cupcake universities have a saxophone program today," he says—and now many of *their* students are also teaching. His protégés span the idiomatic spectrum, from David Sanborn in pop, to Ron Blake in jazz, to Harvey Pittel and John Sampen in classical. His own mentor was Marcel Mule.

In his nearly half century at Northwestern, Fred has witnessed a remarkable surge in the quality of playing among his students. He can document that progress by using his own performance career as a standard. During his junior year at the University of Wisconsin, he went to France to study with Mule and became the first American to win the Premier Prix de Saxophone at the Paris Conservatory. Not long after he returned, he was asked to play a new concerto by the composer Lars-Erik Larsson that reached high into the altissimo range. "It scared the crap out of me," he says. "So I worked hard to learn how to play altissimo. Well, today, kids coming out of high school can do this—as well as play a whole range of multiphonics. It's standard operating procedure."

After graduating from his program, most of Fred's students go into performance. Most are capable of executing any piece—from the work of French spectralists to a concerto by Saint-Saëns. Some have found satisfying careers in military bands. Many end up supporting their gigs with a teaching job. Many get jobs in concert bands. "In the band world, the saxophone is so accepted you can play almost any kind of literature," Fred says.

Because the saxophone is a forward-looking instrument constantly in search of new modes of expression, academics can never get too comfortable, says Fred. They, too, must be able to master new techniques—"and some of this stuff is hard on an old man." Over the past few years, Fred has created an entirely new category for saxophone literature. "My thing is now saxophone and pipe organs," he says. "I search out great pipe organs in churches around the world. The two instruments are marvelously compatible and people love the sound."

The dynamic range of the saxophone is so broad, there are so many new notes and extensions to discover that "it behooves us as educators," Fred says, "to reach a little further all the time. Modern composers love to see what can be done on this instrument. When you show them something new, the next thing you know, you have a piece filled with that new sound.

"If we limit our re-creations to the old stuff, then we'll be no better off than the symphony orchestras that have become museum pieces. The saxophone may have been invented way back in the nineteenth century, but it's still a new instrument. It's still the instrument of the future."

In 1957, when he wrote *All Set* for alto and tenor sax, trumpet, trombone, bass, vibes, piano, and drums, Milton Babbitt felt he was writing for the instrument of the future. A mathematician turned composer, Milton was known for introducing mathematical terms and ideas to the theories of serial, or twelve-note, composition deployed by composers such as Webern and Schoenberg, whose writing has provided him with a lifetime of inspiration. "I had an uncle who played Schoenberg for me when I was ten," he says, "and I've never stopped trying to find out what the hell was going on."

Although the coupling of higher math and the saxophone, the people's instrument, may seem an odd one, it seemed natural to Milton, who won a lifetime Pulitzer Prize in 1982 for his contributions to twelve-tone music. Born in Philadelphia in 1916, he grew up in Jackson, Mississippi, where he played alto and soprano saxophone in dance and jazz bands.

"I started playing when I was eight," he says from his home in Princeton, New Jersey, late one night. He is approaching his tenth decade and doesn't sleep much, and he'd asked that I call him after midnight. "Socially it was the instrument to play," he says, his voice deep and animated. "I picked up money for anything, from country-club dances to pig-stand bands—they were drive-ins that served barbecued pork and had entertainment on Sunday afternoons. When I was fifteen, I went to college. To the pretentious people who conducted orchestras there, the saxophone was a poor sister. So I put it aside."

Years later, with his snooty professors in mind, Milton decided to include an alto and a tenor saxophone in *All Set*. He had always admired sax players' musicality, which in many cases he credited to their lack of training. "Saxophone players were often the real intellectuals of the band—they would get very excited about a new opera they'd heard, for instance—but at the same time some were almost musical illiterates," he says. "They could hardly read music. But they were extraordinary musicians. They could pick up anything by ear."

Milton likes to think *All Set* was an early contributor to the kind of repertoire Jean-Marie Londeix declared the saxophone should have—modernistic, challenging, conceptual music that can't be played on any other instrument. But although it's a high-concept piece, he is loath to have it linked with what he thinks of as avant-garde saxophone music. "That's French conservatory music," says Milton, who still teaches a composition class at Juilliard.

Then, threatening to kick off a new chapter in the concert-saxophone culture war, he adds, "It used to be that études were what came out of the conservatory. Now it's absolutely vacuous virtuoso pieces."

Tonight, following my lesson with Michel, my band assembles for its weekly jam. As a low-technique, highly physical drummer, I've managed occasionally to work myself into a dervish-like altered state, perhaps something like what the febrile tarantella dancers experienced when they twirled their way across Europe in the Middle Ages. Captured by the steady drone of a new beat, my mind kicks way back, like a computer shifting into sleep mode. I play effortlessly—perhaps the way I would if I'd ever learned to play properly—almost unconsciously. Oddly, when I'm caught up in one of these fugues my body often torques to the left until I'm looking behind me and I'm flooded with a blood-warming sensation I can only describe as pure joy. And then it's over, usually in less than ten seconds, because I start to fall off the drum throne—literally— or my ever-vigilant cerebral cortex jars me back to awareness. It's as though I've glimpsed the perfection behind the blinding electric godhead and the limited tolerances of my merely human neural network trip the circuit breakers in my brainpan before I fry myself completely.

Then again, maybe there's something wrong with me, like that Russian singer who could induce an epileptic seizure simply by listening to the aria of Zaren Berendej in Rimsky-Korsakov's Snow Maiden.

For the past half hour now, I've been playing the saxophone, and I can't believe how lucky I am. Here I am—blowing the hell out of my fabulous Super Balanced Action as my pals allow me to lead them into strange sonic territory that could be pioneered only by someone unburdened by much technique or knowledge of music theory. Backed by a drum machine, Craig on guitar, and Dan on bass, Ortley and I put the bells of our horns together and blow. Ortley happily accedes to the common denominator of our pooled talent, which my contribution lowers considerably, and generously plays around me, supporting my efforts with little harmonic filigrees as I search for interesting intervals on the E blues scale that Michel has just taught me.

And tonight something special is happening. I've been hitting strings of lucky notes all evening and have now found a gorgeous little melody that Ortley quickly picks up and harmonizes with. It's a mournful little run through the money notes—all of the sharps—of the C-sharp minor scale in the second octave. I've learned how to modify the pitch of my instrument by adjusting my embouchure so that we're perfectly in tune. We chorus over and over as the rhythm section—the drum machine and Dan's bass—grinds behind us. The big tenor, which my fingers have struggled to support and play at once, loses its heft, fairly floats in my hands, and the beautiful sound I'm contributing to this duet now issues from deep in my belly. It's that oneness feeling I had when I first picked it up, a feeling I've been unable to recapture with the same intensity until now. I'm singing through this crazy brass medium just the way I've read about, the harmonics are perfect, and it's utterly glorious. That familiar warm flush creeps over me, the godhead winking a dazzle of light, jazzing every endorphin in my head. I ride out the high, knowing that I've experienced my last drumming ecstasy, which now seems so crude and primitive. The saxophone is now my path to the altered state.

Every day, this thing finds a way to strengthen its grip on me. It really is like being madly in love.

14. BODY AND SOUL

At a dinner party one night, I was blathering to the woman next to me about my saxo-centric view of the world when I noticed a tear fall down her cheek. She apologized, brushed it aside, and then told me a story about her father.

He was a gentleman, a classics professor at a prestigious southern college, loving father of four children, devoted to his much-adored wife. Not long after his fiftieth wedding anniversary, when he was in his mid-seventies, he began to show signs of forgetfulness. He couldn't remember where he put his keys, his wallet; he would get lost while driving to the office he had occupied for thirty-five years. He was sent to a neurologist, who gave him a simple test of cognitive skills and found that he had difficulty telling time and making change for a dollar. He was diagnosed with Alzheimer's disease.

Medications slowed the disease's progress, but over the next couple of years his faculties gradually abandoned him. The once-voluble professor could no longer speak, confined within a cocoon of fragmented thoughts and meaningless locutions. Occasionally he would gesture beseechingly, and his wife and children would try to guess what he wanted. Water? A candy? A walk in the garden?

One day, her father held out his hands to my dinner companion and she had an idea. She pulled an alto saxophone, itself silenced for the past twenty years, from a closet, rigged it up, and handed it to him. When he was younger he had played in a small community band, she remembered. His eyes seemed to sparkle when he saw the instrument. She strapped it around his neck and helped his fingers find the keys. He blew. His shallow breath wheezed through the horn. But he blew again and again until he eventually got his old saxophone to speak.

Within a couple of weeks, he was confined to his bed; his legs just gave out. But every night, for the last month of his life, his wife lay beside him and he would play her a simple lullaby on his saxophone, the tiny region of his brain inhabited by the voice of Sax still vital and whole.

Next to his heart, it was the last thing in this sweet man's life to go.

Adolphe Sax was convinced that playing a wind instrument was beneficial to one's health and could prevent, among other ailments and diseases, tuberculosis. In an article published in *Dwight's Journal of Music* in 1862 (which first appeared in *La France Musicale*) titled "How Wind Instruments Affect the Health," he wrote, "Persons who practice wind instruments are, in general, distinguished—and anybody can verify the statement—by a broad chest and shoulders, an unequivocal sign of vigor. In the traveling bands that pass through our cities, who has not seen women playing the horn, the cornet, the trumpet, and even the trombone and ophicleide, and noticed that they all enjoyed perfect health, and exhibited a considerable development of the thorax? In an orchestra a curious circumstance can be noticed, and that is the corpulence, the strength which the players of wind instruments exhibit, and the spare frames of the disciples of Paganini. The same may be said, with more reason, of pianists."

Of course, violinists and pianists had none of the messy hygienic issues that wind players had to manage. His feelings about the salubrious benefits of thoracic development notwithstanding, Sax was concerned that a much-played saxophone was also a perfect incubator for pathogens. Keenly aware of and interested in the revolutionary germ theory of disease being developed by Louis Pasteur in the mid-nineteenth century, he devised his own antidotes for horns that had been colonized by microbes. The inventor of the Goudronnier Sax, which infused households with an atomized antiseptic solution, also designed two different systems for keeping wind instruments sanitary. One schematic provided instruments with an inner double jacket that could be filled with antiseptics. The other called for lining the inside of saxophone tubes with substances that would sanitize the air, so that if the player inhaled through the horn he would be assured of a healthful breath.

Sax's concern about the saxophone's impact on a player's health is shared by some modern musicians. "I've discovered that we don't live as long as other players, the lifestyle notwithstanding," says John Handy. "Among my colleagues I've observed this myself. So I don't use all my energy blowing like I did. You wear yourself out—your lungs, muscles, lips, teeth.

"Many of us used to play rod-rubber mouthpieces until the Environmental Protection Agency outlawed them. And who knows what's in all these metals we're breathing through and what happens when they break down. One thing I never understood about the popularity of the C-Melody: the neck has a hump, and if you don't keep the horn angled downward, all the residue, the spit, comes spilling back into the mouthpiece. It's disgusting. It's got to be bad for you."

The horn can be harmful in other ways, too—at least according to John Purcell. When he was in his early twenties, John developed a tumor near his voice box called a laryngocele. Had it been allowed

to progress, the nonmalignant growth would have closed up his larynx and eventually suffocated him—the fate that also awaited
Adolphe Sax before he was cured by the mysterious Dr. Noir. Unlike
the father of the saxophone, John didn't seek alternative medical
treatment for his condition; he had an operation to remove the tumor. But his promising career as a musician was interrupted for
three long years, during which time he resolved to understand why
playing the saxophone had jeopardized his health.

He studied human anatomy, from both an Eastern and a Western
perspective, and acoustical science. As his knowledge grew, he began
to realize that just as every player's oral cavity and body are unique,
no two saxophones are exactly the same, and finding a compatible
match between body and horn can often seem impossible. Most
players understand this intuitively as they focus on finding the perfect mouthpiece. But John delved into the problem more deeply, en-
listing the help and support of Joel Harrison, the developer of the
disk hard drive and founder of Quantum Computer. John studied
the nature of sound, the porosity of metal, and the relationship between the two, particularly how they all affected the human body.

Although he has played in his own bands and assumed the seat
occupied by Julius Hemphill in the World Saxophone Quartet after
Hemphill died, for the past twenty years John has devoted most of
his working life to helping other musicians find an instrument that's
a comfortable fit. He has worked extensively with fellow WSQ
member David Murray, Wayne Shorter, and Michael Brecker, who
also needed an operation, to repair a blown-out larynx. Whenever
David Sanborn is in town, the two huddle for hours over Sanborn's
horns, as though fine-tuning race-car engines.

An early research exercise enlisted the drummer Jack DeJohnette,
who would play his cymbals while John played a variety of saxophones. "We found that certain instruments would just collapse,"
says John as he sips seltzer in my living room. "I'd blow into the instrument and it would close down. Some instruments couldn't handle the increased level of vibrations. I identified it as like taking a car

and pushing it into overdrive and having it rattle. Many times a saxophonist will take an instrument or mouthpiece or reed that is overpowering the metal in front of it and the same thing will happen."

John has since developed formulas to identify an instrument whose "response factor" fits a particular player. Two important variables are the playing style of the musician and the vibratory action of an instrument's metal. "If you have a low-velocity player—*velocity* referring to air speed and pressure—like Lee Konitz, Joe Henderson, or Johnny Hodges, you need an instrument that vibrates quickly," John says. "A high-velocity player like Coltrane, Sonny Rollins, and Mike Brecker needs something that vibrates more slowly. The co-relationship is baseball: the faster the pitcher, the thicker the catcher's glove."

Many musicians have sensed the importance of these relationships even if they haven't understood them. "Stan Getz said if he didn't feel the F vibrating in his fingers, he couldn't play," John says. "When Joe Henderson's instrument was stolen he almost gave up playing because he couldn't find another that was compatible." In 1966, John Coltrane stopped playing for several months after making minor alterations to his favorite mouthpiece and ruining it. Every time he tried to play, he said, he felt "discouraged."

The mouthpiece, John says, is just a "mirror image of the mouth, reversing what we have naturally." The two must conform in shape and size to each other. "If you have long teeth, you should play a mouthpiece with a small opening and vice versa," he says. "It all relates to the back of the throat. If you have long teeth and a mouthpiece with a large opening, you're stretching the back of your throat too much and asking for trouble. A lot of players have this fallacy that a big mouthpiece and a hard reed will produce a big sound. Meanwhile, they struggle."

When a player blows into a saxophone, he sets off a continual process of vibratory call and response between him and the hunk of metal in his hands, John says. The "kickback" travels back through the cranium into the inner ear, which determines whether the sound is flat or sharp, enabling the player to make the minor adjustments in embouchure to bring the horn into tune. But the kickback also travels through the rest of the body. "And because the body is already vibrating from the simple act of breathing and being alive, you have these two vibrating entities that need to be connected. When they're out of phase, it's like a differential tone is produced and you stress the body."

His research, John says, has enabled him to identify specific ailments and how they relate to the horn. "If you have a problem in your throat, the resistance is farther up in the instrument," he says. "If it's in your back, it's farther down the instrument. If you have a problem in your liver, there's kickback in your right hand. Heart problems, respiratory, kidney, groin, ankles, and knees—all can be traced to a problem with a specific part of the instrument.

"If you don't know what you're doing, playing the saxophone can be dangerous to your health."

It may also be dangerous to your psyche. In a monograph titled "Jazz and Aggression," which appeared in *Psychiatric Communications* in 1958, Miles D. Miller, M.D., articulated what he described as the "repressed hostile and aggressive impulses" in horn players. He cited Freudian dream symbolism in suggesting that the playing of a wind instrument "can be an unconscious symbol of masturbatory movements and is closely associated with auto-erotic stimulation." When he plays his horn, Miller says, a musician can experience the same aggressive pleasure an infant does in spitting and sticking out its tongue, both expressions of disgust or disapproval. "In a subliminal way he is literally spitting through his horn and 'spraying' the notes over the crowd. Instead of becoming incensed at the effrontery of his aggression, the audience seems to gain some of these same pleasures through unconscious identification with the musician in the same manner that they identify with the aggressor in any other conflict." In discussing technique, he maintains that the smearing or bending of notes unconsciously refers to "anality and sphincter control." When a musician stoops or raises a leg as he strains for a note, Miller claims he is actually indulging in "anal sadistic aggression." Who knew that the simple pleasures of music could be so violent and hateful?

Although a fair amount of research has been done on medical issues relating to musicians, few researchers have limited their focus to the saxophone. A review of the medical literature turns up few citations: one paper describes an orthodontic device designed to ease pain in saxophonists who experience embouchure and lip irritation; another is a case study of a student who experienced severe headaches while playing the saxophone.

Hoping to bring the literature up to date, two music researchers, Michael Thrasher of North Central Texas College and Kris S. Chesky of the University of North Texas, initiated the UNT Musicians Health Survey, which has obtained information from thousands of musicians around the world. Their early findings, obtained from a random sample of eighty-two saxophonists, turned up significant differences in the incidence of problems suffered by classical and nonclassical saxophonists.

Of the eighty-two respondents, sixty-two of whom were male, twenty-nine described themselves as primarily classical performers. Their average age, twenty-nine, was almost four years younger than the average age of the nonclassical musicians, who also had less formal music instruction and professional experience than their counterparts. The study found that, in all cases, classical performers reported more problems related to the neck, right wrist, right upper back, and right and left fingers. More than half of classical performers suffered from depression, and a third from acute anxiety, compared with 30 percent and 25 percent of nonclassical players, respectively. Blackouts and dizziness were reported by 38 percent of classical musicians, weight problems by 35 percent, and mouth lesions by 38 percent, compared with their counterparts, whose numbers totaled 15 percent, 24 percent, and 11 percent, respectively.

Still, judging by information presented in a brief monograph by Frank Patalano, a psychologist at St. John's University in New York, the classical players can expect to live longer than the mainstream performers. Patalano, after studying the biographies of Coleman Hawkins, Lester Young, Dexter Gordon, and Stan Getz, suggests that high psychosocial stress may have contributed to the saxophonists' shortened lives. The main stressors, he says, were "severe substance abuse, haphazard working conditions, lack of acceptance of jazz as an art form in the United States, marital and family discord, and the vagabond lifestyle that most jazz musicians lived." He then compares the mean ages at death of 168 jazz musicians rated as "legendary," including ten women, with one hundred renowned classical musicians who were their contemporaries. Unsurprisingly, the legends lived for an average of fifty-seven years while the longhairs held on until they were seventy-three, on average.

Nearly 140 years after Adolphe Sax first raised the issue, the question of saxophonists' longevity was broached again in December 1999 when the *British Medical Journal*, an esteemed peer-reviewed publisher of scientific research, printed a "short report" titled "Unsafe Sax: Cohort Study of the Impact of Too Much Sax on the Mortality of Famous Jazz Musicians." After examining data pertaining to the lives of 813 musicians born between 1882 and 1974, the authors, Sanjay Kinra and Mona Okasha, both public health specialists, found that saxophonists had a higher risk of dying prematurely than other musicians. To a smaller extent, they also found that players of woodwind instruments in general and being an American carried a higher risk of earlier mortality. Saxophonists who led their own bands, they determined, lived less hazardous lives than journeyman saxophonists, although they still had a higher mortality risk than other musicians.

The report identified a "plausible" biological explanation for saxophonists' diminished life span: circular breathing. Increased pressure in the neck, they said, can reduce blood supply to the brain, causing a stroke or brain embolism.

The *BMJ* paper produced a flood of letters from worried saxophonists. A saxophone-playing molecular biologist pointed out that other musicians, such as trumpet and trombone players, also use the circular breathing technique but do not show the pronounced high death risk of saxophonists. As did John Handy, he suggested another cause: exposure to toxic metals, particularly copper, in worn brass mouthpieces.

A radio producer and professional musician weighed in with the suggestion that a thin neck strap, supporting as much as thirty pounds of saxophone, might be to blame. Before he switched to a strap that runs over his shoulders and attaches to his belt, he said, he would experience occasional visual distortions and loss of the center of his vision in one or both eyes for as long as twenty minutes.

A plastic surgeon related that after lengthy alto solos, he experiences a minor degree of "velopharyngeal insufficiency," a condition in which air escapes through the nose during speech, causing a nasal resonance. By acting as a safety valve, he suggested, the condition may prevent dangerous pressure from closing down blood vessels in the neck.

A hematologist wrote to say that the authors may have overlooked the possible connection between the melancholic tones the saxophone is capable of producing and depression. Those who are attracted to the instrument are more likely to be depressive personalities, he suggested, and depression is known to be linked to cardiovascular morbidity.

In the discussion section of their report, Kinra and Okasha tipped off skeptical readers to the seriousness, or lack thereof, of their study. Although their research techniques hadn't been used before, they went through "extensive validation procedures," they said; "100 percent of the authors' friends who were asked their opinions on these measures agreed that they were a 'good' or a 'very good' idea." As music lovers and epidemiologists, they nominated themselves for further research. "Attendance at a number of national and international concert venues would resolve this issue," they wrote, "and the researchers are currently seeking funding for this." In conclusion,

they said that "health promotion campaigns encouraging saxophonists to declare themselves as leaders of their bands should have a significant impact on their mortality."

The report, which appeared in *BMJ*'s year-end issue, was a spoof.
The saxophone, long known for its humorous personality, was now
comically subverting medical science—a fact few of the journal's
readers detected. In their concluding remarks, the authors probably
should have included a gentle admonition to members of the medical community who also play saxophone: Keep the day job.

15. GABRIEL'S HORN

His voice was thin, raspy, fatigued—what you might expect of a ninety-six-year-old man who had spent almost eight decades blowing life into the evolving saxophone, inspiring it, like a musical Geppetto, with a playful personality and haughty dignity, but whose once inexhaustible life force was now guttering out, depriving him of the will or energy to play. About six weeks before he died, I reached Benny Carter at his home in Los Angeles. Benny, one of the handful of early innovators who not only found a unique voice on the saxophone that became a model for several generations of players but wrote and arranged some of the finest music ever written for the instrument, politely declined my request to interview him. There wasn't enough time left, he said softly. Respecting his wishes, I asked if he wouldn't mind telling me just one thing: What happened to him the first time he picked up a saxophone?

"I felt incredible joy," Benny said, "and every time I've played it since has been a religious experience."

A similar kind of power appears to be embracing the man onstage right now at the New Jersey Performing Arts Center in Newark. Even as he sways jerkily on arthritic knees, the mouthpiece and much of the neck of his tenor saxophone buried in his great snowy beard, Sonny Rollins inhabits an aura of immense strength. A blousy silk sport coat draped around his large frame, his eyes hidden behind dark sunglasses, he is still the embodiment, both physically and artistically, of the *Saxophone Colossus*, the extraordinary 1956 post-bop recording that justified its grandly eponymous title. As he locks onto a new composition that rides jauntily atop a calypso beat, he holds his saxophone at what for most players would be an uncomfortable arm's length, effortlessly fingering its keys, the bell of his horn, and his eyes, pointed toward the heavens. He churns through several choruses, tilting from side to side, out of time almost, obeying a rhythm only he understands. The long, velvet tones pour out of his horn as he leans back and inflates his broad chest, his horn twinkling and glistening and atomizing stage light like a magnificent jewel. The notes begin to come fast and furious, assaulting listeners with the unmistakable sound of Sonny, and a curious thing occurs. The faster the tempo and the greater the complexity of the music, the less Sonny seems to respond physically. He continues to extend the horn like a gift to the gods while swaying from side to side, but his huge body has retreated into the background and the saxophone, suspended like a pendulum in a dazzling cone of light, seems to be playing itself.

That's pretty much how he explains what's going on, too, when we talk after the show. "The music takes over," he says in a husky voice, "and I'm just a conduit. I can't tell where it's coming from. I'm letting the music play me. There are times when I'm playing really well and I'm looking down at myself standing there, playing, apart. I would ascribe it to some kind of definite higher power without trying to get too ecclesiastical about it. But there is something spiritual going on, otherworldly, no doubt about it."

Sonny believes the horn's transcendent powers have partly to do with its conical form. "There's something about the shape that comes out of animals," he muses, "the conical horns that grow out of the ibex or bulls. I always felt that. I used to know people who worked at slaughterhouses. They'd often retrieve the horns and put little mouthpieces on them. If you see pictures of the devil or a man-beast, you see conical horns, which is maybe why the saxophone has been called the instrument of the devil's music. But I see the conical growth as coming out of the brain, the center of higher understanding. Or as an antenna, picking up cosmic signals, or messages from angels."

Sonny, according to George Avakian, who produced several of his records, is the "real philosopher" among jazz musicians. He has disappeared from the recording world for years at a time—to learn the violin or study yoga, Zen, and the Bhagavad Gita in Japan and India, where he would play by himself in a cave. According to George, his highly developed awareness results in odd things happening when he puts the horn in his mouth. George remembers a session in 1964 when they were recording *Now's the Time*. Sonny was in the middle of a blazing solo and suddenly stopped. "'Did you see that?' he asked," George recalls him saying. "I said, 'What?' He said, 'There was a flash of light that just streaked across the stage.' And I realized I *had* seen a flash of yellowish white light shoot through the room, but it had registered only on some subconscious plane. He believes very strongly that people relate to each other on a level they don't understand, and that persuaded him we could be friends. Sonny's music expresses that, because he's at times a player who's carried away by what's going on inside himself rather than strictly thinking about what's going on musically."

That's been happening ever since he first picked up a saxophone. Born in 1930 in Harlem, Sonny saw his first saxophone at his uncle's house when he was six or seven. It was like confronting the oracle. "My uncle had it under his bed," he says. "The case was lined with purple velvet, really beautiful, and the horn was all gold. It sort of looked to me like a beautiful woman, with the shape and curves. I could feel it reaching out to me."

His mother bought him an alto and a couple of years later a King Zephyr, the same model that Louis Jordan saw in the window of a nightclub across from his school.*

The first time he played the saxophone, Sonny says, "I got that buzz. I could be happy playing all by myself, completely happy. I would start practicing and would go into a reverie, I'd just lose myself. It wasn't something I was trying to do, it just took me over and I could be there forever. I was into heaven, another place. And to a great extent that happens today. I don't have to be playing with a group, I'm quite content to be playing all by myself. It puts me in a very special place. That's why I still look forward to practicing every day. If for some reason I can't play for a few days, I get physically out of kilter. When I get back to playing, I get back to feeling physiologically normal."

Onstage, Sonny is known for his extraordinary and lengthy improvisational runs, such as the one I had just witnessed. Now well practiced at inducing an altered state, he knows how to get there quickly. "I start off by playing some tried-and-true things, something akin to clichés, in a way," he says, "just to get into what I'm doing. Then when I'm into it, my mind goes blank and I don't think about anything. The music takes over. When I'm improvising, things are happening so fast I don't have time to listen to myself, I can't really catch on to too many notes I'm playing.

"It's all involuntary. Something else is in charge."

Do saxophonists develop some special conduit to other realities? After he cleaned up in 1957, John Coltrane clearly took dictation from some higher authority.† Under Trane's influence, Albert Ayler and

---

*Like Sonny, Jordan felt the instrument reached out to him when he first saw it. In *Honkers and Shouters*, Arnold Shaw reports that Jordan told him: "It was a saxophone in a store window. I could see myself in the polish brass—that started me off."

†Since 1971, the Saint John Coltrane African Orthodox Church in San Francisco has invoked Trane's spirit during three-hour weekly services that culminate in live performances of *A Love Supreme*.

Pharoah Sanders produced albums—*Spirits, Spiritual Unity*, and *Witches & Devils* by Ayler, and *Karma* by Sanders—that coaxed an ecstatic spirit from the horn. Dozens of saxophone players have followed their paths. Charles Lloyd, who had one of the best-selling jazz albums ever in the sixties (the enchanting *Forest Flower*, with Keith Jarrett, Jack DeJohnette, and Cecil McBee), spent the next two decades playing only long tones on the saxophone, searching for the horn's "essence" so that he could make a "divine offering." Odean Pope formed his nine-piece saxophone choir and wrote the music for the ensemble's record, *Epitome*, with the singular goal of recapturing the sound and spirit he heard in the Baptist church he attended when growing up in Ninety Six, South Carolina.

Even when they don't try to trap the saxophone's old soul on tape or CD, many more musicians, like Benny Carter, become entranced by the "incredible joy" of playing the horn. Almost every accomplished player I've talked to acknowledges being swept away by the saxophone's transcendent power, although most don't want to put a name to it. "No one really knows how to describe it," says the soprano saxophonist Jane Ira Bloom, who often finds herself swooping and twirling about the stage like a possessed dervish. "You don't want to talk about it in detail. There's the worry that if you talk about it and put it into the other side of the brain, you'll demystify it. So people refer to it as 'that thing, man.' They use the most common word to describe the highest possible experience."

Many players of all instruments acknowledge music's ability to induce a state of ecstasy, the mystical change in self-awareness that Samuel Johnson described as "any passion by which the thoughts are absorbed, and in which the mind is for a time lost." But saxophonists, according to my anecdotal research, seem to have a special passport to other realms, although sometimes, like Charlie Parker, they find themselves trapped between them. After he married Charlie Parker's widow, Phil Woods says that "there was always a bird in the house, flying through a window, an open door." He also recalls that when Jackie McLean opened Bird's saxophone case for the first time after his death, "all the pictures fell off the walls."

My own sense is that the intimate union of player and horn and the very human sound the marriage produces goes a long way toward making "that thing" possible. Few other instruments require the player to insert the sound-producing mechanism in his body— melding the body and horn into a unique hybrid, a musical cyborg. The clarinet's mouthpiece is similar to the saxophone's, but the tone it produces (because of its cylindrical shape) is uniform, distinctly other—unable, despite its potential for great beauty, to evoke many human characteristics. The conical oboe produces a rich and human sound but is so difficult to play and sends such a jarring kickback into the brain that it's impossible to forget you're playing it. (So I'm told by oboe players who also play saxophone.) The saxophone's easy ability to project a player's persona, but to do it in a nonverbal way, on the other hand, seems to offer a gateway to new levels of perception and experience.

Although Adolphe Sax invented his horn with military bands and symphonic orchestras in mind, the saxophone, with what Georges Kastner described as its "sublime and priestly calm," was recognized immediately for its ability to interpret "works of a mysterious and solemn character." Hector Berlioz composed his *Hymne* for Sax's new instrument, premiering the work in 1844, the same year Kastner wrote the saxophone into his opera *The Last King of Juda*. Ambroise Thomas transcribed *Ancient Chants of Peru* for saxophone trio in 1865 and later incorporated the instrument into his Mass. In 1868, Adolphe Sax played in a quartet of saxophones at the funeral of the opera composer Gioacchino Rossini, who was a fan of Sax's invention.

In the twentieth century, as the saxophone became the most prominent instrument in jazz, the devil's music, it came to be considered a poor choice for religious music. In 1903, Pope Pius X wrote the *Motu Proprio on Sacred Music*, which prohibited certain instruments "that may give reasonable cause for disgust or scandal"—that is, the saxophone—as being "unworthy of the House of Prayer and of the Majesty of God." Still, in its inimitable fashion, the saxophone managed to turn this liability into an advantage. By representing the profane, it found its way into such major compositions as *Job: A Masque for Dancing* (1927) by Ralph Vaughan Williams, and William Walton's *Belshazzar's Feast* (1929), an orchestral and choral masterpiece that pitted good against evil. The saxophone had found a back door into the symphonic orchestras that had worked so hard to keep it out.

As jazz put some distance between its early associations with the bordello, composers rediscovered the saxophone's connection to the sacred: its similarity to the human voice, its ability to express yearning and despair, made it an easy fit with the traditional vocal music of the world's religions. It became a regular participant in jazz vespers, New Age solstice-worship services, and Holy Roller prayer meetings. Paul Horn recorded the saxophone in a number of sacred environments, including the Great Pyramid in Giza, Egypt; the Temple of Heaven in Beijing, China; the Kazamieras Cathedral in Lithuania; and Monument Valley and Canyon de Chelly in the American Southwest. The recording he made inside the Taj Mahal in India sold more than a million copies.

In India, Kadri Gopalnath, known as Saxophone Chakravarthy (Emperor of the Saxophone), has adapted the saxophone to play South Indian—Carnatic—classical music. As a child, Gopalnath was considered a prodigy on the nadhaswaram, a long, conical-bore double-reed wind instrument considered to be *mangala*, or auspicious, within the Indian classical tradition. Its sound is thought to be enjoyed by the Hindu deities, so nadhaswaram musicians often accompany marriages, religious festivals, and temple processions at which the blessings of the gods are desired. After receiving lessons from a member of a British brass band, Gopalnath began using the saxophone as a *mangala* instrument and performed at marriages and other religious rites.

First, though, to make the saxophone capable of important subtle aspects of Carnatic expression, he had to modify the instrument. He removed many of the springs that open and close the pads on the tone holes and replaced them with rubber bands so that he could perform *gamakas*, or the slides from note to note that are essential to the genre. He also replaced many of the flat pads with convex pads, which helped him produce smooth slides as the pads enter the holes. Gopalnath is now known as the first saxophonist to be recognized in India as a true master of the country's classical music.

In Japan a similar displacement has occurred. Ryo Noda, a composer and saxophonist, plays traditional shakuhachi music on the saxophone. The shakuhachi, an end-blown five-holed bamboo flute that dates back to the seventh century in Japan, is used by Buddhist monks to induce meditative states. Like Indian music, shakuhachi music incorporates slides between notes and pitch bends of up to a minor third in either direction—not a problem for the highly flexible saxophone. As its earliest proponents predicted, the saxophone has reverently answered its call "to the highest destiny."

It can also get you high—particularly the tenor, says David Murray. "Because it's the closest thing to the human body, or the sound of the human body," he says. "Have you ever put on earplugs and listened to your inner self? The pounding of your heart, the fluids flowing through your body? The tenor has something to do with that, it's close to the body's pitch. You don't have to be playing it to recognize that sound. The tenor can make people wake up and sit up out of a drunken stupor. The tenor can make a woman change her direction and walk toward you."

Since he began playing as a boy, David has been captivated by the saxophone's mystical powers. "Sometimes when you're playing, like Sonny says, you feel like you're sitting there watching it," he says as he stretches out on a couch in a friend's loft in downtown Manhattan. "You can't tell whether you're playing the saxophone or it's playing you. Sonny gets into that realm better than anyone else because his technical facility just helps bring it on. The first time I heard him he was playing a solo at the Berkeley Jazz Festival and he was in that zone already. That's why he's so important for me. I was eleven and playing alto. The next day I got a tenor."

David first played with his family band in the Church of God in Christ, home to the fire-and-brimstone Holy Rollers, as David calls them. His father, who played guitar, was head deacon of the church and superintendent of its Sunday school. His mother played the piano, his brother the clarinet, a cousin the trumpet. Ignoring the saxophone's reputation as a "profane" instrument, David's father encouraged his selection. "We were into praising God and nobody was going to say what instrument you couldn't play," David says.

Within a few years he was using the horn to conjure up both sacred and profane spirits. "When I was fifteen, I used to play in this dive on Saturday nights with Carol Doda, San Francisco's most famous striptease artist," he says. "I'd put on my mustache and go up there and play behind the screen. The next morning, I'd play in church, because that's what it was all about. Sometimes you see the same people on Saturday night you see on Sunday morning—they're just a little more red-eyed, that's all. You need both to be a complete person."

The night before we spoke, playing in a small theater in the basement of Carnegie Hall, David began his set with "Fantasy Rainbow" (or "Sparkle"; he still hasn't decided on the name), which is dedicated to Curtis Mayfield, and followed with "Steps," a piece he wrote in homage to John Coltrane, before premiering his six-part *Aleksandr Pushkin Suite*, which will be part of a movie score about the patriarch of Russian literature, who was of African descent. David was backed by drums, bass, piano, and a large string ensemble. A month before, he was in town with his Cuban big band. A founding member of the arty World Saxophone Quartet, he's comfortable working in every configuration and genre, whether exploring the music of Senegal or divining the spirits in the Music Revelation Ensemble or playing Bach transcriptions or hip-hop. Educated at Pomona College in Los Angeles, he now lives in Paris, where he runs his own record label.

Near the top of just about everyone's list of great contemporary saxophonists, David, a medium-size man with a broad chest and warm, soulful eyes, has made hundreds of albums since he recorded his first tunes in the 1970s.

At every juncture, his goal has been to try to "hook up with the universe" and find sounds in the saxophone no one has heard before. "There are a million tones in the instrument," he says, "all the interstitials inside of notes from tone to tone—quarter tones, sixteenth tones. You have to make a decision if you want to explore the overtone system of the horn and look for all those sounds in between. They make you who you are. No other instrument offers those opportunities. A hundred years from now, people will still be discovering new sounds on it."

That process of discovery, though, can also make you a little crazy. "I was listening to a live recording one time when I played a certain kind of note I'd never heard played by anybody. It was a high note but it created a chord that was maybe seven notes. It vibrated against itself, and listening to it, I recalled how transporting it was when I played it. I kept playing it back and tried to do it again and again and I couldn't. I was like a junkie chasing his first high. I worked about three days trying to get that sound and realized that it had been there, at that moment, in the heat of the action, and I couldn't re-create it and never would."

At such moments, when "that thing" reveals itself, the sensation is a lot like that of being "saved," David says. "It feels like it's out of body, but you're actually receiving the Holy Ghost. It's a feeling of tranquillity, very close to the most enlightening experiences of your life. Whenever I'm at my best I'm in that zone, and it's the most peaceful moment I might receive. I'm doing something I like, I'm happy with myself, and other spirits are helping guide me. Those forces exist in our midst and we just have to conjure them up. When I'm playing the saxophone, I'm not asking for that and I don't get there all the time. In a concert I'm lucky if I get there for one moment. It doesn't last long, but while it does, you just have to be happy to be there."

———

As Vernard Johnson pulls up in front of the North Texas Intermediate Sanction Facility in Fort Worth, Texas, he says a little prayer, asking the Lord to provide him with the strength and inspiration to reach the hearts of the troubled souls incarcerated inside. He'd be grateful for the same guidance he received a couple weeks earlier at a prison in Huntsville, where he persuaded the warden to let him and his saxophone onto death row so he could help the men "in the final hours of their ultimate decision on whether to accept God in their lives." He concludes the prayer with a little nod, then recalls how, standing behind a yellow line on the floor, safely out of reach of the doomed prisoners in Huntsville, he made his way through "Amazing Grace." "When I was done," he says, "someone yelled out, 'Play it again!' Now, if you're on death row and someone tells you to play it again, what would you do?" He ended up working over the classic anthem of sin and redemption for another hour.

Vernard, a boyish-looking fifty-five-year-old man whose friendly features suggest both Richard Pryor and Cuba Gooding, Jr., grabs his black Keilwerth alto, tucked away in a custom-made Louis Vuitton soft-sided gig bag, and gets out of his car, a 1993 Mercedes sedan. He unzips the bag and makes sure he has the necessary identification papers required to enter the facility, a huge, windowless, hangarlike building made of corrugated steel that is situated between a Harley-Davidson motorcycle plant and a computer-parts manufacturer. Discreetly identified on the outside only as NTISF, the prison appears to be just another warehouse in this suburban industrial park.

Inside, Vernard is greeted warmly by R. J. Gray, chaplain of NTISF's Sons of Trouble Community Church, who directs the "man of God" to her office, where he sets up his horn. "We're going to have a good turnout this evening, Dr. Johnson," says Chaplain Gray, a rotund, bespectacled woman whose eyebrows are arched in perpetual worry. Glancing at the horn, she says, "The Lord has placed a ram in the bushes."

Vernard, dressed in black pants and a black and white silk pullover, smiles and hands Chaplain Gray his saxophone case. "If it's like last time, it will be a blessing," he says. A few weeks before, on the night of the Super Bowl broadcast, his concert drew about fifty men. Halfway through the "service," one of the prisoners stood up and shouted, "The other men think they're watching the Super Bowl in there. But the Super Bowl is out here tonight. They say they need three more yards for a touchdown. But Jesus has already run the touchdown!"

After preparing his horn, Vernard, surrounded by Chaplain Gray, the warden's secretary, a security guard, and a couple of trusties in tan fatigues, makes his way onto the prison floor, which is divided into two huge steel-barred cages the size of circus tents. The cages are subdivided into eight "tanks," each of which contains bunk beds, concrete dining tables, bathroom facilities, and one television— twenty-five inmates to a tank. To the rear of the building are eight solitary-confinement cells, currently unoccupied, with thick steel doors. The men spend most of the day in lockdown in their tanks, sprung only for daily exercise or, for the Sons of Trouble congregants, regular worship services with Chaplain Gray, who also arranges the occasional visitation from the Vernard Johnson Concert Ministry.

Inching down the corridor between the two cages, careful to stay between the two yellow stripes on the floor that guarantee safe passage, Vernard begins summoning the prisoners to the service, which will take place in the "chapel," a conference room with a dais, plastic chairs, a huge sound system, a drum kit, and a giant cross mounted on the wall. He plays a few phrases from "To God Be the Glory," machine-gunning the prisoners with a hail of upper-register notes that ricochet wildly throughout the cavernous space. "What y'all doin' tonight?" Vernard asks the men as he passes by each tank. "Come be with me." The inmates, in green or tan pajama-like prison garb, look up from their chess games or remove television earphones as he passes. Some shake their heads and look away. Others nod and extend their hands through the bars, riveting their eyes on the sinuous black spirit-summoner—the erstwhile voice of Sax, which, in another remarkable display of its flexibility, has now shape-shifted into Gabriel's horn—hanging around Vernard's neck. "Send me!" someone cries as Vernard plays a few more bars.

After making his way through the prison, Vernard retreats to the chaplain's office and asks for a little quiet meditation time. Meanwhile, the sound system in the chapel begins to crank with a bottom-heavy beat as one of the prisoners plays along on the drum kit. One by one, the Sons file into the chapel, some with a Bible irreverently tucked into their pants at the small of their backs. About a hundred men, a quarter of the prison's population, have chosen to attend the concert. Racially mixed, ranging in age from about thirty to sixty, they take their chairs in orderly fashion. Most are festooned with tattoos; a few have a pasty medicated look. All have served time for serious crimes, from child molestation to murder, and have been remanded to NTISF for sixty to one hundred eighty days for parole violations.

Now, as the sound system thumps an instrumental backup to "I'll Fly Away," Vernard makes his grand entrance into the chapel, two wired microphones attached to his horn, blowing wildly as the men jump to their feet and begin clapping in time. A one-legged man in a wheelchair sways from side to side, his stump bobbing up and down to the music. Vernard sings a few lyrics—"Some glad morning, when this life is over, I'll fly away. To a home on God's celestial shore, I'll fly away"—blows a few choruses, and, as the song winds down cries out, "Does anybody out there believe in God?" An affirmative roar shakes the room. Vernard chants the question again and again, then launches into "Lord, Help Me to Hold Out."

Often called the greatest gospel saxophonist in the world, Vernard has been playing his horn "for God" since he was seventeen. "I'd had chronic asthma all my life," Vernard told me before the concert. "The saxophone was my therapy. One day I was walking down the street and I had an attack that was so bad I had to crawl home. I just felt empty and hopeless. I said, 'God, I want you to change my life. If you will touch my lungs and take this asthma out, I will blow for you the rest of my life. And that day God began to convict me of my sins and I gave my heart to him. Two weeks later, I was practicing in my bedroom and I blew this note so long that I passed out and fell on the bed. While I was out, through my mind I heard something say, 'Vernard, check your lungs now.' When I woke up, the asthma was gone and I've never had it since."

One of nine children born to a Kansas City, Kansas, Pentecostal preacher (two of his brothers also have ministries), Vernard began playing in tent-show revivals in places like Bearden, Arkansas. "When I started blowing the horn, that tent would be empty," he says. "I'd blow those high notes a long time and all of a sudden Negroes would start coming out of the woods everywhere and jam that tent. Then the elder would tap me on the shoulder and say, 'I got it now.' I was the summoner." Since then, he's recorded sixteen albums, gotten a doctorate in composition, and played concerts around the world, from New Delhi to Jerusalem.

Now he wraps up "I'm Alive" with some freak notes, one hand on the upper horn, the other waggling a scolding finger in the air as he crouches down, his knees almost touching the floor. His technique relies heavily upon a thick vibrato on slower tunes, fiery honking on the fast ones, and a lot of fervent body language. Absent the religious lyrics, which Vernard delivers in a soulful voice reminiscent of Wilson Pickett's, he'd be solidly in the idiomatic camp of the R&B honkers and shouters. "Oh yeah, we're havin' a party in here tonight," Vernard tells the prisoners as sweat pours down his face. "God is not ashamed to be having a party with you."

Over the next hour, Vernard builds his spiritual platform, raising the tempo, pitch, and praises with each song. But just as he eases into "Jesus, When Troubles Burden Me Down," the PA system crashes. As a couple of trusties scramble to fix it, Vernard nods his head and says, "Every time the devil tries to stop me, it reminds me of that time in Chicago."

"Yes, sir!" somebody says, recognizing the opening of a confessional sermon.

"Let me tell you a story," Vernard says.

"Come on, now!"

"I was blowin' my horn in church on Sunday and in the clubs on Monday and a man heard me and offered to be my promoter."

"Uh-huh," a few men murmur.

"He said, 'I'll put your name in lights.' See, that was the devil talking to me."

"What he say?"

"He said, 'I'll get you anything you want. You want a Rolls-Royce? I'll get you one. You want to go to Hollywood and be rich and famous and have all kinds of women? I can get you that.' The devil can sound mighty good."

"Yes, he can."

"And I was getting ready to take that first step. I got my foot in the air, it was just about to come down, and I thought of that day long ago in Kansas City, where I was born, when I walked into a band room in school and saw a saxophone. I had terrible asthma, see, I could hardly breathe, but something inside me said, 'I got to blow a horn.'"

"All right," more men say.

"But the man there said, 'You don't have no way to blow a horn.' And I said, 'I know somebody who sits high but looks low, and he'll help me."

"Uh-huh."

His voice rising and quivering and shifting into the rhythmic cadence of an old-time gospel preacher, Vernard says, "My mother prayed for me-uh. She prayed for me to be able to play that horn-uh. Just like tonight-uh. Somebody's praying for you-uh."

The men jump to their feet and begin clapping. "That's right!"

As the sound system comes back to life, Vernard fingers his horn and yells, "The reason you're not dead tonight is that somebody's praying for you!"

The men roar and surge forward as the man of God begins to play "I Believe I Can Fly," then segues into "Lord, Help Me to Hold Out." On cue, the inmates chant, "I won't be back, I won't be back, I won't be back—no more!" Vernard stands in their midst, thronged, as security-detail trusties mop sweat from his brow and nudge the prisoners back. "I know it's going to be all right!" Vernard screams. "Will somebody shake my hand and say, 'I know it's going to be all right'?" A dozen men touch his shoulders, arms, and the horn. He resumes honking as the Sons of Trouble, arms raised and palms open, with tears streaming down their faces, cry out, "I know it's going to be all right!"

Now Vernard eases softly into "Amazing Grace," the prisoners singing the lyrics. With each chorus, Vernard climbs a little higher on the instrument, sweat spilling down his face, crouching and writhing as he reaches for the notes. Then, playing only with his left hand, he cups the cheek of a Son next to him with his right, drawing the man's head toward the plaintive cries coming from the bell of his horn. As though he'd been electrocuted, the man crashes to the floor, "slain in the spirit." Vernard lays his hand on the forehead of another Son, draws him near for his saxophonic benediction and— bam! Another huge tattooed man topples to the floor.

At the rear of the room men stretch their arms across their fellow inmates' shoulders, trying to reach the man of God and his sacred instrument. Like a sixties soul singer who leaves nothing onstage, Vernard is now wilting, exhausted. The prisoners pat the sweat from his brow as he continues to blow, he and his horn a medium between these lost Sons and the promise of salvation. By now, the bodies of a dozen Sons are strewn about the chapel, heads resting in the laps of fellow inmates, but Vernard plays on, his saxophone, the devil's horn, now dedicated only to delivering God's grace.

The saxophone, everyone says, is easy to learn to play but a lifetime's work to learn to play well. Nonetheless, after my first year, I have a repertoire: "In a Sentimental Mood," "St. Thomas," "Watermelon Man," "Naima," the theme from The Pink Panther, *"Summertime," and, as long as I tongue it about half as fast as Coltrane, "Mr. PC." Oddly, I feel a need to commemorate the first anniversary of my new enthusiasm and decide to stage my own "recital"—albeit in a subway station. It's the perfect venue: I won't have to suffer the embarrassment of inviting anyone, yet people are guaranteed to show up.*

I open my gig bag on the floor, set up, and begin to play a string of arpeggios at the far end of the station. The sound in the cavernous tiled space is amazing. Sensing the unusual acoustic environment, the Super Balanced Action, like a racehorse at the gate, seems eager to be cut loose; I can feel its gathering energy in my hands. I practice some rhythmic fingering exercises on the low notes and let her roar. The long tones carom off walls and pillars and collide with themselves, overtones and har-

monics and partial tones seem to replicate and build up to a dense blast of sonic feedback. Now blowing freely amid these great waves of sound with my eyes closed, floating from crest to crest, I have no idea what I'm playing, but it doesn't matter, because it all works. I feel utterly transported. It's like someone has taken a giant syringe filled with an aural narcotic and plunged it into the center of my brain.

When I open my eyes, a man is standing before me. I stop playing; the waves of sound fade to a ripple as they scatter into the subway tunnel. "You're the guy I've heard practicing," he says. I brace myself. This is obviously my neighbor, owner of the disembodied voice that has repeatedly reminded me to close my window whenever I discover a new sound on the horn and proceed to play it for an hour.

He drops a dollar into my gig bag. "You've gotten a lot better."

BIBLIOGRAPHY

Austerlitz, Paul. *Dominican Music and Merengue: Dominican Identity.* Temple University Press, 1997.

Badger, Reid. *A Life in Ragtime: A Biography of James Reese Europe.* Oxford University Press, 1995.

Balliett, Whitney. *Collected Works: A Journal of Jazz 1954–2001.* St. Martin's Griffin, 2002.

Banks, Margaret Downie. *Elkhart's Brass Roots: An Exhibition to Commemorate the 150th Anniversary of C. G. Conn's Birth and the 120th Anniversary of the Conn Company.* Shrine to Music, Museum College of Fine Arts, University of South Dakota, 1997.

Bro, Paul Alan. "The Development of the American-Made Saxophone: A Study of Saxophones Made by Buescher, Conn, Holton, Martin, and H. N. White." Ph.D. diss., Northwestern University, 1992.

Cohen, Paul. "Vintage Saxophones Revisited." *Saxophone Journal* 10, no. 2; 10, no. 3; 12, no. 4; 14, no. 5; 14, no. 6; 15, no. 1; 19, no. 2.

Crawford, Richard. *America's Musical Life: A History.* W. W. Norton and Company, 2001.

Critchley, Macdonald, and R. A. Henson, (eds.) *Music and the Brain.* William Heinemann Medical Books, 1977.

Dawson, Jim. *Nervous Man Nervous: Big Jay McNeely and the Rise of the Honking Tenor Sax!* Big Nickel Publications, 1994.

Deans, Kenneth N. "A Comprehensive Performance Project in Saxophone Literature with an Essay Consisting of Translated Source Readings in the Life and Work of Adolphe Sax." Ph.D. diss., University of Iowa, 1980.

Dickinson, Malcolm. "The Closing of the American (Saxophonist's) Mind." *Saxophone Symposium*, fall 1991.

Erenberg, Lewis A. *Steppin' Out: New York Nightlife and the Transformation of American Culture, 1890–1930.* University of Chicago Press, 1981.

Ferron, Ernest. *The Saxophone Is My Voice.* IMD Diffusion Arpèges, 1997.

Frankenstein, Alfred V. *Syncopating Saxophones.* Robert O. Ballou, 1925.

Giddins, Gary. *Visions of Jazz: The First Century.* Oxford University Press, 1998.

Gushee, Lawrence. "New Orleans–Area Musicians on the West Coast, 1908–1925." *Black Music Research Journal* 9, no. 1, 1989.

———. "Steppin' on the Gas: Rags to Jazz, 1913–1927." Liner notes to New World Records 269.

Habla, Bernhard. "Darstellung von Saxophonen in der Werbung" ("The Iconography of the Saxophone"). *Pannonische Forschungsstelle Oberschutzen* 12, September 2001.

Hagert, Thorton. "Come and Trip It: Instrumental Dance Music 1780s–1920s." Liner notes to New World Records, 80293.

Haine, Malou. *Adolphe Sax: Sa vie, son oeuvre, ses instruments de musique.* Editions de l'Université de Bruxelles, 1980.

Hemke, Fred L. "The Early History of the Saxophone." D.M.A. thesis, University of Wisconsin, 1975.

Hester, Michael Eric. "The Saxophone Soloists Performing with the John Philip Sousa Band: 1893–1930." *Saxophone Symposium* 23, 1998.

Hindson, Harry Burdette. "Aspects of the Saxophone in American Musical Culture, 1885–1980." Ph.D. diss., University of Wisconsin, 1992.

Horwood, Wally. *Adolphe Sax, 1814–1894.* Egon Publishers, 1983.

Howe, Robert. "Invention and Early Development of the Saxophone 1840–55." *Journal of the American Musical Instrument Society* 29, 2003.

Ingham, Richard, ed. *The Cambridge Companion to the Saxophone.* Cambridge University Press, 1998.

Jones, Andrew F. "Black Internationale: Notes on the Chinese Jazz Age." In Atkins, E. Taylor, ed. *Jazz Planet.* University Press of Mississippi, 2003.

Jones, LeRoi. *Tales*. Grove Press, 1967.

———. *Blues People: The Negro Experience in White America and the Music That Developed from It*. William Morrow and Company, 1963.

Jost, Ekkehard. *Free Jazz*. Da Capo Press, 1994.

Juslin, Patrik N., and Petri Laukka. "Communication of Emotions in Vocal Expression and Music Performance: Different Channels, Same Code?" *Psychological Bulletin* 129, no. 5, 2003.

Kaeppler, Adrienne L. "Airplanes and Saxophones: Post-War Images in the Visual and Performing Arts." In *Echoes of Pacific War*, Deryck Scarr, Niel Gunson, Jennifer Terrell, eds., Target Oceania, 1998.

———. "Reflections on a Tongan Noseflute." Smithsonian Institution, 2002.

Kelly, John-Edward. *The Acoustics of the Saxophone from a Phenomenological Perspective*. Daedalian Music, 2001.

Kinra, Sanjay, and Mona Okasha. "Unsafe Sax: Cohort Study of the Impact of Too Much Sax on the Mortality of Famous Jazz Musicians." *British Medical Journal* 319, 1999.

Kochnitzky, Leon. *Adolphe Sax & His Saxophone*. North American Saxophone Alliance, 1985.

Kool, Jaap. *The Saxophone*. Trans. Lawrence Gwozdz. Egon Publishers, 1987.

Merz, Charles. *The Great American Band-Wagon: A Study of Exaggerations*. John Day Company, 1928.

Millstein, Gilbert. "The Sax Comes Up the Moskva River." *The New York Times Magazine*, 23 April 1961.

Morgan, Ralph. "Does the Material Used Make Any Difference in How Mouthpieces Play?" *Saxophone Journal*, February/March 1995.

Murphy, Joseph McNeill. "Early Saxophone Instruction in American Educational Institutions." Ph.D. diss., Northwestern University 1994.

Noyes, James Russell. "Lefebre (1834–1911), Preeminent Saxophonist of the 19th Century," DMA Manhattan School of Music, 2000.

Patalano, Frank. "Psychosocial Stress in the Lives of Great Jazz Musicians." *Perceptual and Motor Skills*, February 1997.

———. "Psychosocial Stressors and the Short Life Spans of Legendary Jazz Musicians." *Perceptual and Motor Skills*, April 2000.

Pirker, Michael. "Pictorial Documents of the Music Bands of the Janissaries (Mehter) and the Austrian Military Music." *RIDIM-RCMI* newsletter 15, issue 2; fall 1990.

Purdue University. "All-American" Marching Band Handbook, 2002–2003.

Restani, Donatella. "Music and Myth in Ancient Greece." *Music & Anthropology: Journal of Musical Anthropology of the Mediterranean* 2, 1997.

Romero, Raul R. "Musical Change and Cultural Resistance in the Central Andes of Peru." *Latin American Music Review* 11, no. 1, University of Texas Press, 1990.

Schuller, Gunther. *The Development of Jazz, 1930–1945.* Oxford University Press, 1989.

————. *Early Jazz: Its Roots and Musical Development.* Oxford University Press, 1968.

Selva, Riccardo, "The Saxophone in Sacred Music." Ph.D. diss., Northwestern University, 2003.

Shaw, Arnold. *Honkers and Shouters: The Golden Years of Rhythm & Blues.* Macmillan, 1978.

Škvorecky, Josef. *The Bass Saxophone.* The Ecco Press, 1977.

Smialek, Thomas W., Jr. "Clay Smith and G. E. Holmes: Their Role in the Development of Saxophone Performance and Pedagogy in the United States, 1905–1930." D.M.A. diss., University of Georgia, 1991.

Stewart, Jack. "The Mexican Band Legend: Myth, Reality and Musical Impact; A Preliminary Investigation." *The Jazz Archivist,* December 1991.

Stoddard, Tom. *Jazz on the Barbary Coast.* Heyday Books, 1998.

Street, William Henry. "Elise Boyer Hall, America's First Female Concert Saxophonist: Her Life as Performing Artist, Pioneer of Concert Repertory for Saxophone and Patroness of the Arts." Ph.D. diss., Northwestern University, 1983.

Sudhalter, Richard M. *Lost Chords: White Musicians and Their Contribution to Jazz, 1915–1945.* Oxford University Press, 1999.

Thomas, Tony. *Music for the Movies.* Silman-James Press, 1997.

Umble, James C. *Jean-Marie Londeix: Master of the Modern Saxophone.* Roncorp Publications, 2000.

Vermazen, Bruce. *That Moaning Saxophone: The Story of the Six Brown Brothers.* Oxford University Press, 2004.

Walser, Robert. *Keeping Time: Readings in Jazz History.* Oxford University Press, 1999.

Wen, Andy. "Performing Ryo Noda's *Improvisation I*: History and Traditions of the Shakuhachi and Japanese Music." *Saxophone Symposium* 23, 1998.

Wilmer, Valerie. *As Serious As Your Life: John Coltrane and Beyond.* Serpent's Tail, 1992.

ACKNOWLEDGMENTS

When Kris Dahl, my agent at International Creative Management, first secured for me a deal with John Glusman, the brainy editor who bought this book, she suggested that I was going to "have a blast" reporting and writing *The Devil's Horn*. Although excited by the opportunity to explore the mysterious affinity I felt for the saxophone, I was also exceedingly daunted by how little I actually knew about the subject I had proposed— and, for that matter, music in general. An amateur drummer whose limited knowledge of music was pretty much confined to rock and roll, I wondered whether my vast ignorance would be so immediately apparent that no serious musician would agree to an interview.

Actually, of the more than two hundred players, scholars, critics, technicians, and other saxophone fanatics I sought to interview for this book, I think only one turned me down. ("Don't you understand the meaning of *no?*" the crusty old tenor player asked before hanging up.) I'm grateful to all for the help and insights they provided, but some deserve special mention. Early interviews with Tom Smialek, Tim McAllister, and Bruce Vermazen provided huge amounts of information about the saxophone's "legit" and pre-jazz history and set me on my way. Ralph Morgan spent two days with me, explaining how the saxophone worked and illuminating its extraordinary role in the development of instrument manufacturing, both abroad and in Elkhart, Indiana. Jim Maher sifted through his eight decades' worth of accumulated scholarship and wrote up thirty-two pages of invaluable notes regarding the saxophone's role in the evolution of American music—and in American social history—a remarkably generous and selfless effort on his part. Robert Howe shared with me his extensive research on the invention of the saxophone well in advance of its eventual publication in the *Journal of the American Musical Instrument Society*. Jean-Marie Londeix invited me into his home in Bordeaux, France, to share his many insights into the mind of Adolphe Sax and on the saxophone's importance to European avant-garde music. The terrific baritone player Roger Rosenberg brokered some important interviews for me with otherwise reclusive stars, as did George Avakian.

In Europe, I greatly enjoyed the three days I spent with François Louis in Paris and Belgium talking about the aulochrome, traveling to museums, and drinking a lot of good wine. I'd like to thank Norbert and Nathalie Aretz-Brackmyn, his wonderful neighbors in Ciplet, for putting me up. I'm also grateful to Dave Leppla, Bill Kisinger, and Kathy Matter for welcoming me into the Purdue University All-American Marching Band. I hope my performance didn't permanently tarnish your stellar reputation!

Several people did me the great favor of reading my manuscript, correcting technical and historical information and pointing up linguistic "clams." They include Bill Morris, Tom Smialek, Robert Howe, François Louis, Bob "Professor Jocoserious" Bell, and Jim Maher. I'd also like to acknowledge the great songsmith Jerry Leiber for suggesting a fine-tuning of the title and to thank Shawn O'Sullivan, a photo editor at the New York *Daily News*, for her help gathering the book's photographs and art. Dave Sokol, owner of the fabulous Euphoria Studios in New York, generously provided me free use of rehearsal space for my weekly lessons.

Finally, I'd like to thank my Tuesday-night buddy, Ortley, whose name is really Tom Richardson, for helping me jump-start this adventure, and my teacher, Michel Gohler, for enabling me to develop a few chops to make it even more fun. You two are some heavy cats.

INDEX

Twice nominated for National Magazine Awards, Michael Segell's work has appeared in a variety of publications, including *Sports Illustrated*, *The New York Times*, and *Esquire*. He is the author of *Standup Guy: Manhood After Feminism* (Villard, 2000) and editor of the anthology *A Man's Journey to Simple Abundance* (Scribner, 2000). He currently works at the New York *Daily News*, where he is lifestyle editor. For the past thirty-five years, he has sung and played drums and (more recently) saxophone in Las Eratikas, a quartet he and the other band members formed when they were students at Williams College.